PRAISE FOR
BOUNCE OFF THE WALLS –
LAND ON YOUR FEET

"Merrie Lynn's recipes – taking the biggest lemons in life turning them into the best lemonade – lives between the covers of this book. Read this book, enjoy, and learn invaluable life lessons."
Howard Wills – Internationally renowned healer and Peacemaker

"Best book this side of the Moon."
Buzz Aldrin – Astronaut, Author

"Merrie Lynn, a wise woman, helps us enter into the vast radiant emptiness TO know you're free – TO play and dance – TO be happy and make others happy – just by being you."
Ed and Deb Shapiro – Authors "Be The Change."

"Funny Wise Lady, Merrie Lynn's inspiring book…I guarantee will change your everyday life. I love her for capturing the Happiness Code. Hearty-est book since Moses wrote, 'Dropping two tablets and I don't mean Excedrin'. Trust me, get the book!"
Paul Ryan, TV Host/Producer/Author "The Art of Comedy."

"Merrie Lynn Ross is one of the gems of this world. With her mother's heart, star's beauty, wise intelligence, and a healing touch, she shares useful ideas with an easy, interesting, and personal flair that is certain to engage, uplift, and lighten the burdens of readers."
Sharon Janis, author of Spirituality For Dummies, Secrets For Spiritual Happiness, A Modern Quest for Eternal Truth

"A gift for all of us - for parents and teens to learn the value of heartfelt communication, enhancing family and community bonds."
Diane E. Watson – U.S. Congresswoman

"*Merrie Lynn is a delightful beacon of light for all of us trying to find our way on this journey called life. An inspiration to those who have lost a loved one, she has found the strength and courage to turn her tragedy into a message of hope and with love and joy guides us to create change. I am truly blessed by this beautiful spark.*"
Donna Visocky, BellaSpark Productions

"*Merrie Lynn's heart to heart message brings a contagious enthusiasm... for us to live a healthy and happy life.*"
Cheryl Saban, Ph.D.

"*I LOVED IT ... for anyone who is 'stuck' at any juncture. It's an amazingly inspirational journey. Merrie Lynn offers a golden parachute of lightness and laughter to gently guide us out of varying heights of despair or resistance. Her talent, passionate insight, and wisdom resonate within as a clarion call, calling forth our own Higher Selves to join in.*"
Diane Miller – Philanthropist

"*Bounce to success by reading how to effectively and effortlessly 'Land On Your Feet'.*"
Mark Victor Hanson – co-creator "Chicken Soup of The Soul".

"*Merrie Lynn's uncanny ability reached the depth of my spirit. You'll be lovingly supported by her practical techniques. Her approach is brevity, lightness, and laughter, but make no mistake...this is the real soul stuff. She brings us into her world of understanding and you simply don't want to leave. It's comforting to know such a voice exists—to return us to the truth of ourselves.*"
Kim Castle, Brand –U

"*Just when you thought that everything has been shared about personal transformation comes a book of shattering authenticity and depth. Merrie Lynn radiates compassion, carrying us beyond our comfort zones to the dark corners of suffering where the capacity to heal originates.*"
Alison Rose Levy, HealthJournalist.com

"Merrie Lynn's book is written with all the love, inspiration, and pain we go through in our lives. It's filled with all the lessons we need to know. I want my children to read this book.
Deanna Lund, actress/artist, author, "Valerie in Giant Land"

"Merrie Lynn Ross is a friend to the world. You will feel a core connection by reading this inspirational book. An oracle of wisdom, it offered me a feeling of comfort and freedom to make amazing life changes."
Heidi Beyer – CEO Global Wealth Management

"When art and heart meet, magical change occurs. Merrie Lynn opens up that magical portal for creative and joyous living."
David Streets – Art curator

Merrie Lynn has done a remarkable job of indulging us in a playful dialogue to help us turn our lives around. I highly recommend this book."
Sirah Vettese, Ph.D. – Author of Spiritual Makeover: Ten Practices for Falling in Love with Your Life

"Most real book this side of illusion's lens. Helps take off the blinders, opening your mind and heart to Love, to be Happy and to live your truth."
David Paul...photographer/artist

"Merrie Lynn's hilarious humor inspires you to transform your life instantly in a multitude of exercises in this book. Enjoy a blast of self-love and authentic joy."
Deepika Avanti, author Embracing the Miraculous, Attaining Optimal Health on All Levels.

"This book is a refreshing, energizing tonic. Merrie Lynn shares practical and profound ways to integrate body, mind and spirit...to uplift you into living a healthy, balanced, and joyous life."
Suzan Hughes, Herbal Life and Hang 10 founder.

"This is powerful and insightful life-transforming material. Merrie Lynn guides us out the darkness and into the light, illuminating the best of who we can be."
Dr. Caren Caty, Psychologist

Bounce

Off the Walls
Land on Your Feet

by
MERRIE LYNN ROSS

THE HAHA's
Morph
Havoc & Hassles
into
Harmony & Happiness

Library of Congress Control Number: 2010927920
ISBN 0982736649

Ross, Merrie Lynn
Bounce Off the Walls – Land On Your Feet: How to Morph Havoc and Hassles into Harmony and Happiness/Merrie Lynn Ross.

--1st ed.
p.cm

ISBN 978-0-9827366-4-7

Printed in the United States of America

TABLE OF CONTENTS

I always knew my beloved son Byron had deeper knowing than me. He came in as an old soul, a whirling dervish, joyous and enlivened. As he departed this earth on February 27, 2008 at only 22, a part of my soul went home…with him.

In the minutes, hours, days, and weeks that followed my heartbreak, I had to come to terms with the loss of a young life taken before the expression of life's fulfilled potential – the unspeakable, the unthinkable, the unfathomable.

All of us, at one time or another, face finding our way back into living with purpose. My personal process is intertwined within the pages of this book. I wrote about grief even before Bryon's passing, and it has taken me on an inner dimensional journey – gracefully guiding my commitment to live fully in his memory – bringing to life his wish for me always - "To be real, laugh and love. "

Imagine having a child who cheered you on to your own greatness, supporting it at every turn. Now in my darkest hours, his voice rings out, stirring my soul with a remembering. Months before his passing Byron had prodded me, "Mom, please get your book out, it will help a lot of people." It is from his ardent wish that I offer this to you, in the SPIRIT that you will benefit and grow, to live your truth, "To be REAL, LAUGH, AND LOVE."

INTRODUCTION

You can morph HAvoc and HAssles into HArmony and HAppiness, and the HA HA HA of sweet laughter. You can take control of your destiny and juggle a balance between rigidity and buoyancy. Living your potential in an ever-present, feel-good, do-good zone requires a shift in mental, emotional, and spiritual gears in self-awareness and personal commitment. The offering within these pages involves a celebrated, life-transforming process, a quantum leap know-how, called *MORPHING*.

You may be bouncing off walls, aimlessly floating in boredom, or baffled in resignation or defiance. Not knowing your life's purpose, you may be bouncing from one thing to another, feeling empty, always searching. Or your tolerance level may have plummeted to zero-point, where problems seem insurmountable, and life has imploded or exploded.

This is IT – *you are bouncing off the walls*. Clearly, you aren't centered or sure-footed, and Chicken Little is screeching, "The sky is falling. Doomsday gloom!" No matter what you do, it's out of control. Solutions and options are obscured by chronic upheaval.

It could be that you are vexing in the turmoil of chaos, fear, or stress. You may be a nervous wreck over finances, juggling kids, a broken heart, gridlock, allergies… Stop already!

Our issues, life challenges (whatever bugs us), zap us from enjoying life and cause us feel like bouncing off the wall or burrowing a hole six feet under. We are tossed about like a ball, landing here or there, crushed or done-in, with no respite or finish line in sight.

I've learned that at life's crossroads, in times of great crisis or challenge, I've teetered on the precipice of the greatest breakthroughs. Whether you are facing a divorce, illness, or emotional meltdown, a soul-call rings out to reinvent yourself.

This is the opportune time to begin the Morph Process and land on your feet. It's a special gift – those who have used it have related:

♥ "It's a way to actualize and to enjoy the fruits of transformation."

♥ "I was fat and a broke shopaholic. Through Merrie Lynn's Morph sessions, I found the courage to be responsible for my life. I lost twenty-five pounds, and I have a savings account for the first time."

♥ "I felt lighter – my fears and pain dissolved."

♥ "Ever since I followed Merrie Lynn's recipes for tuning into my heart, I'm happier and I laugh more."

Now dear reader, it's your turn. Start your mojo engine…fast track to a Happy Life.

♥ ♥ ♥

In 1995, I co-created the Morph Process and coined the term *morph* that is in the common vernacular today. An executive at Microsoft acknowledged our unique use of the term for personal transformation, and Microsoft became a sponsor for *MerrieWay Community*.

On a national TV broadcast, I appeared with Al Gore, who was on a crusade to stop media violence. He blasted the *Mighty Morphin' Power Rangers* for the gratuitous violence impacting kids. In the broadcast, I debated his assessment and provided a solution: our *Morph America's* media literacy program that teaches parents, kids, teachers how to improve children's TV viewing habits. What a launch for Morphing!

Morphing, as I coined the term, is a continuous process of self-awareness, growth, and skill building, bringing on significant, exponential life changes.

Let's take a leap of faith together. It's time to jump off your fear-base, your procrastination haze, your couch potato slump, and leap for the target. WAKE-UP TO YOUR TRUE SELF – your enlightened essence – expressing your soul's purpose and dreams.

The Morph "wild card" encompasses the heart and the higher spirit within, illuminating virtues such as compassion, generosity, patience, kindness, forgiveness and respect, all vital building blocks for creating a 21st century cooperative society. By reclaiming reverence for nature and sacred rituals we are guided through life passages, such as entering manhood, womanhood, old age, and death. Synthesizing a holistic balance we can shift between a technological world into our hearts and intuition.

Landing on Your Feet – You Could Sport a New ID

Following the guidance in this book, you will learn how to "risk all to get all." Give up the nasties and chaos controlling your life. Dissolve limited concepts, emotional hurts, and muster courage to delete *stuckness*. Recalibrate the humdrum of existing and reboot a natural flow into full-blast living.

Landing on your feet, you are able to move forward, focusing on what you have instead of what you don't have. Knowing you're okay **as you are**, you are free to live your heart's desire and stand in your truth. Hop aboard your retro-caddy, frolic like a mermaid, or take charge like a cow-daddy.

I stumbled upon my "new ID" by following my heart. Little did I know at the time how profound my transformation would become, as a series of miraculous and gut-wrenching experiences challenged me to find a way to land on my feet.

Morphing a SOAP DISH onto a SOAPBOX

As an actress, I morphed myself into amazing characters, including Julie Nixon (President Nixon's daughter), Marion Davies (silent film star), and the outrageous Emma Lutz on *General Hospital*. Imagine having 40 million people watching you play one of the wackiest characters on TV, and being recognized as daytime television's first comedienne. Emma was adored for wearing her heart on her sleeve and for her infectious giggle. People would grab me on the streets to hug me, squealing, "I love you!" My raspy voice isn't easy to mistake or forget. In a fitting room at Saks, I once asked the salesperson to bring a smaller size (heh heh). From nearby stalls voices roared, "It's Emma

Lutz!" – and then fans charged into my dressing room, snatching a glimpse of me butt-naked.

♥ ♥ ♥

Starring on *General Hospital* and in umpteen TV shows and films, my love affair with show biz lit a taste of fame. However, affecting other personas lacked something. Solid in my craft, I longed to put my mark on something more.

Doing a soap opera was a retirement tactic *par excellence*. I became pregnant and opted to have quality motherhood time instead of living on a set 14 hours a day nursing my baby. After leaving the show, the need to sequester myself in a search for privacy diminished, and my lustrous love affair with fame took a back seat.

Morphing a "soap dish onto a soapbox" had a direct correlation with motherhood. In a split second, my life view changed. In a courtyard outside my son's 3rd grade classroom, a small girl was lying on the ground. As I approached her, I was appalled to find her chewing on the bark of a tree. Gently lifting her into my arms, I carried her limp body into the school office. Explaining what I saw, an apathetic assistant retorted, "She probably missed her meds. Kids do it all the time." With the exasperation of a mother, I cried out, "What meds, what is going on here? Who is caring for this child?"

While drowning in unanswered questions, my heart exploded with a passionate conviction to help our children, including my own son. I grappled with the impact of societal challenges faced by our kids, pained by the decline of ethics, troubled by the removal of arts programs from our school system, and horrified by daily reports of escalating youth violence that sent me reeling into insomnia.

I was propelled to look deep inside to find my heart's calling, a clear vision of our society as peaceful: uplifting humanity in a supportive learning community. Fueled by an irrevocable conscience, I climbed upon my self-proclaimed soapbox and took a stand – joining the ranks as a child advocate.

Plotting a reformation front for children's and teens' challenges, I mobilized concerned folks in the film industry and philanthropists, and founded *MerrieWay Community*, a nonprofit organization that brings arts and ethics back into our schools. I co-wrote the nationally acclaimed *Morph America* and *Peace Smarts* curriculums (grades 5-12), which continue to cultivate creativity and harmony as change-agents. In a spirit of collaboration, *competition* takes on a new meaning, and being *successful* is based on humanitarian values, as well as material accomplishment.

I was a keynote speaker and sponsor of the historic *Stand for Children* in Washington D.C. How I got there and what I shared with thousands of young people and communities can be summed-up in one word: *morphing*. **Morphing is about taking Right Action in any given circumstance – about making proactive, positive, supportive choices for others and ourselves.** With all of us working together, we can create a more ethical, sustainable, and peaceful world.

However, before we can help the world and others, we must first look into our own lives, our own shadows, and transform whatever is required in order to bring about the Light.

The Essential Ingredient – YOU

The Project is about YOU – in Action. Can you imagine that *you* are the project? Can you give the same attention to yourself that you give to work, partying, parenting? Are you bouncing off the wall about an issue in your life? Are you fed up with life the way it is, or are you on a positive roll and want to ensure that it keeps going?

Recognize that YOU are the most important ingredient. Your creativity, ingenuity, and participation are a critical part of the whole. You can postulate, recreate, and transform the life you choose to live. Stop being the doormat of your emotions, the slave to addictions, or the victim of misunderstanding. You can learn, grow, and change right now – inside and outside. You can Morph apathy into enthusiasm, ineptness into mastery, and chaos and misery into joy, love, and laughter.

Your journey spirals from inside out, affecting your family, business associates and community. Through your knowledge, your heart, and your efforts, a great mission can be accomplished.

Bounce off the Walls – Land on Your Feet (or on your butt, your head, or hanging from the rafters – it's your choice.) We will deal with the Facts! The practical, the doable. There is no panacea on the way, friends. No magical pill to swallow. No one shoe fits all (Cinderfella proved that point). **There is no pot of gold at the end of the rainbow because there is no end, only a spiral of life weaving a unique tapestry – YOU – with no specific destination, only a journey that is fantastically YOURS.**

In this book, we will gobble delicious delicacies for thought: how to laugh at the drop of a hat, cry during a moment of truth, dump what you don't need, and keep what works. Take off your seat belts; this journey is not for the fainthearted, slackers, know-it-alls, or ball-busting bitches or britches that do everything to prove life doesn't work. Eating "right" works – if you eat healthy. The Know-How, formula works – if you commit and do it. It's your choice to let the air out of the tires or to fly high in a balloon to touch the *Eagle's Lair* – the place of wisdom, right thinking and joy.

Morphing **HA**voc (chaos) and **HA**ssles (misery) into **HA**rmony (peace) and **HA**ppiness (laughter) has a few ground rules:

♥ SHOW UP like a child ready to play, learn with beginner's mind, eat the goody snacks.

♥ Leave your ego on the other side of the opening page.

♥ Begin with a clean slate – a blank page with no expectation for results other than what will serve your higher good.

You may feel resistant to bust through the emotional, mental, or spiritual blocks preventing a desirable life. New insights and innovative tools will open the locks of imprisonment – debugging and reprogramming limited attitudes – providing you with a jumpstart and expanding your awareness, intuition, and perceptions. For some, it will feel like stepping into the fresh air of freedom – liberating a new and creative life.

Once you enter the Bouncing-off-the-Walls zone, I will be there too, as your tour guide, sharing my life-tremors, lessons, and foibles. To share my launch point, I began the process of Morphing before I had a name for it. It came in part in a dramatic way when I was hit by a bolt of lightning – literally. This was a physical transformation without any intention on my part. It was an act of God, an act of nature. It shifted my Consciousness.

After a day's trek in search of water on a property in Colorado, Wilk, a geologist friend, my then four-year-old son Byron, and I, stopped at a small diner in what felt like the middle of nowhere. Inside the diner a Native American man announced, "The Thunder

Beings are coming." I asked Wilk what the man meant. "It means a storm is brewing," he replied. A few minutes later, we left the diner. Crossing the parking lot, a startling bolt of lightning flashed from the sky, hitting Wilk in the temple, missing Byron by only a few inches, and then crackling onto the ground.

During the loud thunderclap, I felt dizziness. Then, as if time had stopped, I seemed frozen in space. I realized the crashing bolt had also hit me. The only visible injury was a minor scalp burn caused by a metal barrette fastened in my hair. Wilk heard an instant ringing in his ears, which has continued on-and-off since the incident. How lucky we were to survive and to be able to tell the tale.

From that moment on, I sensed alterations in my body. I had an acute awareness of what someone would say before they spoke (recapturing a repressed childhood trait). I experienced altered perceptions, unusual sensations and intuitions about people and events that would become true.

Shortly after the occurrence, in a fortuitous meeting with *Ayurvedic* doctor, spiritual leader, and author Deepak Chopra, he related, "Being hit by the bolt, the body receives amperage that instantly changes the molecular system. Symptoms following a blast of electricity into the body can intensify abilities in the realms of the paranormal." Examples of this include clairvoyance (in the waking state or in dreams), clairaudience (hearing other's thoughts), and increased intuition on many levels. The abilities to scan the body of a person with an illness, to diagnose the symptoms, or to develop healing hands (a magnetic field that has been measured by scientists throughout the world) are other possible effects of a molecular system transformation.

In many indigenous traditions, the lightning bolt is a sign that the Seeker is ready to receive an initiation – to become a healer of themselves and others. Destiny then unfolds without conscious thought, and the person exhibits paranormal abilities. Lightning bolts are not the only means of instant transformation, yet the jolt has been revered as the most instantaneous and powerful.

Shortly thereafter, I was in touch with hidden parts of myself, such as having lucid dreams with three-dimensional (holographic) images and an awareness that I was dreaming. Many otherwise overlooked messages were seen more clearly. Life lessons I needed to learn were presented to me very quickly in both my dream and waking states. My creative mind flourished with ideas, new ways of looking at life and new ways of being. There was less apprehension to step out of my norm and just BE. I witnessed nature and animals in a fuller sense. I could touch a tree and connect with its strength or gaze at a mountain and be one with its stillness. I felt the vulnerability in all living creatures. The pain in life – physical, emotional, intellectual, and spiritual – had a gentle sweet sorrow that I too could embrace.

This honeymoon period, as I call it, changed me — it gave me a platform to reinvent myself and claim my place in the world. It became an unfolding filled with challenges and surprises, shifting how I viewed everything. The recognition that "We are all One" was established inside of me, as it is in all of us when we become conscious of it.

Not everyone gets a whack on the head to perceive life anew. Your personal lightning bolt may come as a near-death experience, a divorce, loss of a loved one, an illness, or even winning the Lotto, but the outcome could affect you in a similar way.

Examining the lives of people who have contributed something significant in the world, and who have, in a sense, Morphed "life as it is" (whether from devastating or privileged backgrounds) into something truly great, I realized it wasn't enough to just paint a rosier future for oneself – in one's mind. **To transform, we need to identify, confront, and understand our internal shadows, mistakes and successes; we must heal hurts, forgive ourselves and let go of the past.**

By expanding limited beliefs you release outmoded behavioral patterns. What doesn't work dissolves into positive resolution. To actualize mastery for a balanced life that has staying power, you will learn to embrace your present circumstances and become anchored in the NOW. Then you can move on to envision a blueprint for change, formulating and implementing a future plan with a Can Do, fun spirit – inspiring a claim to work miracles in your life. You may choose to amp your creativity and joy, become a practical common sense problem-solver, add passion in your work, acquire more money, get better grades, improve health, or attract and keep loving relationships.

The purpose of this book is to inspire you to find your highest truth within, to actualize your potential, and then share it with the human family as unity in community – to enlighten others, to love yourself, and to love all beings.

When people ask me, "What is it that you do, it is so inspiring? What is your path?" I simply share, "I am on a LightHeart Path™ – the path of Love. To be Love. To live in Love." Morphing your life puts you on a LightHeart Path™ – knowing all is LOVE.

It's okay to smile right now. You might feel relief that transformation and unconditional Happiness is possible, and you are embarking on a unique and fascinating journey. Using the tools and focusing on the guidelines in this book, you can Morph a quality of life for your family, friends, and community beginning with YOUR willingness to explore and BE YOURSELF. The One you have been seeking, your true nature connected with universal intelligence – filled with HArmony and HAppiness – **a LightHeart Path™ of wisdom to BE Real, Laugh and Love.**

NOW is your time.

Merrie Lynn Ross

PART I

The Big Picture

"Who said you weren't perfect? Time to perceive all of YOU…Reach into the core of your being….Roam in that greatness, in that Perfection. YOU - reflecting all you think, say, and do. "

CHAPTER 1

HOW TO GET TO THE PROMISED LAND

While crying, broken-hearted over the insurmountable loss of my son, I asked myself, "What counts most to make this a life worth living?" First, I realized that we need a belief, an internal connection, whether we call it God, a higher power, or the divine source. Second, I realized that no one is an island, and we need a support system: family, friends, and cohorts. We can flourish by tuning into that higher source and staying open to the support and love from others, while returning the same.

Creating quantum life-changes entails cutting to the truth, facing it square on, and shifting our perception. We begin with ourselves, and then we SPIRAL outward into our greater spheres of influence (family, friends, co-workers, community). Morphing doesn't stop with us. **Any forward step we take, any change we make, creates an impact on others and influences events and our life's destiny**. The intent of Morphing is to increase our awareness and take responsibility for that impact.

But first, how do you change YOUR life? Do you want to change it? Or is it changing in spite of you? Change is scary, inevitable, with no guarantees. It means letting go of what was, surrendering to what is, and embracing what could be. Maybe you're caught up in "all talk and no Action." Some people are satisfied to complain about their miserable existence, lousy job, or annoying spouse, yet won't do anything real to change their misery.

Consider these two themes: Comfort-people would rather be comfortable – even to the point of suffocation. Change is usually uncomfortable. Routine-routine is comfortable, even if it is stagnant, depressing, and oppressive. However, if you are driven to change, create, or rock the boat, staying in a fixed situation is not a viable option.

Our journey starts with the first step.

Change One Thing – Change Everything

Roy, a talented businessperson, attended a Morph Group where he committed to "change one thing." He chose to Morph his work situation. Although he liked his job and excelled at it, he could not stand his boss's demeaning tactics. Initially, Roy had injected new blood into a staid organization, but his boss met the radical and creative ideas with either scorn or sabotage.

Fed up with his boss's daily head hammering, Roy decided to look for a new job. Before bailing ship, he met with the company recruiter. Roy related, "I'm ineffectual working with this man. I'd fire him if I could." The recruiter questioned, "Fire your boss, how so? What are your strengths compared to his?"

Roy was candid. "I'm a people-person, and he's a number cruncher. This position needs a motivator – that's me." Reviewing Roy's strong track record and potential value to the company, the recruiter checked with upper management. He came back with a synchronistic, unique spin that matched Roy's idea. "Why don't we find *your boss* a new job? There just happens to be one he'd jump for," the recruiter suggested. And jump he did. Roy was then promoted to boss and accelerated in his "new" job.

The Morph was successful from the standpoint of making one change. One change often creates a trickle effect, spilling into other areas of our lives. Even if radical change may not be feasible due to tenure or a family situation, internal changes such as reframing your attitude and how you think about your job or changing your workspace environment in an office are small steps that can turn the face of misery into the smile of satisfaction.

Problem-solving is paramount in every aspect of life. As problem-solvers, we are trained in a limited linear fashion, embodied by algebra questions like, "Find X." We spend our lives looking for the X – the solution to the problem – when, in fact, life's challenges are complex, and each problem may have many possible solutions.

Morphing is a quantum leap exploration, an inventive possibility-transformer, engaging seemingly unsolvable problems. It bumps beyond the wall of *can't* – as in, "It can't be solved. I can't change it. We can't do anything about it." – into the realms of, "Why not? What can I learn from this? Let's go for it!"

Change Perception

How we perceive something becomes our belief system. We operate out of this belief system, proving it over-and-over to be true, creating our reality and circumstance. Our skewed perceptions are rooted in emotional circumstances that were erroneously formed in childhood, perpetrated by family dynamics or hypnotic societal influences. This entire book is filled with doable steps, techniques, and tools to alter those misperceptions – to see anew – reinventing the life you choose to live.

Parallel Universe Trek

Imagine looking at yourself from the moon, a tiny speck at best. With all your challenges, envision a parallel universe where you are totally free of your concerns.

♥ To feel the effect, stand up, experiencing being locked in your current issue or dilemma. Feel the emotions, frustration, and limitations.

♥ With the intent to drop all concerns, enter the parallel universe of happiness and inner freedom by taking a step forward, back, or sideways. Leave the old Self behind. Bring the best of you along.

♥ Do you feel a shift, a tingling sensation, or lightness? In this new self-awareness, the challenge is not about controlling everything. The best of you naturally thrives. You are free to do what you love – your health is great, your relationships are fulfilling, you are peaceful, and you're functioning at an optimum level.

Shift in perspective is the change. When you feel life is a choking constraint, take a Parallel Universe Trek and blow out stagnant trappings. Jump into the NEW YOU.

The Power of Belief

Many philosophies agree that a positive attitude can heal an illness or radically change one's life. The challenge is staying anchored and consistent in that affirmative belief. Our subconscious psyche can overpower our conscious awareness by flooding it with doubt and negativity. It's an insidious process that overtakes the best of us. Morphing offers a strategy to break this chain of *thought failure*, which is simply a lag or block in the belief system.

Lindsay, an attractive, middle-aged art consultant, baffled her friends when it came to her love life. She married young, had a child a year later, and realized early on that her husband was irresponsible and immature, rather than an equal partner. Lindsay's rock bottom belief was, "Nobody in my family gets divorced." Ironically, her parents had divorced, wreaking HAvoc in her childhood. She declared, "My heart broke in two and I vowed never to do it. "

Finally, when her daughter was seven, Lindsay and her husband separated. For the next five years, Lindsay made no move to divorce. "I've been stuck in emotional turmoil, holding on to 'not wanting my family to fail '. Virtually single, I act like a married woman. I've gained weight, not caring if I'm desirable to men. Even though I'm alone, I'm really not alone or available, as long as we aren't divorced."

Examining her chronic procrastinations one by one, none of her lame excuses held up in the Morphing mirror. Faced with the daunting power of incremental fear – one fear feeds another – she viewed her excuses: "I'm afraid to be alone," "I'm a failure," "My protective barriers thwart a new relationship." Lindsay made a commitment. "I can't wait another precious second 'getting ready' to end my so-called marriage. The outer legal work for the divorce seemed overwhelming until she did the internal work – superimposing a solution over a problem.

Lindsay took the first step by calling a good lawyer, and from that all else followed. The divorce was settled amicably. Afterwards, she claimed, "I'm more energetic than I've been in years. I've lost weight and feel free and light." Soon, other areas of her life were moving forward. Lindsay aligned belief to Action, while uncovering and removing the sabotaging twin forces of doubt and delusion. Stretching limiting beliefs shifted her awareness into a more enlightened state, allowing her to flow and embrace the unexpected.

Commitment

Commitment is a key ingredient in growth; it activates progress. You commit to engage and explore a serious issue in your life, in your world, to come up with solutions to put into Action.

In India, Brahmin priests begin their sacred fire ritual, *yagna*, by rubbing two sticks together. (This practice is also rooted in other cultures such as Native American, and African spiritual traditions.) The friction of two sticks rubbing together creates energy, and this energy is expressed (or released) in fire. Delving deeply into the nature of your challenges creates a friction that releases that fiery energy, and awakens the inner kernel to promote change.

Your commitment is this fire in potential form. It helps you stay the course, to keep experimenting with solutions until you find one or creative multiples that fit.

I have worked in 102-degree temperatures shooting one hundred pages of a script in a day on *General Hospital* because that's what was required, and I vowed, "The show must go on." Crazy as it was to attempt completing the day, my work ethic and sense of responsibility chose no other option – not even to faint. I remember using every bit of energy to read the teleprompter, which ordinarily violated my acting creed. Would I do that everyday? Absolutely not. Yet, as a pro, I spun on a dime of flexibility. I got through it. That was my standard, my surrender, my let-go. Where do you draw the line on staying the course? What is your let-go? What limits do you impose on giving 100%? What expectations do you allow yourself and others to impose on you?

Intention – The Core Energy that Motivates Action

Intention is the root of all Action, words, and deeds. Intention vibrates in the subtle energy or messages we send to others. **Intention (conscious or unconscious) affects each moment of our lives and creates our destiny** – from tying our shoes, to being faithful in a relationship, to living a noble life. All these are the products of our intention in Action. Examining why we do what we do, why we say what we say, why we are moved in one direction and not another, provides clues to our real motivation.

When making an intention, life lessons are often revealed. If you want more love in your life, an awareness of not being open to love may surface, showing how you push others away or close off. Or if you are seeking more success, you might encounter ways you self-sabotage and wither into unworthiness. Confronting the challenge and limitations makes a quantum shift and helps to actualize the intention.

Rather than reserving good intentions for a New Year's resolution that will be forgotten in a week, honor a daily contemplation. Speaking your intention into being, writing it down to be seen and reread, releases the power into the quantum field of intelligence to be fulfilled.

♥

Intention can shape how you view the beginning of the day, whether you expect a miserable time or a glorious adventure. Remember you choose your state of being – choose wisely.

♥ ♥ ♥

As the youngest, newbie member in "Women in Film," I was the recipient of a generous scholarship for USC film school from Tichi Wilkerson Miles, founder of *The Hollywood Reporter*. After taking a few classes, I got the bug to produce a film. Not even knowing the full responsibilities of a producer, I began my quest. Finally, after hounding everyone, a filmmaker I worked with succumbed with a proposal, "You want to be a producer? That's easy – raise the money for my next movie."

Luckily, I hadn't heard all the nightmarish fundraising stories, so in my mind I held a vivid image of my name as producer on the screen. With a definitive "Yes," I had a clear intention to raise the money. I didn't know the *how* or the *who*, but I had *what* indelibly imprinted in my consciousness!

I put the word out to friends and business acquaintances. About thirty days later, a prominent lawyer invited me to lunch. He had a client with him who had recently sold a music company. He was bored and antsy for something new to do. With great enthusiasm I told him the movie plot, acted it out, he laughed a lot, and we agreed to be co-producers. It was a slam-dunk. The next day, in the Polo Lounge at the Beverly Hills Hotel, we signed our agreement in conjunction with the filmmaker, and the movie was funded. The rest is history; it launched my film-producing career. I learned how **a clearly defined intention promotes certainty and transforms short and**

long-range goals into results.

Intention gets your Attention, exacting a *stop-look point* that energizes the direction you are about to pursue. It's like shouting "Stop and look!" to a kid who is about to dash into the street; there is no hesitation. The target is clear-cut from start to finish.

♥ ♥ ♥

We held a Morphing seminar as the finale of the Girl Scout's executive annual retreat. I joined our trainers in the East Coast woodsy haven. Primed to expect the best of everyone, the day's events began in the great room of the lodge. For icebreakers, we ran a series of warm-up techniques. Within minutes it was obvious there were two reluctant participants. One was extremely rowdy and the other turned her back on me. Perceiving that their intent (for whatever reason) was to disrupt our efforts, I proceeded with, "Now, take a moment to ask 'what is my intention for coming here? What do I want to take home with me?' " Then I stated, "Our intention is to ignite your creative spirit with techniques you can replicate. What we want from you includes honoring your intention to be here. Second, we expect a mutual support from everyone and respect for our time spent together. Last, we expect a big can-do attitude from all of us, including me."

I invited the woman who had turned her back on me to state her intention. Surprisingly, she said, "I'm really disappointed. I came all the way from Atlanta and not one session delivered the arts and crafts they promised." I asked, "Are you good at art and crafts?" She laughed, "It's my specialty."

"Great," I said. "We need your help. The day wraps up with sharing artwork, skits, and music as a creative expression of what you learned. Can I count on you to help shepherd it?" Her face lit up, signaling a big "Yes." Then I added the kicker. "But we need your energy with us…it is very powerful. I need you to be present here. Is that a deal?" She agreed.

First, I heard her concern and need for creative input. Then, as it served the whole, I guided her back to her original intention to take innovative techniques back to the community. At the end of the day, the props she designed brought a theatrical flair to the group skits.

Themes vary with the individual needs in a group dynamic. Isn't it the variance, the blend of musical notes, which make a symphony magical? In the same way, having respect for differences in a group allows the unique blend to flow, inspire, and flourish.

Invoke Your Intention: Focus on a chosen area of your life – on a goal, a relationship, health, or a personal tendency. Ask yourself, "What is my intention?" Let the feeling and sensations arise. State aloud what comes to mind. What stands out? Write it down, as doing this integrates the physical aspect of mind/body/emotion and catapults your intention into the universal energy field.

Reflect on your Intentions/Goals/Progress: This practice deepens your CONVICTION. Conviction breeds passion and steadies your goal's pathway. Clarity is a focus device to engage your energy field 100%. When that awareness is triggered, energy aligns and opportunities can surface with synchronicity to attract what you've intended. Conviction helps us all to KOKO (keep on keeping on).

Creative Spunkiness

Creativity springs forth in every step. No two times up at bat are the same. The curve of the pitched ball is different each time. In that nuance, creativity lives in each moment. Do you know how creative you truly are? Appreciate your creative supermarket budgeting, getting the most for your buck. Relish your soaring glee at the sight of squirrels chasing each other up a tree. Notice the playfulness while rubbing styling gel into a coif, rejoice when you have taken the short path to Rome and still pleased the boss.

Let's get down to the nitty-gritty of creativity. Creativity is a way of life, a way of being, flowing, and responding. The spontaneity of a creative spirit connects, touches, and inspires others. It generates revolutionary ideas, inventions, and solutions that erupt like geysers one after another. Morphing is a spigot opening the natural flow of your creative process.

Enlist to be a maverick of creative living: your response must penetrate thickheaded thinking – yours, your family's, friends', colleagues', or your boss's. Stop convincing yourself that you are not the "creative" type. You were a kid; you played in the mud, sloshed out sandcastles, or concocted unique ways to cheat on a test. So, how about owning-up to, "I am Creative." Each of us is prone to dry spells, funks, physical challenges, boredom. When creativity seems beyond your reach, ask yourself, "If I am not creative inside, how do my cells multiply, how do I magically wake up in the morning, how did I learn anything from tying my shoes to twirling a baton or riding a bike?" Practice, repetition, and rote learning, are part of the mix, but creativity is your special way of doing something.

Playing your life-song belts out joy for a fun-filled life. Your special way can be blessed with humor, enthusiasm, and spunkiness. Bring on the imagination, the creative One inside of YOU. Listen to the calling – on the wind of your breath... Breathe in the creative wonder – all inside and outside bursting forth.

Illumination: the AHA! Wild Card

Illumination – the AHA! – can occur at any step in the Morphing Process. *AHA!* is an instant breakthrough, a transcendental moment when your perspective shifts, transforms, and penetrates your fixed notions, opening up the realm of possibility, eliminating the do-or-die, stuck-forever syndrome, or the fear that "This will never pass."

The AHA! awareness frees our feelings of bondage and issue-trappings. Even before the circumstance changes we can envision a state of well-being. Our altered attitude is accompanied by the feeling that we "will be all right" no matter what the outcome. The cognition, the light bulb, turns on in your head. It may turn on gradually, as a flickering of information, or it can happen in a nanosecond as a burst of light, with the overview apparently all in place.

The exhilaration that accompanies discovery is the Mother of Invention, manifesting the magical. Experiencing the AHA! moment elicits, "I Got It! That's It! I never saw it that way before." **The AHA! serves as a catalyst, a pivotal aspect of the whole. It gets to the instant truth. Doubts cease. Clarity of purpose is aligned with right Action.** With newfound awareness, creative insight prompts distinct changes in brain activity that is not found in normal problem-solving. Your purpose and direction, your decisions and solutions for change infiltrate the practical and spiritual aspects of your life. AHAs can fly you to the moon, and there are others that tweak your consciousness – or keep you on the edge of discovery.

Getting "IT"

As a soul-searching young writer, pursuing the mysterious "Who am I? Why am I here?" I wrote and produced a comedic play, *Getting It*, filled with hilarious AHA! moments. We landed rave reviews, and I was compared with Neil Simon at his cutest, with a Frank Capra pace. The lead character, Diane, my alter ego, whether popping bubbles in a bath or enraptured in a sensual French kiss, viewed AHA! heart connectors as life's turnkey, merrily exclaiming, "I got it!" Then, upon a knockdown (her boyfriend cheating, her deceased grandfather screeching disclaimers from his urn), she tumbled into a momentary abyss – trying to off herself in the commode. Seduced by another AHA! she rallied, chasing life's illusive "IT."

On closing night, the cast took a final bow. Through the applause, I heard an elderly woman commenting, "That's the funniest play I ever saw." Her friend answered, "I laughed my head off, but what the heck was it about?"

"Right on," I thought. Explaining life's meaning in one snapshot is tough. I sure couldn't. Some AHAs are connectors to our true nature, a connection with the infinite. For me, writing *Getting It* was a cog in the wheel of self-discovery, exploring truth's revelation, and playing in the NOW.

CHAPTER 2

7-STEP MORPH 4 LIFE

The Sky's the limit…until you're on the Milky Way. Create from your truth; dive into to the freedom zone. Dump the trash. Jumpstart your personal quest with the 7-Step Morph.

We use the 7-Step Morph to solve any pressing issue or concern, from the practical to the sublime, to determine options, and illuminate your visions and goals. It wiretaps both your *imagination and unconscious* (right brain), and *analytical or conscious* (left-brain) to problem-solve your query. Creative solution finding ignites ongoing success and resolve.

Don't fret if you are slow or clumsy and trip on steps – take one at a time. If you usually skip up steps two or three at once, leap on to the next. There is no right or wrong way. You are the dealer of your deck of opportunity. It's your game. Play alone, with a buddy, or a support group.

Step 1. DREAMSTORMING
(Discovering your issues, visions, goals.)

Step 2. INFORMATION GATHERING
(Learning more about your challenge, dream, and goal.)

Step 3. CONTEMPLATE
(Going deeper.)

Step 4. INCUBATE
(Entering the Heart of the issue.)

Step 5. MORPH SOUL-U-TION
(Discovering the answer.)

Step 6. ACTION
(You're Morphing.)

Step 7. EVALUATE-APPRECIATE
(Patting yourself on the back.)

STEP 1: DREAMSTORMING – A FUN AND CREATIVE PROCESS

Dreamstorming opens your imagination to unlimited possibilities. You can Dreamstorm future goals, identify issues or problems, and discover the underlying truth or root essence of *what* to change. It prompts positive expectations – an "anything is possible" mind-set.

Dream connotes uncensored visual images, symbols, and metaphoric impressions. Unexpected ideas pop out, expanding your everyday understanding.

Storming refers to an accelerated energy that increases idea flow-speed. It can burst forth like an explosion, blasting all you need to know about your predicament.

Dreamstorming taps your unconscious from the wildest to the most practical aspects of an issue. It opens a portal of creativity where genius resides, enhancing intuition, and heightening perceptions.

Studies have shown that animals subjected to repeated shocks without any hope of blocking them will develop learned helplessness. (Helpless and hopeless feelings are a basic textbook definition of depression.) In the same way, we can learn to be optimistic and hopeful through Dreamstorming, by increasing our faith in possibility and creating hope and well-being. It really is that simple.

People preparing to watch a funny video, an obviously pleasurable experience, were found to have lower stress hormones and stronger immunity before they watched the video. This reaction indicates that even anticipating a positive event can be health-enhancing. Because Dreamstorming anticipates a change for the better, the very process of engaging in this activity begins to relieve stress around the issue, triggering a shift in perception.

Dreamstorming is much more than coming up with ideas. It's an Act to take responsibility for engaging an issue:

♥ It promotes courage. We risk that our idea might not be workable or ideal in an effort to arrive at one that is.

♥ It's an exercise in faith. We hold a vision for arriving at a solution.

♥ It's an exercise in detachment; not being "right," perfect, or attached to an outcome. We are participating in a discovery process.

♥ It elicits generosity, giving ideas freely without judging "good," "bad" or "mediocre". A simple idea might prove a most valuable solution, and the most obvious path could lead nowhere. A slight twist on a failed idea can translate into success.

Why Dreamstorm?

You may not know your issue until you say it. Your mind is a jumble of ideas like a drawer stuffed with clothes. The thing to do is to dump out the contents to see what's inside. One idea stimulates another. A so-so idea can give birth to an innervated one, and an old, tired idea can generate a new one.

Come up with ideas, impressions, wishes, problems, and issues. Dump your mind's contents, allowing the unexpected to pop-out. Bounce Ideas off the Wall, and let them sail all around you. Open up the sky and let it rain ideas. Shout out whatever comes into your mind. Take risks. Think the unthinkable. Find humor in the absurd. Dreamstorming is like swimming. You can stand around the pool practicing every stroke and kick, learning every rule of water safety, but if you don't jump in the water, you'll never swim – so dive in.

Dreamstorm Guidelines

DREAM BIG. Let your imagination fly and flow. It's cornuco-pia time. Hold off evaluating the ideas' worth. No censoring. Don't judge, even if you think the issue is unchangeable, hopeless, or weird. Look at current challenges in your life, or your life-dreams. Write everything that comes to mind.

Review your list. Is it the obvious or too "off the wall"? A private fear? Something too Great to dream about? Go with your first impression, and select the ones most important to you. Pick one or two issues to Morph.

STEP 2: INFORMATION GATHERING

Start with yourself. Explore personal knowledge, feelings, opinions, biases, and personal experiences about your issue. Asking a variety of questions stimulates a productive energy that leads to exploring more compelling questions and ideas.

What is the most pressing issue in your life NOW?

Focusing on the issue can bring up frustration, fears, pain, sadness, joy, confusion, exhilaration, and a variety of impressions. "Listen to Your Own Voice." Getting in touch with our inner voice expands and directs our consciousness toward Morphing our goal or problem. Be free of justifying or explaining yourself to yourself or anyone else. Anticipate the best.

Create a safe environment for your intimate exploration. Whether indoors or under a wish-fulfilling tree, remember that you are with your best friend – You.

Allow, trust. Tune-in. Breathe deeply. Then ASK Yourself:

♥ What does my challenge, goal, or issue mean to me? Why is it important?

♥ How can I better understand it or gain clarity to change it?

♥ What do I already know about it?

♥ What do I need to know, learn, or do to Morph it?

Sit quietly, write down thoughts, and let them flow without editing.

Additional Information Sources

♥ Consult friends, experts, and mentors regarding their knowledge or experience.

♥ Utilize knowledge systems: the Internet, library, books, magazines, articles.

♥ Role-play with a partner or group. Improvisation fosters a deeper relationship and understanding of the issue. Let the intuitive/ right brain create images, symbols, feelings, sounds and sensory awareness. Look for symbols to activate your imagination – accessing information in surprisingly accurate and wonderful ways.

♥ The information gathered will lead to solutions, Actions – a shift of your goal. At this stage, your logical mind wants to sort the diverse, random, and chaotic information to classify and prioritize. Ways to accomplish this are to ask, "What are the pros and cons? What is the upside, the downside?"

♥ Take the issue apart (or an aspect of it). Visualize it in your mind's eye. Is it a jigsaw puzzle that has missing pieces? A roadmap with detours?

♥ Look at the issue from every angle. Turn it upside down. Draw it.

STEP 3: CONTEMPLATE – GOING DEEPER

You have used your mind to come up with ideas. Let's go beyond the mind to a place deep inside yourself, your Heart Truth, where you can tap into the source of all inner knowledge and wisdom. Take some "alone-time." Listen to relaxing music.

Be open to Receive. Deep Breathe. Inhale deep, exhale long (two+ minutes).

Focus on issue, challenge.

ASK: God-self, higher power, infinite intelligence.

♥ What is it I need to know about the issue to expand my awareness?

♥ What garnered information will benefit others and me?

♥ What path will lead me to what I want?

TRUST: All you need to know is within you. Let whatever comes up, to come up.

KNOW: Whatever was revealed is perfect for now, although consciously you may not understand the message, or may think that you didn't receive one. Reflect on your experience. Write it in your journal.

STEP 4: INCUBATE – ENTERING THE HEART OF THE ISSUE

Digest facts, impressions, and feelings – all of the data discovered up to this point. Allow your subconscious mind to take over. During this stage, give your mind a rest, allowing the place where genius is born to percolate. Trust that innovative solutions are on the horizon; that the unforeseen, the hoped for, will be revealed.

Live life as usual. Have FUN! Laugh. Do what you love. Take a soak in a Jacuzzi. Play tennis. Learn to juggle. Remember – life is a hoot! Blow a whistle or make a sandcastle.

The timeframe for the incubation stage varies, depending on the nature and complexity of the issue. Your timeframe could be quick – overnight, or a weekend of down time (which often provides a more in-depth discovery of viable solutions).

STEP 5: SOUL-U-TION

Soul-u-tion expands our concept of potential positive solutions.

- ♥ Now is the time for convergent thinking: narrow down great ideas, prioritize possibilities. What is the most practical, doable, to provide results? Clarify, evaluate, or redefine options. How does this new awareness affect your options?

- ♥ Select the best one or two possible soul-u-tions.

What if you're not getting what you expected? The answer/solution may seem unattainable. It's like trying on a new suit of clothes. Don't judge its validity just yet. Wear the possibility for a day. Feeling blocked? Innovative tools throughout this book expand your INSIGHT and problem/solution-finding style.

STEP 6: TAKE ACTION – YOU'RE MORPHING

Now you are moving things forward, taking a step, a leap, or something in-between. Action is the final step, a concrete manifestation, moving a project forward. If your Action isn't working, fizzles, or backfires, select another option.

Overcome the fear of getting "right" results, "right" answers, doing it the "right" way. The trick is that there is more than one right answer, one solution or way of doing something. You're creating the skill of flexibility, opening to the unknown, the unexpected – the Morph.

It's OK to say, "I don't know how to do this." Action is an

adventure, an exploration, and a learning process that is as important as the result.

Agreements

Solidify your Commitment. Copy the following **Action Agreement.** Put it in a place where you will view it. Read it daily as a refresher and energy boost.

SELF-PERMISSION AND COMMITMENT
AGREEMENT TO TAKE ACTION:

I_____, give myself permission to take Action on_____ (issue). I commit to begin now_____ (date). Completion _____ (date/timeframe).

Add other elements. For example, create a support team or a buddy (to keep you accountable). If you choose to do it on your own, be patient with yourself by saying, "Know I know."

STEP 7: EVALUATE – APPRECIATE

What did you learn? What is working? What isn't? Get feedback. Fine-tune. Have gratitude for your learning. Acknowledgment is currency for future learning.

In addition to the 7-Step Morph, a viable tool to assist your journey is to create the following:

Life-Path Journal

This tool serves as a soul guide or reference point, a progress recorder, a listening ear, a creative outlet, and an invaluable accomplice for inner/outer growth. Journaling connects us with the intuitive, higher self. Years of writing in journals document the life shifts I've made. Witnessing the trials and tribulations from illusion, anger, hurts, and the misunderstandings, blocked knowing and living in truth. It's amazing how differently I perceive life today. I'm no longer hung-up or affected by old issues, for they have blossomed into a deeper understanding. I've become comfortable in my own skin.

- The key is to WRITE with the RIGHT BRAIN, without thinking or judging.

- When pondering an issue or a situation, write a question. Simply answer it by writing. The answers are often startling and profound.

- We can carry on a conversation with loved ones, even those who have passed on. We can forgive, heal, and treat the journal as a best friend or an oracle.

- Write down experiences and impressions you receive during meditation, night dreams, reflections, and contemplations.

- Include your Action Plan. Stretch your perspective and share it with a friend or group (or keep it private).

Journaling is spiritual and practical, serving as a record and revelation of your transformation process, providing heightened awareness of who you truly are. This is your magical journal ride, trip, and adventure.

Use it to explore your moods and attitudes, brainstorm a solution or Action. At the week's end, review what you've done and see what has changed. If you are stuck, switch from words to pictures or vice-versa. Use obstacles as opportunities to define the next step.

Heidi, an "on the move" entrepreneur, felt that writing was burdensome, and opted for an **Audio Journal**. Using a pocket-sized recorder, she was good to go, wherever and whenever.

Without editing, speak into a tape/digital recorder (or any device you use for recording). State questions, record impressions, and/or experiences. Don't judge how you sound or what you say. Allow YOU to speak YOU. Automatic speaking releases your intuitive voice.

If you're visually oriented, you may choose to make a "DVD Journal," a "Morph Your Life" reality show. Set up your video or camcorder, step into the frame and talk. Pick a specific issue or randomly speak (utilizing the "Audio Journal" technique above). Chunk it down into a doable timeframe – thirty-second tips or a one-minute realization. Watch it a few days later. Are there changes in your demeanor? What has expanded or contracted? What are you learning about you?

CHAPTER 3

THE "GO FOR IT" ACTION PLAN

The "Go for It" Action Plan is not an overwhelming step. In fact, taking Action is liberating. Remaining in *inaction* is the source of overwhelm. Just take your head out of the sand, or put your Action where your mouth is. One Action, whether it's having that bold conversation at work or confronting the reality of divorce, can unstick an entire belief system, kick-starting transformation. When a commitment is made ("I will change my job" or "I will go back to school"), although we can't predict the exact outcome, a positive shift will occur. Recognizing the demarcation point, the AHA!, activates and facilitates our process.

To a film and television actor the word *Action* literally means ACT. When the director shouts "Action!" the scene comes to life and the camera operator starts shooting. Although you've done your preparation, put on makeup and costume, if you don't show up when the director calls "Action!" none of that other stuff matters. If you freeze-up, muff your lines, or go crazy and start throwing props (and believe me, it wouldn't be the first time), you'll either be fired or the scene will end up on the cutting room floor.

♥ ♥ ♥

What challenges or adversities are you facing? I have hem-hawed by stalling or putting a vital issue on a back burner, but it doesn't disappear. When I reframe "difficulty as opportunity," I jump on the fast track to learn lessons, build character, and develop fortitude. Results are the sum-total of what and how we choose to participate and play the game. What qualities do winners have to achieve maximum results?

Cultivate Winning Qualities

♥ **Optimism/Positive Expectation:** Passion and the belief that you can accomplish your goal are vital. Optimists not only cope better with stress than pessimists do, they live longer!

♥ **Desire to Achieve:** Have a clear intention on why you want to reach this particular goal. Be mindful of this desire and keep its flame alive in your heart.

♥ **Patience:** Life has a natural rhythm, and events unfold in their own time. Some people call this "God's time." Don't confuse patience with inertia. Keep putting forth effort while waiting, trusting it to bear fruit.

♥ **Determination:** Set and reach your goals. Find your limits and exceed them.

♥ **Perseverance:** Hang in there. Don't get sidetracked from the goal.

♥ **Self-Discipline:** Refer to your Morph list daily. Rehearse your Action Plan. Change negative emotions and attitudes into positive affirmations.

♥ **Commitment:** Throw yourself into an Action – live it in the moment. Recommit daily. Share your commitment with others. Don't let anyone talk you out of or negate your goal. Believe in it 1000%.

♥ **Dependability:** Meet the goals you set for yourself. If you consistently fail to do so, maybe you are aiming too high. Set smaller, reasonable goals and meet them. Show up, remind yourself: "I can be counted on."

♥ **Integrity:** Keep your word, and if you have to change it, be willing to renegotiate it. Some people unethically say, "No matter what it takes." "The end justifies the means." Keep ethics in place. There is no stronger force than character. It precedes all you say and do, residing at the core of your Truth, reflecting who and what you truly are.

♥ **Self-Awareness:** When we are self-aware, we attune to doing our best. Know when you are shirking responsibilities or taking detrimental shortcuts. Awareness alerts us to make corrections, adjustments, and improvements. By deceiving ourselves or ignoring the consequences of our Actions, we'll pay the price later on. Self-awareness safeguards us from self-deception.

♥ **Humility:** Be willing to admit you are wrong. Give the opportunity for someone who is right to be right. Don't be afraid to say, "I don't know." Back it up with, "Let's find out."

♥ **Flexibility:** Keep an open mind; be creative and receptive. Learn from others, and use what you learn. Don't be stuck with one way to do it. Shift instantly into 'what is' true.

♥ **Resiliency:** Durable yet pliable. Long-haul, strong-minded to weather the perfect storm.

♥ **Consistency:** Walk your talk. Practice what you preach. Sometimes we start a project or noble intention with great enthusiasm, and then lose interest. Don't slacken. Rekindle your enthusiasm every day.

Morph Your Attitude
What's so Difficult about Taking Action?

"I can't take action." "I'm afraid of what will happen if I do." Sound familiar? If you feel stuck, the first Action is to Morph your perception of your capabilities – what you *think* you can do is a self-fulfilling prophecy from the get–go. Stanford University psychologist Albert Bandura calls this quality *perceived self-efficacy*. It's the I-think-I-can ability of *The Little Engine That Could*. This feeling has a powerful effect on people's ability to act.

Do you think you can take the next step? If you answered, "Yes," go ahead – take it. If not, why don't you think you can do it?

♥ Is it "too big" to change? If so, pick one smaller aspect to begin.

♥ Is it "too hard" to do alone? Get someone to help you. Have a friend rehearse the Action with you, especially if it involves another person. Play with various scenarios, such as how he/she might respond. Then go for it.

A confident attitude is a jumpstart to success. It's time to take Action and play your goal FORWARD.

Define your natural Action mode: Find an action word to describe a special quality (core essence) you have to offer others. My action word is *to inspire*; yours may be to teach, learn, contribute, create, feed, entertain or love. (Oops, *to love* is #1 for me.) Of course, we all have many action-abilities, but for this step, choose the main one. Your action word can change over time, from *dealmaker* to *dreammaker*, for example. The best action words focus on what you have to "give" more than what you want to "get." Contemplate your word when doubtful, losing focus, or for an inspirational boost.

Action Begets Action – The Ripple Effect

When you toss a pebble into a pond, the pebble skips across the water, creating ripples. Each ripple expands outward and causes more ripples. This ripple effect keeps spreading, crisscrossing, expanding in many directions.

Every Action you take generates a ripple effect, creating more results, more possibilities. Every new Action builds on that initial Action. Every reaction you have and everything everyone else does in response to your Action creates more ripples, attracting more opportunities for growth and change.

Bottom Line: Once an Action has begun, a cascade of events will follow.

In my own experience, the cycle of Action generated by taking a stand as a child advocate was filled with the exact amount of bountiful energy needed to do it. The initial undertaking was to design the

Morph Curriculum, supporting the mission "to bring arts and ethics" back into our schools.

It was my job to launch Morph Vision into Action with the first step: I had to take a stand and speak out. No one else could because it was in *my* head. I could brainstorm with colleagues, but ultimately I had to begin the process. It was a doable vision, and by holding it strong, the decision-making process sped up.

My commitment included bringing to the table my strengths and capabilities, while identifying and attracting the missing links. Recruiting the best talent and needed skills provided a leg-up and a trajectory for the planning process. This doesn't magically happen. It takes an Action Plan and clear goal: "Where are we now and where are we going?"

Action is Energy

Thought and Action, Action and Thought – both are energy. Thought is held within us, Action is energy externally directed and converted into results. **For creative energy to bear fruit beyond a lofty plan or dream, concretize it in the now with Action.**

We're constantly in Action, from small things like walking, driving, eating, and speaking, to complex actions such as work, family duties, and recreation. Before an Action can take place, we must have the intention for it to happen. Then we convert the thought or intention into results (because they are also energy).

One thought, one intention, one Action at a time. To walk across a room you must first have the intention to start at point A and end up at point B. You may have to walk around a couch and a table. Those Actions are simultaneously processing through your five senses at nanosecond rates of speed – a measureable form of energy.

By committing to an Action, a quantum energy field is initiated, igniting our conscious and unconscious awareness. Examine the energy expenditure needed to execute results.

Rehearse the Action

♥ What Action are you about to take? Does an emotional memory affect your approach?

♥ Focus on the details. Let the sequence of the Actions run through your mind as if watching a movie.

♥ Make it real. Focus on images, sounds, smells, or tastes. What feelings come up?

♥ What thoughts or beliefs permeate anticipating the Action?

♥ What is your energy level? Do you feel empowered or energized, drained or deflated, comfortable or strained?

♥ Are you over-efforting, or are you complacent?

♥ Are you confidently completing what is required? **How does completion feel?**

♥ Jot down the most vivid impressions, thoughts or feelings.

Is your strongest impression positive or negative? Transmute the negative by acknowledging it. Then create a positive affirmation, such as "I can do and have this NOW."

Morphing Energy Fields

Emanating a human jet stream, we can leave a 360-degree energy trail. Our thoughts, deeds, and intentions flow outward and affect outcomes and others in our path. Energy extends beyond the subtle and gross, whether it is meek or lambasting, subservient or dominant. **A one-hundred-pound physical weakling can stave off a four-hundred-pound crocodile by staring it down with the focused energy of intention — not backing off and remaining fearless.**

A mother of five said, "Each one of my kid's is different. Lucky for me one of them is an energy monster. He wears out the other four, giving me rest-up time."

Merrill enters a room and suddenly the computer jams, or the phone clicks out – electrical equipment of any kind short-circuits. Her energy field apparently zaps energy grids.

Matthew's gentle, calm energy enters a room and instantly everyone feels relaxed.

How does your energy affect your environment?

Where we focus our energy, we become one with it. Like a magnifying glass, what we focus on becomes larger, dominating our reality. We can invoke positive, negative, or neutral responses by focusing or rewiring our energy field, which holds the key to our Action. If we're scattered, our outward actions lose power.

Energy Grid – Fine-Tune It

Our thoughts, feelings and emotions evolve outward and inward as quantum particles in flux. These subtle particles have measurable frequencies and their effects range from regeneration (healing) to degeneration (disease). The energy frequencies of tension, stress, and resistance produce immune system weakening toxins, blocking life's natural flow. For good health and balancing a positive state of mind, let's release the toxic energies.

♥ Ask yourself what thoughts or events trigger toxic feelings (headaches, lethargy, short breath)?

♥ Focus on the toxic feeling independent of the thoughts or events that trigger it. Imagine the toxic feeling filling a giant ball, then shrink the ball. Hold it in your hand and continue to shrink it until everything in it has disappeared, dissolving all toxins.

♥ Focus on what you want. Visualize a new ball that is huge in size and fill it up with positive expectations and feelings. Feel a *light energy* permeating you. Sit on top of the ball – gaze around at the beautiful vistas of opportunity.

♥ Recycle your energy. List "Ways I Waste My Energy" and "Things I Could Do To Recycle It." Include excuses, complaints, procrastination, gossiping, etc. Include Actions to recycle energy productively to accomplish your goal. Stop excuses, complaints, procrastination, gossiping. This frees up energy accomplish your goal.

♥ Influence others by consciously extending your energy light field

Visualize a wheel (you are the center). Draw who and what you want to influence on each spoke. Extend your energy grid around the planet – see it reach out into the universe. Trust this connection is in place and the energy will flow to your designated point. Choose when, where, and to whom to send uplifting, healing, light energy. Let go and trust that the receiver, as they choose, will receive it.

One trick is to discern, "Where to put my energy?" I practice discrimination to choose the high road. Following my intuitive intelligence, I'm guided moment-to-moment. Swirling in life's drama, I'm capable to know what is best. Saint or no saint, no one gets out alive, so why not ask, "Will this Action bring me closer to God (highest good) or further away from God (lowest choice)?" **Make discrimination your companion. Intuit it. Know it. Walk with it. Keep in mind that "energy flows where attention goes."** It's essential to focus on what and where you want your energy to flow.

Power of Words

Words are powerful energy frequencies. The primordial sound AUM pierces our heart core, opening to all of existence. Once uttered, a word's frequency blasts into the cosmos.

♥ Mindfully choose words. Be Aware how words affect you and others. Kind words empower. Unkind words annihilate.

♥ Repeat 3 times out loud: Harmony, Peace, Laughter, Love.

♥ Repeat it silently like a mantra. How do you feel?

♥ Choose an Uplifting word: ' Happy' or Joy.' Repeat fast. Feel lighter? Honor the Power of your Words as a daily practice.

"Right Action"

Think like a woman of Action, act like a man of thought. No gender pun intended – it's simply cross-pollination, the yin-yang balance. We all contain both male and female energies and finding a balance can improve our lives, to make right choices and take right Actions.

What constitutes "right" Action varies from person to person, or situation to situation, but virtually all traditions agree that Right Action means a righteous path to follow in life. In Chinese philosophy, for example, it is called the *Tao*, or "the Way." In Sanskrit, it's *dharma*, and in Hebrew, it is *derech eretz* – literally, "The way of the land."

Right Action is done for the highest purpose, carrying out our duty with a pure intention to the full extent of our abilities. It means taking Action when needed and refraining from Action when necessary – performing whatever is right and proper according to the occasion. This does not suggest negating or ignoring obligations, work, parental responsibilities, paying bills, meetings, or work deadlines, nor does it mean blaming others (like your parents, boss, or bad luck) for your lot in life. It takes into consideration the ethical motivation behind all intentions, words, and thoughts – knowing you are 100% responsible for all of your Actions.

The same Action can be performed out of a multitude of motivations. Motivation colors how you perform it, including specific steps you choose to take. You may need to satisfy your ego, take revenge, one-up someone, or benefit others and improve a situation. Thus, the importance of examining your impetus for Action: *what* and *who* are you doing it for?

Others perceive your intentions and they can be inspired by your commitment, belief/faith, passion, or a good plan. Demonstrate desirable attributes and they will more readily follow you and support your goal. If you're having trepidations starting your Action or reaching your goal, reverse the negative and visualize a positive.

Some people make things happen, some people watch things happen, while others ask, "What happened?" Which one do you choose to be? Get plugged in. Without Action, ideas wither and die.

Action without Attachment

During the INCUBATE part of your Morph journey, you practiced letting go of *efforting* – and allowing the natural process to unfold. In yoga, this phenomenon is called *non-attachment* or *non-doership*. Non-doership doesn't mean to stop acting, but to act free from attachment, fear, and ego. Doership is an ego-based activity. I can attest that an overly inflated ego creates disharmony. Whenever I thought my feats were greater, more impressive than anyone else's, this thought backfired with a swig of humility. I learned, "We are but a drop in the ocean of grace."

Attachment also swings to the opposite pole of self-doubt or self-recrimination as in the "I'm not worthy," "I've failed" syndrome. Or we give too much weight to the opinions of others. We perform Actions for approval rather than self-satisfaction. I love the following sayings: "Go beyond praise and blame," and "Our enemy today could be our friend tomorrow, and our friend today could be our enemy tomorrow."

We won't please everyone in this world. Those dictating little voices in our heads – mother's, dad's, or society's – scream, "Do it this way, Fool, or I won't love you." **What are you giving up for**

approval? Your authenticity, power, or self-respect? How about becoming a renegade and doing things your way, taking your power and owning it?

When overly attached, you get in your own way, trip over your shoelaces, and self-sabotage. You can't control everything (as control freaks know), nor make everything perfect (as perfectionists have found out). Let go and see what happens.

Balancing between Action and non-doership, our best work blossoms. An art teacher told his 10th grade class, **"When you think, 'All my painting needs is one more thing,' stop! Stop before you ruin it."** A publisher told his editors, "You can always make it better. But if you never stop making it better, you won't produce anything." Perfectionism is one form of ego-based doership. So consumed with the work coming out a certain way, we never let it be.

Effective Action vs. Activity

In a virtual, fast-paced world, we view Action as activity and inaction as equivalent to failing. We keep busy, constantly in motion, but where are we going? In taking Action, be purposeful and intentional. Action isn't mere busy work or the antidote to depression or desperation, as in, "I'd better keep busy, or I'll bounce off the walls."

Performing Actions for the sake of keeping up, "If don't keep going I'll be left behind," or "I'll be lost, be too old, it'll be too late," is like treading water. Obviously, the purpose of treading water is to keep us from going under, but it doesn't propel us forward. Action is swimming.

I clean my home before I write because tidying-up prepares my writing brain. My friend cleans her house as avoidance. She scrubs the doorknobs and matches unmatched socks if she's having writer's block and is then forced to abandon her creative writing for a teaching assignment. Seven years later, she's still saddled with an unfinished manuscript – no closer to her goal. **Be mindful of your tendency to opt for *activity* over *Action*.**

List the areas where you spend time. Include work, family, caring for yourself and others, leisure activities, community service, etc. What percent do you give to each category? When multitasking, prioritize what needs to be completed first. Leaving tasks undone is like a hanging participle leading to stress and mounting pressure. Is there an area that is out of balance or one where you need more time?

Being mindful of your energy output and input (from others and situations) leads to time-mastery.

DO YOUR BEST. Whatever task you perform, be in the NOW. Totally immerse yourself in your career, your family, and all your activities. Remember the exhilaration you feel when totally immersed, whether touching your cooing baby or running the last mile (past the point of exhaustion), and enter into the *zone of oneness* with the activity. Becoming a witness to the activity rather than being the doer offers the freedom of nonattachment and a sense of play.

Making Time You Time Your Friend

Does your issue seem insurmountable to tackle, such as having a high-interest $20,000 credit card debt and being clueless how to pay it off so you ignore it, hoping it will go away? Of course, it won't.

When on overload or overwhelm, feeling blocked or hesitant about taking Action, give yourself a moment to regroup. Stretch or take a walk. I use a purse-size mini-massager. In a few minutes, it works miracles on my tense neck and shoulders. Then I'm good to go. **Create a habit to rejuvenate yourself and appreciate the revitalization.** You can take this time to rethink, get to the root of the matter, gain an overview and readjust, or bring an expert onboard.

The old saying, "If you want to get something done, ask a busy person," is true. Busy people have schedules and stick to timeframes for a particular project. They know how to expedite it, and if they commit to do it, they'll get it done. They prioritize, do the necessary tasks first and say "NO" when they are on overload and set boundaries for what they will or will not do.

What are your boundaries or off-limit areas? What will you not do that means a "NO" for you? Lending your car? Bailing out a friend or a family member's debts? Doing your kid's homework? If you do not have "NO" boundaries, make them and keep them, or remain prisoner of a resentful "Yes." I learned to say "No" by framing it around my needs, limits, and capacity. I say the truth: "I'm not doing that anymore." "It doesn't work for me – nothing to do with you."

Time is elusive. Are you caught-up in time compression, where stress lives?

Each second counts, multiplying, making time a most valuable asset. **Make time your friend. Don't waste it. Time is one**

commodity we can't buy back.

What is your time tally? Are you sleep-deprived or sleeping too much to avoid activities? During a "global promotion" of a film, not having a day off in a month, I hit burnout. Lying in a hotel bed with a raging fever I realized, "I'm human!" It doesn't matter if you're Donald Trump or Beyoncé, burnout can gobble you up without hesitation. For optimum health in a fast-paced life, I needed time off – just to BE.

Maximize time-management by being and doing things ON TIME. Prioritize details, honor to-do lists, and get rid of clutter. To avoid rushing and getting sloppy, create a doable timeframe. Strategize an optimum method to do the job. A great example is when Abe Lincoln was asked, "How much time would it take you to chop down a tree?" Lincoln replied, "I'd spend ninety-percent of my time sharpening the axe, and the other ten-percent hacking the tree."

"Actions speak louder than words." Great ideas or a glut of information are useless and don't change anything, until they are put into Action. What incompletes do you have on projects that were started with good intentions and ended up just taking up headspace? This cycle weakens your potential in other areas. List your incomplete projects, either personal or with others, where you are slacking. Writing an *incomplete* on paper zips it out of your mind into physical reality: the Commitment zone.

Go For It Action Plan – Nuts & Bolts

The *Go For It* Action Plan is a blueprint for personal and community goals, as well as a template for business plans. For optimum success, begin with a positive expectation: "I will succeed at _____ by_____ (date)." Be specific. "I will raise $25,000 by the end of our first quarter." Make a habit to revisit and evaluate, improve or modify the strategy in your plan.

1. Write a Mission Statement

What is your purpose? What values are important to you? This applies to an individual, business, community organization, government agency – anyone and anything.

2. Ask Yourself Action Questions

Who? Who will take the Action, and who is going to benefit?

What? What Action are you going to take? What steps need to be made? With what activities are you involved? What are the obstacles that must be overcome?

When? When will you start? How much time will you offer? How often will you perform it? On a regular basis? Once-in-a-while? Or, is it a one-time act?

Where? Where will the Action be performed? If it's an event, where will it take place (what arrangements are necessary, financial and otherwise)?

How? How will you take Action? What limits will you need to place on the activity?

Why? Why are you doing it? What is your overall purpose?

3. Set Your Goals

State the goal(s) of the Action. What's the Bottom Line? Take on a realistic goal. Example: *MerrieWay Community* commits to serve children by creating *Peace Smarts* – a 5-12 grade curriculum that teaches problem-solving and conflict resolution.

4. List Action Points – The Steps Needed to Meet Goal(s)

Prioritize your steps. What is needed first, second? (i.e., *Peace Smarts* Business Plan, sponsors, a website.) Break each Action into sub-steps. Chunk it down. Divide actions into smaller, manageable steps. (Write *"Peace Smarts"* Manual.) Ask yourself, "What do I need to do before I can take this step?"

5. Determine Needed Resources

List what you need and how to acquire it. Be specific. Don't write, "Money." Write *how much* money. You may need an office, equipment, a new phone, computer, tools, a post office box, a hairdo, new clothes, transportation, or childcare. Number your needs in order of priority. Then choose what must – and can – be done first, second, and third. Be creative about how you can get what you need. Example: You need an airline ticket but you can't afford it. Barter with a friend or client for Frequent Flyer miles. Find a fair exchange. Use readily available resources. **Resources become available when you have clarity, commitment, and vision.**

6. Assemble Your Support Team

List people who can help you. Pick successful experts with skills you lack. Give them a reason to support you – barter, help them. Different viewpoints, guidance, and feedback expand options and elicit creative insights for Action.

7. Create Your Goal Time-Line

Set a reasonable timeframe in which the goal can be completed. Prioritize time.

Ask yourself, "What needs to be done right now?" What support or resources would you need to do it sooner? How long will it take to gain that support? Pace yourself. Expanding too fast can backfire.

8. Evaluate Your Progress

Maintain your momentum. Ask yourself, "What have I accomplished? Where am I in the process? Am I over the major humps? What, if anything, could I do now to make things go faster, more smoothly, and ensure success?"

9. Stay on Track

Keep your eye on the ball. Read your Mission Statement and goals weekly. Ask yourself, "How is this working?" If energy scatters, do a focusing technique. Reviewing what the goal means to you helps to avoid burnout.

10. Keep the Ball Rolling

Every week, make a list of Action Points you need to take. Check off points as they are accomplished. Unfinished business rolls onto next week's list. Take three Action Steps daily, no matter how small. Multi-task whenever possible. The early bird may get the worm, but the persistent bird gets ten worms.

Follow up! Follow up! Follow up!

Don't wait for people to get back to you. Get back to them. It's your priority, not necessarily theirs. Caution: Don't be a pest or wait by the phone expecting the call.

Fill every gap. Tie-up loose ends. What knowledge, skills, or support do you need now? Play the "What If?" game: What if she didn't get my resume? What if it rains or snows the day of our event? What if we run out of food? Call or email to insure an important letter, fax, check, or invoice was received.

Shift gears when necessary. Renew your objective, priorities, and your plans.

How can you achieve the goal from this point? Don't let temporary setbacks get you down. Avoid being stuck on one Step or one decision. Prepare a Plan B. Challenges and setbacks come with the territory. Setbacks signal a wakeup call – a learning curve leading to alternatives, ultimately making you more self-reliant, re-energized, or doubly committed.

While viewing alternatives, choose a win-win for all concerned. Evaluate the risks versus the benefits: Ask yourself, "What am I risking by choosing one over the other? What am I gaining?" Celebrate completion of each Step. Give yourself a pat on the back. Now take this success into your next Step. Acknowledging one success leads to the next, building your confidence in the winner's circle.

Entitlement affirmation: *"I will achieve extraordinary and positive outcomes."*

You have now explored the 7-Step Morph and the *Go For It* Action Plan to set a framework to deal with vital issues. Remember: Results occur when you commit to what you want. Make a choice to take Action and move forward.

Now let's spiral outward, digging deeper, looking at life from the "inside-out" to the "outside-in." We'll explore ways to enhance intuition, use tools for communication, live life as an improv, and discern what matters most as we grasp a holistic approach to life.

CHAPTER 4

INVOKING TRUE PURPOSE – YOUR CALLING
Seek and Ye Shall Find

Your life *purpose* (your reason for living on this earth) is the internal guide that makes all you do have meaning. Our purpose may shift overtime, guiding new direction and unforeseen possibility. Many submerged passions or life purposes are not revealed dramatically. A subtle calling of the heart may be whispering. Can you hear it? Your willingness to be silent, to listen, and to hear your Inner Calling requires patience, steadfastness, and flexibility.

Ask yourself, "What is it I need to know about my purpose?" Pray or meditate for guidance…listen to what comes. Listen with your entire body. Pay attention to subtle sensations. The revelation of the unexpected can unfold in the form of a thought, in a friend's example, or delivered in a televised public service announcement. **Knowing your purpose makes your heart sing.** What do you love doing? What excites you? What brings on your passion?

For instance, my calling to "help uplift children" was a meeting of destiny seasoned with every skill garnered throughout my life. The culmination of past failures and successes became the foundation, expediting the launch and perpetuation of the *MerrieWay Community* and the creation of *Morph America* as a transformational curriculum.

My life's lessons were a preparation for the doors that were now opening.

View your skills and abilities. Can they be used to transform your life?

Action Point: Make a skill inventory list. One column indicates skills, talents, and personal strengths. The second column lists personal weak points and tendencies. Your skills may not be directly involved with your life purpose. Your heart may scream, "I want to become an incredible chef!" or "I need to serve mankind and help stop hunger," while your mind may rebel and attempt to talk you out of following a new frontier in your life. Override this limiting voice and continue to allow your heart to expand and speak to your deepest desires.

What is your definition of *winning* in this life? Is it to amass a fortune, get a good retirement pension, raise a healthy family, or become famous? Is winning being satisfied that you did your best, lived a righteous life, loved, respected, and honored yourself and others? Is it viewing others without judgments, witnessing their strife with compassion? Is it to have balance of mind, heart, and spirit teamed with outer success? Does it include having passion and zest and to Love What You Do?

Is passion long lost or not remembered? Now is the time to reclaim it, reshape it, refocus, and relish it. Passion is fueled by inspiration. It's not one big event – like the Olympics – that you are charged up about. It's born in the moment; listening to the bee buzzing, seeing a cloud dance, smelling a crimson flower, absorbing a child's giggle. Inspired juicy living connects passion with the life-force that springs forth in all you do. Allow your heart's passion out...why not? Life is expanding for you, as you.

Tips to Invoke Inspiration

Awareness: Check in. What is your inner state? Are you bored, in burnout, in a rut, stuck in a mind loop? Anticipating your good?

Stillness: Choose to meditate, quiet the mind. Allow the chatter to stop. Inhale freshness of being.

Listen to your inner voice whispering in the silence: The one that knows...the one that inspires.

Focus: on the good, what you love, what you aspire "to be".

Attention: Give yourself to the task at hand, fill moments with your presence, and be attentive.

Risk: Be the outrageous. Do the unexpected. Take a new path to Rome.

Appreciate: what's before you – other people, pets, a project, the air you breathe, the water you drink. All of life's bountiful treasures inspire every step you take.

The Calling Evolves

Like the universe expanding, so are we. Just when we feel we have it wired, the status quo bursts, exploding our concepts to smithereens. We can hold onto a tree branch in a raging storm until a strong wind annihilates our security anchor; then suddenly we are flying debris, which was a fair description of my inner state after hearing the words of my teacher Muktananda: "Give me the parents, and children are cared for."

I instantly flew into a tailspin after hearing those words. I love nurturing children. They are more truthful, more fun, more loving, totally in the moment, and downright smarter than most of us calculating adults. I realized that to serve the children I had to continue working on myself in order to understand them. While resisting and insisting I "wasn't ready," a cohort reminded me that the only constant is change; and I would grow into the challenge. So, with her help, I surrendered.

I took Ted Turner's advice, "Lead, follow, or get out of the way!" Guiding our *MerrieWay Community* team, we hit the drawing board, rethinking and revising our direction. Not everything was easy. It required personal courage to overcome obstacles and sidestep adversity.

Meeting the Adversary

In martial arts, a key tactic is to meet (resist) the opponent with their level of energy instead of using force. Whether your adversary is a fixed belief, a physical person, or general obstacles, identify it. Contemplating my reasons for not "feeling ready" to take Action, I identified my core resistance as feeling overwhelmed. I asked myself:

1. Does this calling seem unattainable? Am I worthy of taking on such a noble cause?

2. Who has done something similar? What traits does she or he have? I added, "I commit myself to adopt those traits, and use them until they're really mine."

3. What non-essential activities can I eliminate that are adding to my feelings of overwhelm?

Picture yourself meeting this adversary. If it's not a person, picture the situation. With full conviction, ask, "How can I meet and best deal with this adversary?" Stillness is where the answer is. Invite inspiration. An Action you need to take may surface. A shift in your awareness may take place (such as having realistic expectations in your relationships).

The Hero Within – Courage

Courage enables us to do the right thing in spite of adversity. Courage directs our attitude, our perspective, and even our moods. Courage empowers us to see what is present or available, rather than what is lacking. What does inner courage mean to you? Is it bravery, boldness, daring, risk-taking, being vulnerable? Ask yourself, "When have I felt inner courage? Where I have shown inner courage? Who do I consider courageous? Why?" Instead of seeking approval or a pat on the head, courage lets us see that our "bowl is full." Courage is the place where our heart and our character meet.

Dancing On a Mind-Mine with Your Hero/Heroine

To allow room within your heart and mind to hear your calling or Divine Purpose, it's important to understand how you operate. How do you handle a fear or challenge? Do you face it? Ignore it? Escape it? It's a natural impulse to want to run away from a problem or avoid it; however, as you become more adept at Morphing, it becomes easier to step up with positive solutions that previously eluded you. Self-effort overcomes fear and limitations, spurring ideas and providing courage.

What is going on in your life right now that calls for courage? You might feel like you are "dancing on a mind-mine" full of potentially explosive negative thoughts – this is when you need the fortitude of a hero to go on.

Envision Your Inner Hero

During one Morph session, everyone laughed when I shared my heroine vision: "Gee, I have a choice of a Munchkin or a fierce Goddess." Actually, both were perfect. Two different challenges were up for me: One involved my son taking a trip abroad with his buddies. I definitely needed the help of a Munchkin's light-heartedness to be heard and to help me relax about the trip. The second was a no-mess-around business contract that would fare well with fierce Goddess energy.

Perhaps your hero is a warrior, a strong Sumo wrestler, or a gentle, wise sage ready to take on and combat your limited beliefs.

♥ In your mind's eye, envision your helper, a comrade of spirit, doing battle to overcome your chosen negativity. See this hero in as much detail as you can. Does he/she tear it into shreds or just slowly squeeze the juice out of it, blast it to pieces or dissolve it with love?

♥ List three qualities you admire that could help Morph this situation. (Creativity, relentlessness, compassion.)

♥ What Actions would your hero take? Remember: this hero is a powerful part of you and knows what to do.

♥ Now visualize the challenge as a crafty cartoonish character (Joker or Catwoman from Batman. Imagine you are dueling them, leaping through hoops as you defeat their negativities.

♥ What did you hero teach you about transforming your situation? Becoming your own hero, you stand strong in the face of adversity, a person of courage!

Going the Distance

How can you pursue your passion while honoring life's responsibilities? Are you willing to exercise the commitment, tenacity, and self-initiative of a distant runner, or have Rocky Balboa's fortitude to hang in against all odds? How can you set priorities with a busy and demanding schedule? Do you juggle it all? Do you differentiate between mundane duties and Actions that support and bring you closer to a lifetime goal?

Change your perception about time use. Are you filling time with tedious activities rather than pursuing your life's passion? Cleaning out a closet for an hour seems useful, yet that same hour spent actualizing a dream is far more energizing, satisfying, empowering, and leads to your goal.

♥ ♥ ♥

"Don't give me an excuse. I wouldn't know what to do with it," Carol screeched when a job was not done. Would you prefer an enabler who agrees with your lame excuses, keeping you down-under and predictable? Do you use business or child-raising as an excuse for not taking a ski lesson or devising a business plan? Are you always saying, "It's impossible; I don't have time or money"? Do you rant the ultimate justifying excuse, "Whoever said 'nothing is impossible' obviously never tried slamming a revolving door shut." When you justify your life away, excuses bring gnawing guilt, lethargy, frustration, and a feeling of being out-of-sync. Ah! But, when you are in-sync and doing what you enjoy, you feel exhilarated and satisfied.

So I don't sabotage myself when writing; if I feel the urge to deviate, I make a deal with myself. Finish this section, and then bake brownies. The creative process requires incubation. I often garden for a change of pace. To recharge, I take a dip in the pool or treat myself to a luxurious bath…my basic think tank.

A cluttered mind seeps into all we do. Clear out the debris. Go within the Silence. Be Still and Know you are THAT. From that expansive space you can feel the tingling creative source that drives passion.

Reserve one hour a day for your dream or passion. Honor it; declare it as a Commitment. Prioritize chores and obligations. Operate over fear or procrastination, and go forward – take Action. Tune out fears that project into the future: "I might fail" and so on. Projections have nothing to do with NOW. Take Action TODAY. Today will take care of tomorrow.

Money – Money – Money

At seven years old, my millionaire mind began churning; I convinced my brother Bill, "If we ask everyone in the apartment building for a dime, we'll be rich." Climbing the stairs to the 5th floor, the dark hallways got a little scary. Gathering courage, we took a deep breath and rang a doorbell. A minute later, lurking from behind the door, an old man with a gruff voice taunted, "What are you wantin' from me?" Bill innocently answered, "Just a dime. We're getting rich." Shushing him, I grabbed his arm, and we scurried away like scarred rabbits. It was a minor setback, but I continued my serial solo-preneur track by selling greeting cards door-to-door. Maybe it was the banana curls, or my tenacity, but I made big sales totaling $128.00 at one dollar a box. Along the way, I realized I loved making the deal, doing my own thing, and money was a by-product. If you want to be rich, make your plan and work it. If you want to be richer, make sure you LOVE what you do. "Ka-ching" may be the sound that lights your fire!

Morph Magnets

"As you think, so it is. As you believe, so it is." Our belief is the power that magnetizes events in our lives. Whatever you are experiencing right now is that belief in Action, resulting as success or failure. All human Action (from the lowest to the highest) is a domino effect from what we hold true and focus on. Our smallest daily choices create our state of mind and destiny.

Our beliefs, thoughts, and erupting emotions spiral outward. As energy pockets, these thought-forms become our life's result: they boomerang from each of us, downloading a "collective" effect on the nature of society. The decline in the morality and fabric of our nation can be perceived by children less than 16 years of age – our Geiger counter – registering as nihilism ("What's the use, the future looks bleak…") and is demonstrated by violence, suicides, drug addiction, and a lack of respect for parents and others. These negative attitudes and actions beg the question, "What are we magnetizing as a society?" Why are we settling, perpetrating degradation, spiraling-down our human potential and spirit? Let's define a noble society as ONE that holds within it diversity – embracing ALL AS ONE. To choose uplifting and humane values is our responsibility and society's salvation.

Create a Morph Magnet

What values are important to you? What do you want to magnetize – a love-mate, joy, good health, prosperity, healthy relationships? What values would you like to magnetize for our society? A peace culture? Equality? What would uplift an energy trend for a new frequency reading on the Geiger counter? This energy starts with ONE and, like a magnet, attracts another and another and another. Hand in hand, heart on heart.

Know It – Grow It – Sow IT

Knowing you can have something you want, believing you can have it, and feeling entitled to it are keys to attaining spiritual and material abundance. The difference between wishing and hoping vs. knowing and believing is claiming certainty in a decision. Certainty is a clear vision, a thru-line to the goal. It's not mired in doubt, second-guessing, or fear that your plans won't happen. Feeling entitled claims your birthright to attain the most beneficial, highest results for yourself.

Acknowledge your right to this privilege. Hold the feeling of entitlement within you. Claim it! "I'm entitled to all abundance, both spiritual and material. When am I entitled? NOW!"

In many spiritual traditions, people pray and perform rituals to God, Goddesses of prosperity, or honor symbols like the Kabbalah's wish-fulfilling tree. A spiritual practice opens us to possibility beyond measure. We petition for specific outcomes; whether to heal, find a loving relationship, or create a better environment. **Aligning our self-will with grace is an act of trust in life's natural flow.** We willingly express gratitude for what we have received, even if it's not what we expected. Gratitude is an attitude, appreciating the simple gifts in our life. Take a moment to appreciate what you have NOW.

Are you waffling on a tightrope with doubts dominating? Bless everything you want and bless those who have it. Blessing removes doubt, envy, and negative beliefs we hold for personal attainment. **Blessing someone who "has what we want" sends positive energy outward (universally) and affects you as well as the people you are blessing.** Blessing a third party bypasses negativity: its powerful energy boomerangs back to YOU, the sender.

List the times when *what* you wanted happened. Were you positive?

Was there a knowing and certainty that somehow you would attain your goal, even though you didn't know how? Feeling certain taps into and generates a quantum energy field of possibility. Ideas flow and inspire, increased focus delivers synchronistic events, the right resources and helpful people show up.

Look into your heart and DREAM. What was your most vivid, exhilarating childhood moment? Was a fantasy fulfilled? Maybe you were older when a wish was realized. Take a moment to recall the experience. How did it make you feel? How do you feel recalling it now? Allow the feeling of abundance to fill you – carry it with you in daily actions.

What Do You Want Or Need?
What Is Your Secret Wish?

Imagine sitting on a giant Santa's knee and rattling off that wish list. Have the courage to pretend, to actualize your dreams. Put on your dream hat, hop into your dream machine, and allow your imagination to speak up. Great inventions (or a windfall of success) are spawned from a vivid vision.

♥ VISUALIZE what you want. Maybe it's a new hybrid car or a job promotion. Put the request in the NOW, as if you already have it. As if watching a movie, see yourself refueling the hybrid or cashing the check with your pay raise. Feel the joy of your attainment.

♥ Not everyone works on a visual level. You may think it or have a sensation. Feelings are powerful magnetizers. To visualize is to imagine, to see is to connect, and to feel is to sense.

♥ Visualizing can be generated by drawing a picture or a symbol. Practice visualizing (we think in pictures): See your front door. Where's the toothpaste? Where are your socks – in a drawer? When you thought of the image, did you picture it?

♥ Remember the key: imagine your objective as already happening. The act of simply writing down, "I have_____", energetically solidifies your dream in the physical universe.

♥ Feel certain about it while letting go of results. With positive expectation, the universe supplies the *how, what, when,* and *where.* The *when* can sometimes be a shocker – our dream project may be delayed, somehow blocked.

♥ Or it may not occur and this doesn't mean your efforts were a waste. View the experience as opportunity and ask, "What is the life lesson?" Receive the lesson as a gift, and then regroup.

♥ ♥ ♥

I was recently presented a Visionary Award for my body of work as a filmmaker. As I held the trophy in hand, gazing at the sea of faces in front of me, I had an epiphany. This audience and these young filmmakers were the highlight of my life vision – for they would carry the dream, the vision, forward. My gratitude speech spontaneously crescendoed, "Please do not lose your dreams, no matter what, no matter who. Don't listen to all the can'ts, the couldn'ts, what won't work. Listen to your heart, follow your vision. Then I paused, "This Visionary award is dedicated to my beloved son Byron, an inspiring, talented filmmaker, my greatest champion."

Watch What You Ask for – You May Just Get It

As a teen anchor for a local CBS TV station, I covered the Beatle's historical press conference in Detroit on their first American tour. The stodgy press foisted zinging questions at them. In response, the boys were charismatic and funny, bouncing witty quips off each other. Being the youngest reporter, I was last. Every imaginable question had been fielded, so I boldly made a statement, "Sounds like your music influence is Elvis and Motown." John grinned, "Now isn't she on to our sound." Paul jumped in, "Bring her right up here, she's the only one who gets us." Ringo chuckled and invited, "Yep, come sit on the stage during our concert." Truthfully, I had never heard of them before the interview and had only listened to a demo.

Alas, that night, there I was on stage right behind Ringo and his drum set. The Fab Four faced a mob of hormonally charged girls. After the first guitar strum, the screaming drowned out the music. Out of control, one girl leaped onto the stage, charging toward Ringo. A policewoman subdued her by wrestling her to the ground. With adrenaline soaring, kids were fainting in droves, carried off by security guards.

Adding to the mayhem, during our earlier TV interview, Ringo said he "loved and wanted jelly beans." As pounds of multi-color jelly beans smacked at us with stinging body blows, I ducked for cover and yelled at Ringo, "Watch what you ask for, you just got it."

From that moment, I knew the downside of asking for something and the importance of being clear on the terms of getting it: The *how, when* and *where* it would serve you best; *who* would give it to you and for *what* price?

I'll admit it – I still totally love jellybeans and Ringo.

PART II

Nitty Gritty

"In the midst of the storm, the winds are hallowing. Tree branches sway in seeming chaos. Through the dark clouds, a glimmer of sunlight bursts forth; revealing a rainbow. Knowing its promise, a bird chirps a Love song...
opening your heart to hear."

Bounce off the Walls Land on Your Feet

CHAPTER 5

HAVOC AND HASSLE BUSTERS

The Shackles that Bind

What do you want to be free of: pain, suffering, endless debt, a boring job, a poor relationship, or playing it safe? Imagine being free of these encumbrances. How would you feel? What would be different? What would you do differently? How would you treat other people? Lift out of your warped mindset and kick-butt out of HAvoc or HAssles. Stop end-of-the-world thinking.

Morph Road Blocks into Detours

The way to freedom and transformation has many paths. In life, there is no GPS directing you where you're going. The best of plans run amuck, bombarded with unexpected roadblocks, construction zones, mudslides, and dead-ends. Before opting for a detour, stop to examine the derailing roadblocks. This is key to actualize your potential.

Common roadblocks:
- "I hate change."
- "It won't work anyway. Why bother?"
- "They don't like me; I am never picked."

Common excuses:
- "The market's down."
- "Bad timing."
- "I don't know what I'm doing."
- "Who cares what I think? Nobody takes me seriously."

When we have negative expectations, we view challenges as black or white, good or bad, all or nothing. We harbor the self-defeating belief, "If I make one mistake, I'm a failure," rather than realistically viewing it as *one mistake*. An accumulation of rejection or failure leads to a negative filtering system, an uninspired attitude, and a tendency to over-generalize failure. But just because you feel it or believe it, doesn't mean it is true.

Stop forecasting negative results! "I can't handle this. It's going to be a disaster." Catastrophic thinking rejects positive possibilities. And if you feel responsible for something you can't control, tell yourself, "It's not real. It's all in my head." The mind is fickled; it wanders here and there, tricking you. Why give it power over your innate knowing? When feeling hijacked at every turn, rather than struggle, stop to listen! What's the message? Plug up doubts and trust you are on the right track.

♥ Red-flag it when a negative mindset is in play. Stop mislabeling yourself a loser, ineffective, undesirable, or inept. Stop doing

Bounce off the Walls Land on Your Feet

the same to others by blaming them out of frustration for their shortcomings. Stop comparing your performance or capability with someone else's. There are those who know their worth...and others who inflate or deflate it. True worth is the unseen magic in every breath we take.

♥ When approaching a detour, become aware when you are operating out of a *should* or *must, can't* or *don't like* mode. When these thoughts and attitudes crop up – say "NO" to *shoulds* and *musts*, and "YES" to *coulds* and *woulds*.

♥ A positive determination shifts the negative roadblock into a positive. **When you say *YES*, a tremendous power flows through. The infinite intelligence hears that *yes* and without judgment vibrates an outreaching flow, moving you toward the potential.**

♥ Bottom line: Overcome the assumption, "What I want is impossible because I don't know how to do it." Find out. Research. Don't take "no" for an answer. Go around it. Pursue a more doable process to success. To overcome a roadblock, Morph it!

Truth Test

It's time to fess-up. Be truthful with yourself. No one else can advise you; no belief system is failsafe. The answers lie within your heart and soul. If it takes more than a few moments to determine the truth, you are over-thinking it. **An overly stimulated mind is a chatterbox of nonsensical dribble.** Let's trash mind dribble, so we can move forward in Truth.

Truth Test:

Check in with yourself to see if you're on the right track. Or discover an unconscious block – a lie you are telling yourself.

♥ Stand up. Say your name. "I am____." Does your body slightly lean forward or backward? By stating your real name, the direction you moved is your truth meter.

♥ Say a false name. "I am____." Did you move in the opposite direction? Test a couple of times to determine your truth measurement.

♥ Now ask a pertinent question of concern. "Is this the job I want?" "Am I operating out of scarcity, fear, or what?"

The art of being true to one's self liberates us so we can freely express our authentic, divine nature. Then we Act. We break free of our shackles and self-imposed bondage.

A Three-Piece Suit and Nowhere to Go

Marshall, 23, armored with a BA in business, took to the streets with all the promise of "America's Success Dream." Embarking on his job finding quest he hit the wall, only to be told, "Been a lot of downsizing." "You're over qualified." Within four months no job prospects were in sight; his suit was wearing thin along with his motivation and drive. Dependent on his family's assistance, he divulged his discouragement in a Morph session, "I lack what it takes. I don't have know-how or whatever you want to call it."

I asked him, "How do you start your day? What do you say to yourself?"

Marshall shrugged, "I don't say anything. I just get up."

"What you say to yourself, think to yourself or believe within yourself is the first know how for success. So when you wake up in the morning, go to the window and look out. Then Open your arms wide and give the world a big hug. Then ask your Higher Power, "How should we face the world today? Should we make this a good, happy day, or make this a bad or sad day?"

He grinned, "I can do that, but I still don't know what to do"

"You don't have to know everything." That's why you have all this inside of you. I tapped him on the heart. LET YOUR TRUTH OUT." Follow what pulls you, what leads you to clarity of your highest vision. I spoke to his inner greatness, reminding him what he had forgotten.

Marshall perked up. "Okay. I got that. I want to succeed. What else do I have to do?"

"Now that *you* are in place, you need to refine your success tools, meet experts, a mentor who leads to contacts. Be relentless, persevere.

Marshall met the challenge, "Have anyone in mind?"

"Depends on what you're going to do first thing in the morning."

He beamed, "I'm opening the window to all possibilities."

I assured him, "Know that you'll be giving yourself more than a breath of fresh air! You'll be breathing in the breath of life."

The pendulum shifted from giving-up to enthusiasm. Marshall's new quest launched, now equipped with a fresh perspective. This wasn't a simple pep talk. Encouraging a new way to perceive challenges, providing support, and giving someone (as well as yourself) the permission to DREAM is a gift – it can kick butt out of HAvoc and HAssles.

♥ ♥ ♥

Remember: You are a CREATIVE being and anything is possible. Walk on the wild-side, play in the rain. Drench yourself in possibility.

Window Streaming: Expand Perception

A window represents an opening – a transparent connection between two realities. Looking out a window creates anticipation, wonder, exhilaration or, in a few cases, anxiety. Keeping the window closed alludes to a protective veil from the unfamiliar or unknown. Opening the window allows fresh air to be absorbed, connecting the inner and outer world. Positive anticipation, an opening to growth and change, is at the core of Window Streaming.

♥

Imagine looking out of a window. Take a few deep breaths, connecting your inner and outer reality. Merge into the present moment. What is the feeling, vision, or sensation that arises? Name your window. Is it the window of opportunity, window of exploration, window into the past, window reclaiming lost hopes and dreams, or window into the future?

♥

Venture into the core of your window's offering. Open the window if it's closed, and climb out. Play with the sensations, tangibles, and opportunities that are displayed (feeling more lighthearted, going to Bali, getting that yacht). Imagine. Let newness engulf you. Let it ignite all the good you can see, have hoped for, and are entitled to.

♥

Window streaming fuels ideas when you feel stale, out of balance, or need another viewpoint; you find a deep message inside you, one that was overlooked.

Who Am I? A Noble Contemplation

Angelique compared herself with everyone – either superior or inferior at any given moment. Proud of her caustic sense of humor, she was clueless how intolerable the bantering one-upmanship could be. In time, she found herself without a social life and making major mistakes in her job. Chronically plagued with mood-swings she attributed to

PMS, suffering from exhaustion that was diagnosed as Epstein Barr (immune-deficiency disease), she sequestered herself as a shut-in.

During her unbearable time alone, Angelique mulled over, "What's the use? What's my purpose?" In one of her bouts of depression, she heard a wailing sound outside. Opening the door, a puppy surprisingly tried to jump into her arms. After a futile attempt to find its owner, she named it "Jumpers." Strolls in her neighborhood created newness through interactions with people who wanted to pet him. Angelique was smiling again, often belly laughing at Jumper's antics. These daily walks were incremental steps to building a new life, as Angelique was able to take her mind off herself. Gradually, the ME fixation expanded into WE. She explored work options and ways to improve her health. She found a natural-path treatment of vitamins, herbs, and deep-tissue massage. Her system slowly revitalized to optimum health.

Sometimes we grow numb to life as if we are the living dead – contemplating our death without fear, even welcoming it. This was part of Angelique's syndrome: she did not fear dying; she feared living life.

Spiritual Emergence – Wake-Up Call

A *spiritual emergence* is often taking place when we are consumed by "What's my purpose? How can I find it?" Internal festering can generate self-discovery: peeling off the ego layers of illusion, delusion, and self-sabotage.

Take heart when plummeting into a personal crisis, for it may trigger a spiritual emergence. You find yourself tumbling into the abyss, experiencing your day of reckoning. You feel like you are cracking up – but you are really opening up to waking up. Your self-image rips into shreds, all you stand for is challenged, and you cling on as a life chapter is ending. Halleluiah! This is the WAKEUP CALL, a connection to your soul's desire and the time to discover a new life chapter: your purpose for being here.

A noble tenet of self-inquiry is to ask and to contemplate these timeless questions. Great sages have said, "Keep your eye on your death and chant God's name." To know it is coming, perhaps in a second from now, can recharge the value of zestful living.

Luckiest Man in the World

The headline in the local newspaper read "Luckiest Man in the World." Racing down the double diamond course in Snow Valley, the teens skied off the designated trail. Byron, the last one down, accidentally veered off from the rest. Visibility was getting worse, a snowstorm was wailing. Byron shared his harrowing experience:

"I didn't have warm enough gear. I was in unfamiliar terrain. I knew I was in trouble. Nightfall was upon me and I prayed for strength and for what to do. Within moments, I stumbled next to a ridge. Like a movie flash, I saw myself digging a cave in the snow. Kicking into the snow pack, I began digging, digging deeper. I crawled into my hovel. Huddling inside, I prayed to God and all the great beings "please come and protect me." Suddenly I saw the cave's walls lighting in a golden glow...warming me. I saw a vision of great souls around me. I thought maybe I was dying, but I felt peaceful and calm. The beings stayed with me throughout the night. At dawn, I crawled out and began yelling for help. The ski patrol found me. And the miracle of miracles, it was below zero and I barely had any frostbite. No wonder they called me "the luckiest man in the world…who almost paid the ultimate price." I am more than lucky…I am touched by God's grace and love."

♥ ♥ ♥

Grace is the indescribable synchronicity that can appear in a time of great crisis. As major HAvoc sweeps through our life, a miracle can appear. It's likened to the wings of a dove in flight – one wing is self-effort, the other is grace, guiding our way.

Cut the Symbiotic Umbilical Cord

When a litter of puppies is born, each of their umbilical cords detaches from the mother. Instantly they become individualized, no longer appendages, although they continue to suckle the mother's milk. Does the mother believe that she is each one of her pups? Nudging the stronger pup, making room for the tinier ones to feed, does she think she herself is starving, or is she detached, honoring a maternal instinct to nourish her young?

Our attachments, ways we cling to or depend upon others, become energetic umbilical cords. Energetically connected we are unable to distinguish boundaries: we project ourselves onto others, erroneously believing the "other is I" and that "we are they" (an ego transference that differs from the spiritual connection of "there goes I"). Similarly, with material possessions or status through our work, it's easy to think that we are WHAT we HAVE or WHAT we DO.

♥

Reflect on someone in your life, past or present, to whom you feel emotionally or psychically attached. When they hurt, do you hurt? If they fail, do you fail? Does your happiness, well-being, or mood depend on theirs? Does their opinion of you count more than your opinion of yourself? Now is the time to contemplate positive *new agreements* with yourself, unleashing the cords that bind.

♥

Imagine cutting the attachment cord. See yourself do it. Bless the cord. In your mind's eye you may choose to bury it in a sacred place, or toss it out to sea, or toward the heavens. Feel the burden lift – setting you free.

♥

Ask yourself the same questions about your job, your position/ status in life. How deeply are you attached to the labels and images of yourself? Acknowledge, "I am not my job," or the titles attached to your name, and then cut the identity cords. Open, blossom into the new, delight in the unexpected and unforeseen.

Shedding the Past

Butterflies change shape during their lives – a complete metaMorphosis. The peacock butterfly lays her eggs on a nettle leaf, and a caterpillar hatches. While growing, it sheds several layers of skin. The caterpillar spins its cocoon, inside its body changes into goo, and finally emerges as a butterfly.

Humans shed one pound of skin per year, flaking off, often

unnoticeably, mixing in with house dust. Similarly, shedding skin or *peeling the onion layers* is what we do when we change our habits, attitudes, and behavior. It is the process of growth, leaving behind the old for the new to emerge. Ridding ourselves of what we don't need brings the surprise of a renewed spirit to our lives – our metaMorphosis.

♥   ♥   ♥

Past habits and addictions stand between our potential Greatness and us. Addictions fester as a real part of us – devouring and controlling our bodies and existence. Lost in a muddled maze, you carry on in delusion – seeking external distractions to fill the emptiness in your core.

To crush unsettled feelings, we self-medicate with sex, food, excessive partying, gambling, or overspending. We become super-moms (or dads), workaholics, adrenaline-rush shopaholics, or drug and alcohol abusers.

Chasing feel-good endorphins (serotonin) to fire you up – **Yes, passionately UP!** You're hooked on a Red Bull adrenaline charge akin to watching the last minutes of the NBA playoffs. Passion is a natural high – A powerful emotion, such as love (lustful sexual desire), joy, hatred, anger. Passion rouses boundless enthusiasm, all-consuming zeal for what we love, fuels fiery devotion for our ideals and strong beliefs.

Healthy Passion can be a 'helper's high' doing good for a cause, loving music and theater, to closing the deal. Or having passion in a relationship that initially keeps you tongue-tied, texting feverishly, or flaunting new lingerie. We often marry our passion-mate, only to discover after the honeymoon the hot flames fizzle to barely a simmer. Addicted to passion we crave sizzle NOW, a quick fix to keep the juicy arousal alive.

Unhealthy Passion – Power tripping, bitchin' and moanin', and testy abandonment are knee-jerk reactions to passion lost. Communication lines are down. Angered like a two-year-old wanting a cookie and getting a carrot instead, we want that sizzle. We want a trippy feeling, reeling out of the ordinary, dronish daily life.

We find dramatic outlets, cheating, sneaking around…the danger – the possibility of getting caught is risky and super-charged with energy. Living a double-dealer reality is worth the consequences, so we think; until the lies explode and crash burn our world. In pursuit of this enigmatic high we fire power-triggers, pushing a loved one to the cliff's hanging edge – threatening the big D – divorce. With adrenaline raging, passion fires up once again and make-up sex is often great.

Fixed beliefs and habits stunt us into a no-growth zone. Fear and denial run the show: "I don't have a problem." "Life's good; I'm okay with how I am." It's an excuse-filled, Russian-roulette mind-set before a meltdown or life-altering crisis takes place. Millions of addict-prone disaster stories haunt us: each one a devastation of a life destroyed, a life robbed of potential greatness.

Early Choices – Fixed Beliefs

- "I've always done it that way."
- "I could never change it."
- "The thought of it makes me sick."

Always and *never* are rigid rather than flowing reactions to possibilities. "Makes me…" is victim blaming – not owning the choice. Keep in mind that no one, no thing, makes us choose. We choose.

Our early decisions lead to fixed beliefs that we habitually act out. Operating in default, we don't give it a second thought. One decision leads to the next, and then we can't remember how we arrived where we are – doing what we're doing. What early choices may be blocking you from your goals? Recognize the interconnectedness of your past, present, and future. A great way to delve into your life lessons is to do a *LifeLine Challenge*.

The *LifeLine Challenge* is a clarifying device that highlights the through-line of your life's tapestry. Reviewing crucial demarcations, gleaning a clear picture of your past successes and failures, disappointments and joys, provides a launch point for self-discovery.

Draw a LifeLine from 0 to your present age. You may recall being in the womb. If not, dig into your memory for stories told to you by your parents and other family members from womb-time, birth, or early years. View your life on your mental screen. What are the key moments? Births, deaths, schools, jobs, honeymoon?

♥ Allow impressions and images to unfold. Go decade by decade. The big events will speak to you.

   1940 1950 1960 1970 1980 1990 2000 2010 2020

♥ Did one particular event or person stand out?

♥ Focus on the experience. Where are you? Who is there? What is being said? How are you feeling? Let the images that come up float by without holding on to them.

♥ Jot down feelings, sensations, or thoughts that come up.

♥ Reflect on the experience. How did your life change? What new beliefs did you develop? What decisions were made that you still hold to be true? *Are they true?*

♥ List what serves you. List what does not.

♥ Choose the most important decision that still runs your life that doesn't serve you. Next, pick the one that still serves you.

Use Morph Steps to help you dig deeper. View the issue you want to change. Select an Action Step or elicit Commitment to transform what is no longer serving you and/or reinforce what is serving you. Can you see how you have become you – the sum-total of the parts that equal who you have become? You have always been changing and Morphing.

In every life experience there is a lesson to be learned. Choose to see the benefit in the lesson – the upside, the character builder – no matter how difficult or earth-shattering the challenge.

My grandmother Lillian built several churches and integrated the first black and white church in Southern Illinois. It took courage to cross racial and ethnic lines. She was brave of heart and she loved with all that was in her.

Lillian gave me the greatest gift. She believed in me when I doubted or shamed myself. **To be empowered with self-worth it only takes one person to know your goodness, to sense your greatness of being and your innate capabilities, even before you know it yourself.** Grandmother was that person for me. Her wise words were, "You are dedicated to God's light, and no matter how far you stray in this life, you will come back to the light." Those words reverberate as a touchstone, providing an arsenal of comfort when I need it most. That is my thru-line.

Future LifeLine

The best way to project the future is to become it. Project yourself into your future. Where would you like to be? Imagine you have lived your life and are looking back on it. View it in vivid detail.

- ♥ What were your three most significant lessons?

- ♥ What would you change, and how would you change it?

- ♥ Take an issue you have been avoiding that requires changing.

- ♥ Project what your life would be like if you never made an effort to improve or Morph this issue.

- ♥ Project how your life would look if you chose to Morph it.

Draw a Lifeline from now to 20+ years in the future. Starting right now and moving forward, create the vision of how you want your life to be. Dictate milestones and demarcation points. How would they change your beliefs and reconstruct your attitudes and life choices right now? What new options would you have by utilizing this unique perspective?

After Byron's passing, creating a *Future LifeLine* seemed impossible to do. Yet, a part of me sensed that doing it would help lift me into another dimension. I will share the following because miracles happen when our multiple dimensional selves intertwine with faith.

Grass Looks Greener until You See a Miracle

At the beginning of January, Byron had been gone almost 10 months and this was my first new year without him. 2008 had ended; he was physically here in 2008. Now it was 2009, and he wouldn't be here physically.

Feeling unnerved projecting into the future, I needed a breather so I took a walk with Oscar and Emmy, my two shelties. Wanting a connection with Byron, I spoke to him from my heart's yearning. "Byron, what can I do without you?"

Deep within I heard a chuckle, "Mom, go up the hill, there's a surprise at the top." Filled with anticipation I started up the hill. A gust of strong wind seemed to push me back. Byron's voice asked, "What's the rush?" Then he prodded, "Look at the air." Not knowing what he meant, I looked ahead seeing only the hillside foliage. "Don't look through it. Really see it," he instructed. I focused, gazing in front of me. Suddenly, dancing light particles appeared, filtering the air space. It was as if bubbling molecules existed without form or shape. The air was alive! Caught in the swirling light show, my mind became completely still.

I continued the walk, relishing each step. When I reached the hilltop, as if on cue, a bird sang out and flew overhead. As it soared toward the heavens, a fluffy cloud formed into the shape of a heart, miraculously glowing in rainbow colors. In awe, I watched the rainbow cloud whisk into magical shapes, dancing hope in my heart. Wanting to share this miracle, I pulled my cell phone out of my pocket and called Byron's father and told him to drive quickly up the hill. He arrived in time to see the glorious sight. Together we shared a miracle of faith, a loving connection to our son.

Scientists may have an explanation for this phenomenon. No one

I know, including me, has seen a rainbow that wasn't arc-shaped or lateral. To witness a rainbow heart is pure magic. (A rainbow signifies God's Promise of Love.) Byron IS my heart angel infusing me with his enlivened spirit, a connection radiating infinite Love, healing, and HOPE.

HOPE ACRONYM:

H - HOLDING
O - OPTIMUM
P - POTENTIAL
E - ETERNALLY

My reality has traversed multi-dimensions — the miraculous connection with the spirit world as well as the grounded and participatory experience *here*, living out this incarnation as fully as intended. My fixed beliefs have expanded, softened inside, lifting the otherwise bound shackles of limitation. I have discovered truth is revealed when you are living it.

Contemplate the HOPE acronym: Write it in your journal.

CHAPTER 6

LIFE: THE BATTLE THAT MUST BE FOUGHT

Our particular deck of challenges reflects the type of warrior we become – maybe fearless or cowardly, a kamikaze or a pacifist. The *spirited warrior* works from the inside-out to overcome inner conflicts. The battle raging with negative thinking, rehashing old hurts and wishing harm on others is ultimately the battle we must win to have inner peace.

Donning the mask of well-being is a jump-start in the right direction. However, the toxic enemies of anger, jealousy, fear, greed, self-doubt, guilt, and self-recrimination must be dealt with as ardently as if you were in battle. The act of surrendering, or letting go of our negative tendencies, is the winning doorway for our beneficial attributes to thrive.

The ACT of SURRENDER is not passive. It does not mean you lie down in the face of adversity and let the truck roll over you, losing spirit or hope. It's an active energy, accepting, "What IS – IS," grasping the facts as they are. Accept "what you can change" and "what you cannot change".

True surrender is a release of what is not necessary: worry, procrastination, lethargy, unrealistic expectations, judgments, disappointments, avarice. This release provides psychic space to find clarity, decisiveness, peace of mind, and true purpose. If you are married, surrender to marriage by making it the best you can. If you are a student, surrender to homework, study for tests, and give your all. If your business is failing, surrender to reinventing or redesigning your product.

Living in denial about your reality makes surrendering to the truth scary and challenging. Recognition and ACCEPTANCE of where you are in life, rather than where you wish to be, launches a promising journey.

Plunging into Chaos and Misery

"Mom's flipping-out," the kids screamed as Lydia whacked the TV with a flying shoe. Lydia collapsed on the floor and paramedics arrived to find her babbling incoherently. The prognosis was lack of sleep, hypermania. The underling culprit was playing cards at home for a few dollars with friends had turned into all night sprees at a local gambling casino. Lydia was a high roller, a winner in her mind, unbeatable. Raising the stakes, she re-financed her house. The money was gone in less than a month. There was not a cent left for bills, or even food. A gambling addiction had taken over faster than a runaway train. The way back was a long haul for Lydia and her family.

Why wait until the wakeup call? Become a warrior and face self-sabotaging behavior NOW. Seek the help you need. Getting out of denial is the first step toward rehabilitation, recovery, and living your potential.

What is on your mind? What are you avoiding? Pangs in the heart, unresolved issues? To release, acknowledge what it is. Not sure? Tune inside, breathe deeply, and stay fixed on your breath. In the stillness, invite truth. Listen. Open. Trust. Go gentle with yourself. Allow the wall of sadness, disappointment, and blame to crumble. A door opens. A fresh understanding flourishes – a journey of hope and resolve. A LightHeart Path™.

Razor's Edge

It has been said, "If you're not living on the edge, you are taking up too much space."

What is "living on the edge"? Some might say it is, "Hanging by my fingernails from a thousand foot cliff," "Plunging into oblivion," or "Embracing joy and pain equally!" "No boundaries."

When a friend and I were horseback riding in New Mexico, instead of taking the trail home he opted for a shortcut, meandering straight down a rocky cliff. My teeth began chattering at a mere glance at the ominous terrain. Without giving me an option to turn back, he started the descent. My horse followed. On the horse's second step, barely able to keep his balance, he teetered, slipping a few inches. Wobbling, he planted his hoof and cautiously took the next step.

Terrified to make even the slightest move, I was barely breathing. It became obvious that to get down the cliff alive I had to trust the horse. Attempting to relax my body, I imagined being a ragdoll glued upon his back. In spite of feeling nauseous, I began a soothing chant, "So Hum."

Each step the horse took was calculated and eternally long. He was in full concentration, stretching what appeared to be his own limits. Slips of the hoof, teetering on tumbling rocks, he made remarkable steady recoveries. This death-defying trek took amazing courage. Let's face it; he sensed that I would chill rather than panic, saving us a tumble into oblivion.

The ride down the cliff was a lesson in trusting. Trust God (or a Higher Power) when it is out of our control. If I had risked dismounting and going it alone, my chances of reaching bottom were questionable. I had to rely on my horse and his belief in himself that he could get safely to the bottom.

"Living on the razor's edge" embraces all that happens to us as part of life's teachings. The *razor's edge* is a state of being which embraces both pain and joy with equanimity. To walk on this edge is tricky; one slip could feel as if you are being cut in two, torn between suffering and peace of mind. By releasing emotional attachments or the belief of "how things should be" and by releasing judgments toward others and ourselves, we can learn to live in equanimity. Our state of mind is likened to the calm in the eye of the storm.

Contemplate TRUST

Trust was born in a lightning storm. The ultimate test: who do you trust? A greater power, yourself, no one? Trusting infinite intelligence opens us to inspiration and greater insight. Our heart-truth guides a deep Knowing, beyond limited concepts, mind-chatter, and emotional wounds.

We grow in Trust: we see and feel the unseen. Wisdom unfolds how to BE, how to live in enlightened Awareness.

We learn to Trust our inner voice, our vision, and inner calling. Rooted in the miraculous daily events flow in HArmony. No longer bound by limited perception and resistance, our energy transforms – We are Free.

Most practically, trust comes from honoring and upholding ethical agreements. Trust is the opportunity "to do the right thing," but from whose perspective – yours or theirs? Do you clearly state ethical guidelines, or do you operate in the void of assumption (a set-up for disappointment)?

Contemplate the following questions regarding trust issues:

♥ What would it take for you to trust yourself? Honoring commitments, risking being wrong?

♥ What tendencies don't you trust? Lies, duplicity, cruelty, abusers?

♥ Which ones do you trust about yourself? Intuition? Honoring your feelings?

♥ What engenders trust in another person? Kindness, caring, truthfulness?

♥ What would change in your life if you lived in trust?

Opening up and becoming vulnerable often sends us into an anxious mode. Gripped by the fear of annihilation, we want to protect that intimate part of our self. Trust may have never been gained in childhood, or was broken by those we loved. The way back to trust is learn to trust yourself, your heart voice that is ever present within you. Open the floodgates of trust…watch the miracles flow.

Let Go – Let Life in Right Now

We want certainty about the outcome of events, when in life, the unknown, the unexpected moment, is the natural creative order. Success in any area of life requires flexibility and being open to change. It's common to feel incapable or on overwhelm as the change button clicks on. Julie, a Morph Group participant, nearly bolted out of the door at the mere thought of letting go. She squirmed upon hearing the opportunity to change is RIGHT NOW. "I feel anxious, pressured to do all these positive actions. Even though my life's like a foggy sleepwalk sometimes, I still have my whole life ahead of me."

I simply replied, "That you do. How long is it that you have to live?"

Julie looked at me with a dumbfounded expression. "No one can answer that."

Exactly! We can live our lives putting it off, waiting for certainty, waiting for a sign to engage – or we can jump in and live right NOW.

De-Sensitize Our Worst Fears

Half asleep, I was resting on a hillside in Ojai, California, listening to Krishnamurti, a spiritual teacher, speak to participants at a weekend retreat. His soothing voice resonated, "You create fear in your mind. It doesn't really exist." In an instant, I understood that our unrealistic, imagined fears range from ludicrous to life-crippling. Most of what we fear never happens. As our mind magnifies catastrophic and disastrous outcomes, we may feel immobilized or shake in our boots – waiting for the onslaught. Fear sabotages progress.

Let's consider the fear of driving in the rain. Moments before going out to a movie, you hear a weather report of a 50% chance of rain that night. Haunted by a previous fender-bender you had in the rain, your mind races into an accelerated exaggeration. "Oh no, it's too dangerous to drive in the rain. *What if* I get in an accident again, and it's my fault, and I'm sued over my insurance limit…I could lose everything. I'll be homeless." Then you erroneously conclude, "Forget it, I'll stay home. I won't risk driving in the rain." Remember the predicted 50% chance of rain? You stayed home, and it didn't rain that night after all.

Maybe you are magnifying the possibility (or ramifications) of losing your job, or that your investments will nose-dive to zero. Trapped in a worst-case scenario, negative projections sidetrack finding a solution. You cave-in rather than effectively respond to the event.

Imagined fears are not based on intuition, logic, or facts. They linger like a splinter and trigger emotional eruptions and behavioral arrests, like anxiety, procrastination, or inaction.

When fear overwhelms into mind-bending chaos, it's time to mind-dump our concerns.

Toning Practice. A healthy energy release through sound.

♥ Breathe deeply. Scan your body from head to toe. Stay aware of tightness, aches, tremors.

♥ Begin humming. Allow toning of high pitched (head)or guttural (belly) sounds to release pent-up emotion.

♥ Without force allow tears, laughter, angst to release on the out breath. Stay aware of the energy shift.

Another of my favorite recipes is Safety Net, a calming, energy release.

Safety Net

♥ Hold your hands up in front of you, palms facing each other, about a foot apart. If you are right-handed, put all your fears and concerns into that hand. Lefties will focus on their left hand. Keep sending thoughts and energies of your fears and woes until your hand begins to feel heavier.

♥ Now focus your energy on the opposite hand. Looking at the palm, say aloud, "I am safe. Nothing can hurt me. All is well." Repeat it three times.

♥ Close your eyes for a few seconds, sense the calm in your breath. Feel the shift in your body, mind, and spirit. You may feel lighter, clearer, at ease, balanced. Practice the Safety Net technique until you own it as a daily habit. Calming your breath may even save your life one day.

Break Through the Fear

The last words our camp instructor uttered as he hoisted the locked food container into the tree was, "No food in the tents, the bears can sniff it out." Byron and I tucked in for the night in our two-person tent and quickly fell asleep. Awakened by a thrust against my body through the canvas, I noticed a giant mound of a shadow outside, illuminated by the moonlight. "My God, it's a bear," I thought. My heart spiked in terror as I moaned to myself, "Oh no, there's a candy in my pocket." Grabbing it, I stuck it in my mouth – wrapper and all – swallowing it whole.

As I hyperventilated loud breaths, I was sure the bear would eat us alive. Byron remained asleep, and I decided the less noise from our tent, the better, so I chose not to wake him. Through my gulping gasps, a loud grunting noise within inches of us drowned me out. The bear was inhaling deep, slow diaphragmatic breaths, "Ahm...Ahm." As I listened to the rhythmic tone, my breath slowed down. Still leaning against me through the tent, this giant creature and I began to breathe in unison, "Ahm...Ahm." Eventually, despite the mental urge to stay awake, I fell into a peaceful slumber. The next morning I awakened, thinking the night's experience was just a dream.

As I shared the dream with Byron and the other campers, our instructor nodded, "Maybe it was, and maybe it wasn't. Let's check for tracks." Byron raced behind the tent and screeched, "It's real! Look! Giant bear tracks!" Grateful for the peaceful connection with the bear, I marveled how I breathed through my fear.

Fear Busters

Exaggerating Fear: Exaggerate the fear to the most ridiculous possibility. Let it grow large. Turn the fear into a giant Dough Boy or the Goodyear Blimp, until it becomes absurd, outrageous, or comical. Say to yourself, "That's ludicrous. THIS IS NOT REAL." Watch the fear dissolve. The fear of driving in the rain will simply ring the awareness bell to be cautious and to drive with care.

Shrinking Fear: Unlike denial, shrinking a fear minimizes its power over you. Imagine the fear is a spot on the wall. Instead of fearing that the spot will increase in size, wipe it off and watch it disappear.

Each fearful moment we encounter must be faced square on. We must go through it, one way or another – to come out the other side: dancing in the light with gratitude for our life. Focus on what can be gained by not having the fear. Imagine risks or consequences of operating in fear. FACE the fear and ACT in spite of it. Relax behind the thought, "What's to lose? – so much to gain." To BE one with fear and peace is an ultimate lesson. Counteract fear's illusion. Truth is your power.

Counteract the Excuse/Fear Syndrome

Recall a time in your past, when starting a project or learning a new skill, that your positive habits were able to overshadow obstacles. Was your curiosity and explorative nature engaged? Recall the learning curve with its setbacks and challenges in becoming proficient. Recall the personal satisfaction of completion, the exhilaration of going the distance.

Completion, finishing the task, is the name of the game. Remember this simple formula: When you want a hard-boiled egg, keep it in the pot until it's done. If you take it out too soon, it's soft-boiled; take it out even sooner and it's a drippy mush. In the same way the egg changes, so does reality. If it doesn't work the first time, do it again! Keep going past fear and excuses. Don't give up!

"Fearlessness" Is Just another Word for Nothing Left to Lose

As mortals we know we're trapped in an amphibian (animalistic) brain. This primordial *fight or flight* survival instinct keeps us in battle or running in the face of perceived danger. Our daily tribulations translate into our survival of the wild: tortuous business transactions, volatile relationships, or even road rage.

Fight or flight is embedded on a cellular level and is triggered by our innate fear – our fear of death or the debilitating fear of full-blast living. A way to harness fight or flight reactivity is to realize that we exist beyond our body, emotions, and thoughts. Recognition of the soul as eternal (it does not die) sets us free to go beyond fear and be fearless.

In a heightened awareness, a glimpse that I was more than Merrie Lynn, the personality in this life, occurred during a self-actualization technique. Our sessions (geared for actors) were facilitated by Dr. Robert Gerard and his wife Donna, and took place in their home. Other attendees included Jack Nicholson (the one and only) and Cindy Williams, the star of *Laverne and Shirley*. Much of the process was sitting quietly and using breath-work, guided imagery, and archetypal symbols.

The altered states of reality were incredibly real – unearthed from our unconscious depths, unblocking fixed beliefs, and liberating creative response. Through this technique, I realized we are more than our bodies and personalities, that we are scintillating spiritual beings, students in residence on earth, learning life lessons to help us remember what we forgot = who we truly are.

In a particular visualization, I saw myself as a frail bird with bulging eyes and long spindly legs, unsure of herself and fearful of taking a step forward in a dense, foreboding forest. It was odd that this fear came up because on a film audition two days after moving to Los Angeles, I had boldly scored a lead in a movie. Unfortunately, driving home after the six-week filming schedule, I fell asleep at the steering wheel and smashed into a divider on the freeway, wrecking my newly leased car. Not wearing a seat belt, I was thrown to the passenger side of the car and knocked unconsciousness. Had I been buckled in the driver's seat, I would have been mangled: the firewall had blasted through the driver's side. When I came to, I had a strange feeling of contentment and peace. I had entered the psycho-synthesis session only ten days later with that inexplicable liberated feeling still inside of me.

Now, while in my visualization, the trek in the forest continued as the frail bird – me – stopped dead in its tracks and observed a sly red fox observing her. The fox was unafraid, plotting and planning its next move. Clearly, I was observing two opposite poles of myself – the fearful and the wily. The vision changed and I was catapulted back into the wrecked car that was teetering on a guardrail over an embankment. I witnessed my body unconscious, but "I" was floating above it, feeling ecstatic and very much alive. I knew, "That body is not me. I am all that is, has been, and always will be. The soul does not die. It is eternal."

My awareness shifted, I sensed that before being born in this mortal life there was an overview. An intention was set: to shed our egos and to reclaim our true essence. We promised to return home, arriving full circle, back to the beginning, a vibrational spirit – knowing that we are the manifestation – God as Love. That we are we akin to a flower that reseeds itself, to a bird that lays eggs perpetuating evolution – all as One, a subatomic energy field pulsating as universal intelligence.

With that cognition my body literally shook on Dr. Girard's tufted chair. Life as I knew it had transformed. The fight or flight instinct had merged into the realm of fearlessness – the liberator of being-ness. From that day forward I was willing to take more risks, to give up being popular, to follow my heart, to standup for what I believed, and to face my life's challenges with conviction and an ever-growing courageous spirit.

And when I falter, caught in the human condition of doubt, pain, remorse, or other naggers, I choose to remember, "This feeling is not me. I am all that is."

Draw a YOU Map

To honor your uniqueness, let's play with the following:

With paper and pen (color markers add zing), draw a circle in the middle of the page. Insert your name. Draw outward lines representing areas of interests, talents or expertise. At the end of the line, circle or label the major categories, then draw offshoot lines that are specific to a category. If you wrote "family", it could include kids (draw stick figures), school and your support team. Keep the ideas flowing. When you are done, reflect on your You Map. Is it predictable, wondrous, tedious, or a revelation of your own complexity and specialness?

Life Chunks – Life's Lessons

Life Chunks are more than age-related passages from childhood to old age. They are events and episodes that have shaped our lives: long-term marriage, school years, job cycles, living in one home, changing residences, moving to a new city, becoming parents or grandparents, changing professions. Observing *Life Chunks* provides a through-line, zeroing in and illuminating your life's lessons.

Within *Life Chunks* (unlike the *LifeLine Challenge*), there is a beginning, middle, and end. Some events are simple, others more complicated. It is not necessary to recall specific details; it's more important to identify the essence and effect of each *chunk*.

A life chunk ends in spite of your attachment or emotional need to carry it forward. However, residual emotional memory lingers with questions, doubts, confusion, concerns or aspirations. Addressing what haunts us or stops us from new ventures is a first step in eradicating unconstructive patterns of behavior – and stimulating positive tendencies.

Unfinished Biz to Wholeness

Calculate unfinished business in a current or past event in your life. Is there something you haven't let go of? Is a block or an underlying tendency, fear or trepidation controlling you? Does it have power over your present actions, or lack of movement?

Pick one event in your life that has a hold on you:

1. Recall the beginning. What was your attitude toward it, your aspirations, your fears and expectations? Were you acting out of need, frustration, desperation, or a real enthusiasm for a positive outcome?

2. Were the others involved in-sync with your beliefs? Were they (or you) realistic regarding your responsibilities? What was your role in the play? Did you make unrealistic promises, commitments, or choices? Did you know it at the time? What other inquiries do you have about the situation?

3. Envision the timeframe. What stands out as demarcations, turning points, positive or negative events, attitudes or situations?

4. What ended it? Were you ready or reluctant to move on? What did you tell yourself you would never do again? What did you tell yourself you would repeat?

5. What message or belief did you hold as your truth? Are you still living that past belief? Does it work for you now? If not, Morph the *Chunk* out of your life and create a new option. Take the BEST. Leave the Rest.

6. What was the lesson in the *Chunk* event? Treat it as if you were reviewing a play. What is the theme? How does the experience or the belief in the theme alter the character's life? Spend time evaluating other possible related themes.

7. Forgive yourself and those involved. Tell them in prayer, a phone call, in person or in a letter that you were wrong, you forgive yourself or you forgive them.

8. Now let the debris flow out of your life. Let go of the unfinished biz and move on.

What Would You Go to The Wall for?

Do you know your innermost convictions? What would you stand up for? Not determining what really counts in life down-spirals into not *walking your talk* – not taking a stand. Evaluate what counts, what is a *must* for you to live your life with that conviction.

When Byron was born, my heart felt like it was wiggling and breathing outside of me. With this innate love and connection, I became a diehard advocate, his *Rock of Gibraltar*. I stayed aware of the input he absorbed from outside sources, including babysitters and TV.

When Byron was four-years-old, I hired a full-time nanny. One day she picked him up from pre-school, and when they returned home, I noticed that Byron was unusually quiet. I asked if he felt well. He blurted, "The nanny got mad and threw me out of the car." Astounded I asked, "She did *what?*" He jabbered on, "I started walking, then I ran fast." Obviously, she picked him up a few blocks later. Stunned, I held and hugged him, feeling both helpless and frightened by the incident. I asked if he was all right and, after a barrage of questions, I was fuming.

I quieted my agitation in an attempt to hear the other side of the story. The woman admitted to making Byron get out of the car. Justifying her behavior, she said, "I wanted him to learn a lesson."

I screeched, "*What* lesson?" My mind raced from A to Z. Nothing computed. Nor did it seem feasible to explain what I expected from her. We were light-years away from what was acceptable to me regarding disciplinary measures. I asked her to leave – a decision that I have not regretted. It was a decision based on my intrinsic recognition that as my child's guardian, I was to protect him from harms way – no matter what. That was the bottom line. I learned that I would *go to the wall* to protect my child.

CC, my friend, recounted what she would go to the wall for. "I was seriously challenged in a life and death situation while scuba diving. We were down at about a hundred-and-twenty feet when I ran out of air. I couldn't survive to the surface without air. My dive-buddy was in front of me. I alerted him with the out-of-air signal, a slash gesture across the throat. In that moment, I knew what I would go the wall for: LIFE ITSELF! I would have done anything in that moment to get air. Anything. I would have killed for air.

As my dive-buddy came toward me, I was desperate. We would have to share his regulator and buddy-breathe. He would take the mouthpiece out of his mouth and give it me – a scary notion for him because then he would be the one without air. From that point onward, we would buddy-breathe to the surface. I reached for the regulator as he handed it to me to put in my mouth. All I wanted was air. A strange feeling passed between us at that moment. Later he admitted, 'I feared you wouldn't give it back.' When we surfaced I ran onto the beach, sobbing, grateful I was alive."

Throughout my life, I have contemplated the question, "What would I go to the wall for?" So many things we do depend on the circumstances with which we are faced. We can't predict our actions, what we would actually do in a situation, until we are pushed to the wall. I learned the humbling lesson, "There but for the grace of God go I."

What would you go to the wall for? Take time to contemplate. Think of an example when you stood up for a value you hold, or for something or someone you care about. List the positive outcomes in taking a stand. Write it in your Morph Journal.

CHAPTER 7

DOWN 4 THE COUNT! WHAT WOULD WIPE YOU OUT?

Uncontrollable events in life can affect your ability to prosper. These unforeseen events can knock you down for the count. An unmerciful twist of fate can be devastating, emotionally or physically – a heavy-duty life-quaker beyond our control, not fixable, and irreversible. That dreaded phone call from the police, the paramedics, or the medical lab. Has an event blasted your equilibrium, put you in a catatonic stupor, and taken away your will to go on? A death, separation from a loved one, illness, a natural disaster, bankruptcy? What is the feared element that could take you out, place you in limbo, denial, a meltdown, or isolation?

Loss of A Loved One

As I now know, the loss of a child is one of life's most unfathomable, cruel, and gut-wrenching debilitations. I was knocked down, annihilated to the core of my being by Byron's untimely death. Wavering on a thin thread, I struggled either to find the will to live or surrender to a broken heart. My grief connected me with other's pain, a mutual healing ground. God's grace invoked deep compassion and a test to live fully in Byron's memory. It is with this understanding that I share the following:

My friend Ron received the dreaded phone call. His son Ben had been in a traffic accident – a drunken friend had driven the car. Ron couldn't comprehend that Ben had succumbed and been pronounced dead at the scene. The funeral was a blur. Devastated, Ron stood over his Ben's body lying in a casket. It made no sense that his son had been taken before his life could unfold.

In Ron's psyche, Ben wasn't really gone – he couldn't be. His room and clothes were still intact. Ron's heart was ripped; his life collapsed. The tears flowed often, providing temporary relief. An internal ache continued to suck the breath out of him, and a deep agonizing grief remained constant.

Ben had done the right thing that night. After having a couple of drinks he chose to be a passenger, not realizing that his friend, the designated driver, was over his drink limit. Because of this, they both paid the ultimate price.

The third young man who survived the crash was not doing well emotionally. He suffered from guilt and remorse that his friends had died and he had lived.

As time passed, Ron found a place within himself, a thread of light prodding him to recapture his life. His loving bond with Ben became a driving force, propelling him to help the surviving boy. A gnawing sensation for completion drew them together.

Gazing at the face of the remorseful young man, Ron saw the lopsided truth: the boy was also a victim, in deep pain, needing to heal. Sensing the double injustice and a need for resolve, Ron took the boy under his wing. Day-by-day, Ron was *there* for him, treating him with kindness, compassion, and understanding, as Ben would have wanted.

It was the beginning of healing the hurts with forgiveness of Self first. To this day Ron feels Ben's magnanimous spirit at play as he continues to help youth in need by spreading that love and eternal bond.

Grief is a real part of life. When someone we love dies, a part of ourselves passes on, too. We will never be the same. In this life, each person we connect with creates a quantum dynamic energy, an entity of its own. We meld into and merge with their energy and share this special-ness of *who we are* with them. Your loved one is still a part of you – in your heart – to share his or her legacy with others.

Chronic Illness – Torn Lives

As family members and friends of Alzheimer's victims, or of the mentally ill, we also experience grieving the loss of a loved one – as we once knew them. We miss and mourn them while juggling the complexities of their illness, learning to adapt and accept without judgment, embracing their true essence. Physical illness and mental illness are thieves that rob us of our loved ones and can creep in unexpectedly, turning and crushing our world.

Kevin was the CEO of a publicly traded company. As the stock in the company plummeted, he complained of severe migraines. Believing it was stress-related; he had a routine physical check-up that resulted in a three-week hospital stay. Kevin had a malignant brain tumor. Marie, his wife, saw their world crumble in an instant. A nightmarish ordeal ensued as she watched Kevin fade away from brain cancer. He had epileptic seizures, memory loss, falls causing broken bones, and numerous brain operations. Chemotherapy, radiation, blood transfusions, natural path remedies, and European cures, didn't work.

Kevin became cantankerous, emotionally unreachable, and even paranoid of Marie's intentions. The horror of seeing her husband disappear day-by-day, took its human toll. Marie was giving-up. She prayed for Kevin to be out of his misery. She prayed she would be out of her agony, living in daily anticipation of his physical death.

We bargain with God at these times: "Let my husband get well, and I promise to be a better person." The frustration and guilt of not being able to alleviate suffering is a profound challenge. To gain an everyday grip, just to get through it, is often as much as one can expect. Yet, when a loved one is out of the suffering, there is relief and hopefully some consolation to hold onto.

Create a Ritual Honoring Your Loved One

A few months after Kevin's passing, Marie created a ritual "to let go and let God." Her goal was not to forget Kevin, but to remember him as the loving soul he was before his illness. She held a vigil of light and gave blessings, honoring Kevin and all others needing support through prayer. She gave each attending person a crystal angel with a pink candle inside as a symbol of his loving spirit.

Near a waterfall at sundown, everyone lit the candles. The crystal angels' glowing rosy pink lights reflected on the sweet faces of family and friends. Awestruck by the sight, Marie was overcome with an unexpected joy, "I saw Kevin smiling and twinkling from each flame." That deep connector began Marie's way into a new life. The crystal angel became a touchstone; she could light it whenever she felt sad or had a need to attune to Kevin. Marie transformed her view of suffering because she believed there was a connection of spirit beyond this world.

A comforting statistic: 60,000,000 Americans report having had a form of communication, whether through a dream, voice, or vision, with a loved one on the other side.

Understanding Grief and Loss

The stages of grief are not linear. There is no timeline or shortcut to grieving. Feelings come and go at random, even daily, or one stage could dominate, lasting for weeks or months.

Denial or shock is usually the first stage. It's incomprehensible that you will not see, talk to or be with the person you love. Denial can serve as a coping mechanism from the initial overwhelm. Your loss may feel surreal, the underlying pain slowly realized.

Anger at the situation often follows, or anger at yourself for not being able to prevent it. Anger at your loved one who passed in an untimely way and left you alone is a natural reaction. Anger sits on top, anchored to the more intense emotions of pain, which are too much for the human psyche and spirit to handle at once. Coming in and out of a foggy mind, we might rationalize and attempt to make sense of the unthinkable. We may call out for justice by blaming anyone or anything associated with the loss. If so, then pound a pillow, scream, yell. Get it out!

We may also dwell on *what ifs* and *if only*, regrets may be in play: "If only we had known sooner." "What if the doctor was wrong?" Bouncing like this, from one emotion to another, can lead to resignation and feelings of hopelessness.

Depression: you can't bare the pain, the loss, the unsettled life. What's the purpose for going on? However, relief can come by dealing with the trauma and by releasing guilt and doubts through a variety of options. Reach out, there's no shame sharing your truth. You're not alone; trust someone else will be there, offering support.

♥ ♥ ♥

To come to grips with my grief I began sessions with quantum healers, Dr. Kam Yuen, Dr. Hector Garcia, Howard Wills, and Dr. Richard Bartlett, each one helping to lift a veil of sadness. I did "Qui Gong" (a meditative martial art) with Master Mingtong Gu for one hundred days to balance the jarring repercussions of loss. I prayed on my knees and wailed in deep agony flat out on the floor as if a stake had been foisted through me. I attended many places of worship. My life turned into a living prayer… seeking relief, seeking respite, seeking to live in God's light.

In our numbed-down society, we are supposed to smile through it all, rise above it, not linger or express pain or suffering, nor feel "down" for more than a moment. Grieving is a process – you must go through the debilitating feelings to heal. Your body and psyche may need to shut down to regroup before beginning the healing process. Stay in bed if you choose. Take a few days off work. If you don't get out of bed for days on end or if you grow weaker in despair, seek help, either from family, friends, or a professional.

Over time, there is a shift in perspective and you realize you are not in control of life. From there, day-by-day, living in that awareness helps rebuild a new life structure.

Acceptance: This is final – your loved one is not coming back. The spiritual perspective is my savior, knowing "the soul does not die with the body." After the death of my mother, I was comforted by a friend's wisdom. "We aren't supposed to forget our loved ones; they live on forever in our hearts."

Connect With Departed Loved One.

♥ Focus on your heart and fill it with light. Expand your chest wide. Breathe deep. Inhale pink heart light. Allow it to permeate your being, filling every cell, expanding.

♥ Invite the presence of your loved one. Image, feel their essence. Allow, what comes or doesn't is fine. Reach out heart to heart. Speak out loud, surrender. Trust they can hear you.

♥ Share wishes, regrets. Release feelings, pent up or buried, "I miss you." "I love you."

♥ You can ask questions: "How are you?" "Is there something you want to tell me?"

♥ You may hear a voice, feel tingly, or chilled. A sign may alert you, a bird may fly and hover at your window. You may feel light-headed or peaceful.

♥ Allow grace to shower you. Thank your loved one for being there. Give gratitude.

Grief Support: Join a bereavement or support group that offers coping sessions for those dealing with specific kinds of loss. Sharing your plight with others in the same situation provides a safe space for mutual understanding and letting emotions out. Tears are healing and so is laughter. Laughter often follows tears, and vice-versa.

Victim and perpetuators' families can come together to heal the hurts, to forgive, and to make peace with their mutual tragedy. A father who lost his son to a heinous crime made peace with the killer and related, "As long as one holds hope in [his] heart, hope exists. As long as one holds hate in [his] heart, hate continues. As long as one holds love in [his] heart, there can be peace. We [have] to forgive."

MADD (Mothers Against Drunk Drivers) supports families dealing with the loss of a loved one from alcohol-related accidents. Voices ring out: "My tragedy is your tragedy. My children are your children. My dreams are your dreams." Forgiveness can be the catalyst to ACT, to reach out, and to help others in their loved one's name.

I started "Byron's Buds" as an offering in his name to support youth's creative expression. Our "Heal the LA River Gala" showcased youth portraying parts of the river – the tide, the ripples, the fish – all swimming in the river of life.

Dark Night of the Soul Revisited

Triggered by various circumstances or crises, the *Dark Night of the Soul* infuses one's spirit and mind with a feeling of dying. The loss of a job, money, relationship or home, is often as disabling as illness and death. The wellbeing of the sufferer is compromised; life loses its purpose and meaning. From this perspective, facing bankruptcy and poverty, coping with a midlife or internal crisis, can send one reeling into the stages of loss and grief, and into a decompensation of self-image and a questioning of life's worth. At this time, the grief model is a viable aid to healing.

♥ ♥ ♥

Jay plummeted into a tailspin when the airline he had given seventeen years of devoted service to offered him a severance package. The six-year early retirement rattled him, derailing his life. Jay spiraled into a dark vacuum, unable to redefine his life. Shut out by younger competition (ageism, the chronic baby-boomer dilemma) limited his options.

In a 'Heal the Hurts' Morph session, Jay spontaneously released deep childhood wounds, feelings of hopelessness and pain. "I felt isolated, obsolete. A part of me was dying – a small shadow of me remained." The internal death process is real; letting go of what was, who we were and no longer are (the boss, wife or employee, etc.), is a tough challenge. Death of "life as you know it" short-circuits your familiar, internal wiring.

Be alert to an inner pull, a creative energy hatching from a seed deep within the darkness. As your world cracks open, rebirth can follow. Reclaiming, redefining, and getting your life on a new track, requires patience and support.

Jay stayed with it, learning that we can die to our old Self many times in this life. He referred to a quote from Franklin D. Roosevelt: "When you come to the end of your rope, tie a knot, and hang on." Jay admitted, "I couldn't hang on, I had to let go. And I kept asking myself, 'What am I supposed to do with my life?' In time, fed up with suffering, the dark cloud lifted, and I resurrected my life. I'm teaching at a nearby flight school. I have the satisfaction of flying and sending new pilots into the sky I love."

When a transformation occurs, it's like becoming a midwife to yourself – eliciting hope against all hope. When you pull yourself up by the bootstraps, you begin visiting the new. Watch what interests you, what attracts your attention; it may be as simple as baking cookies or getting a new pair of golf shoes that walk you into a new life game.

Breaking-Up Is Hard To Do – Heart Breakers and Shakers

Letters and poems from the lovelorn have ripped at our hearts for centuries. What happens when a couple breaks-up? Do they go on their merry way? Or is one left in the lurch, dejectedly consumed with the past and singing the blues? Billions of dollars have been spent on unrequited love tunes. A lyric from Carol Connor's, "With You I'm Born Again" says it all:

"And when love dies, why can't it just die quickly? It ends, but then, I still want you with me. So how was my heart to know? That someday you would go. How was my heart to know?"

Sometimes one loves more than the other does in each relationship. And on the split-up that the "more" lover absorbs the hurt, disappointment, gloom and the potential to obsess and pine over their lost love – doing the work for both of them.

What does loving someone or being loved mean to you? Is it security, intimate bonding, a way to deeply connect with your inner being?

There are as many scenarios as there are lovers: Betrayal. Abandonment. Falling out of love. "I don't love you that way anymore; we're just friends." Whatever! The sex is kaput. The love has dried up. Something's gone wrong.

We have heard the tears, the questioning, and lamenting: "I

gave that jerk the best years of my life." "She ran off with the pool man." "I'll never find love again." "No one ever loved me like that." "We were soul-mates – how could he just walk away?" **Alas! Love remains no matter. Always there, immutable, painted in your heart – the sweet nectar of self-love.**

Betrayal/Infidelity – The Heart Twister

Betrayal implies deceit, seduction, and treason. The betrayed feels duped, taken advantage of, and lied to. They feel like a victim or act-out like an enraged banshee. We hear daily reports of lawsuits and violent crimes caused by incidences of infidelity or fraud in business. Betrayal implies breached ethical or moral expectations. It's within the expectation that we are deceived. In examining our perceptions, we must ask ourselves if there was a clue we overlooked, rather than face a painful truth. "He did it behind my back." **Move out of a victim mentality and have the courage to examine what part *you* played.** Were you naïve, in denial, or set up?

Denial vs. Road to Authenticity

With the intention to add *spice and life* back into her twenty-year-old stale marriage, Barbara joined a Morph Relationship session. Hot issues pervaded when Herb, another participant, confessed to an extramarital affair. Barbara vented at Herb, "You men are all alike." Seizing a growth opportunity, we did a Mirror Image game. Herb and Barbara chose to partner. Facing each other, they silently stared directly into the others' eyes and they began relating the feelings and powerful images that were evoked.

Barbara's painful story poured out. "My husband, Dillon, has been sneaking around for over a year with his twenty-something secretary. I hired a detective, found receipts from hotels, and even got photos of them making love."

Though Barbara had spent thousands of dollars, she never revealed to Dillon her discovery. "He still makes love to me, I am his wife. The other woman is just a fantasy." Barbara was not denying the affair, but she was denying her feelings and covert anger about it. She wasn't living a full life; following Dillon was her 24/7.

Mind-Bender: How many times can we sweep the dirt under the carpet before we smell the stench? Keep sweeping until it becomes dust.

Facts vs. Assumptions

With exploration, Barbara admitted her identity was attached to being a wife and mother. "My self-esteem's glued to my *Super-Mom* status. I'm just like my mother, a martyr...I've sacrificed developing *me* and outside interests."

Upsetting this comfort-zone dynamic seemed catastrophic. Barbara soul-searched and ALTERED ONE ASSUMPTION: "I do not exist without Dillon." She made a Commitment: "It's my duty to rediscover myself." The simple FACT: she would continue to exist in spite of their failed relationship.

While continuing in the Mirror Image game, Herb empathetically connected to her, and it jolted him into a new consciousness. Owning up, he asked himself "What do I really want? I love my affair, not my lover." Next, he stated with remorse, "My marriage is one of convenience."

Herb was open to exploring his issues, which was a big step

forward. He dealt with his inability to commit to a relationship and sought out a relationship therapist. He ended the affair, and his failed marriage ultimately resulted in divorce. Herb is now more honest about what he wants and is engaged in living an authentic life.

Try the Mirror Image Game with a partner: Stare at each other for 2 minutes in silence. Then verbalize feelings and images. You may experience the person's face changing, and connecting on a deep spiritual level. Then, practice naming the facts and facing unreal assumptions. Getting REAL with ourselves launches breakthroughs.

What IS – IS Real!

Sometimes there is no gray in the picture. The car tire is flat. You were fired. Your divorce is final today. Your hair is gray. You won the Lotto. You didn't win the Lotto.

"What Is–Is Real" signifies accepting that which you cannot change. Focusing on what isn't, we stall in delusion and bottom-out in repetitive lies and denial. Facing the truth of "what is", where you are now, instead of where you want to be, is a launching point toward self-actualization and handling life's conditions.

Healing Hurts/Regrets – Make Peace with the Past

Have patience with yourself. It takes awareness not to act-out in old habitual patterns. Allow time for adopting and implementing new viewpoints. If you regress, it's part of the course. Be gentle with yourself.

Remember: "Two steps forward and one step back" offers a solid path to growth.

Regrets deplete your energy, both mental and physical. Regrets anchor you in the past. I didn't have a single regret in my life until Bryon's passing. I felt lucky, as if I had lived ten lives in one incarnation. Yes, I made mistakes, but I could let go, not obsess or beat myself up about them and view them as a growth and learning process.

But when I lost my son, I thought of all the times I could have been more available to his being, his loving presence, instead of operating out of the 'Mom protects and knows best' zone. I strangled my inner heart with gnawing questions about why I didn't take him here or there, or do or say, or not say, this or that. There are so many things, irretrievable moments, I can't get back or change.

Regrets register as sensations in the body. I feel a swirling pit in my gut. What soothes and works best for me is to be available and present in the moment. When I am missing Byron and my thinking rambles into the abyss, I consciously choose to absorb myself in our eternal loving times and carry that oneness into the next moment. I am in a continuing process to understand and make peace with what I cannot change.

Making peace with rejection or regrets, healing past wounds, coping with infidelity and heartbreak, takes time, patience, and perseverance. Don't give up at the first sign of feeling uncomfortable. Growing symptoms resemble the aches and pains of a teen whose legs grew six-inches in four months. A relief remedy is to soak in hot Epson salts baths. Do it. Relax and rejuvenate. **And, keep in mind that the way back to loving is to Love.**

Invite Love...make it a daily practice, in all you say and do. Witness, when you close off like a clam or a turtle hiding in its shell. Choose to open. Invite LOVE

Emotionally Charged – Go to Neutral

Can you keep a level head? "No, I'm ready to blow a fuse." Can you be mindful of your reactive tendencies? Surprise yourself by remaining detached in the moment. Observe yours and others' triggers, explosive or covert reactions. In the middle of a confrontation count to ten – observe. If that doesn't work and you still feel over-reactive, upset, trapped in an unpleasant mind-fix, it's time to disengage your erratic emotions.

When you or someone else is emotionally triggered, overreacting, confused, anxious, frustrated, or angry, *dropping to neutral* disconnects the emotionally charged energy field.

Neutralize Emotions

Take one hand; move it from your throat to your belly button (known as *Chi* midline) and say aloud (or silently) with conviction, "Go to neutral." You will feel an instant shift and the emotional charge will diminish. You can use the same motion – throat to belly button – and command, "Go to neutral" on someone else to drop them to neutral if you are in an emotionally detached state.

Take good care of yourself. Give yourself time to rebuild your immune system. Eat properly, exercise, rest and get a good night's sleep, talk to others or write in your journal – whatever feels right for you to do. Touch opens the heart. Relieve raw emotion with massage and hugs. Being held or rocked like a baby comforts and soothes the soul.

Contemplate **H.E.A.L.** acronym. Feel its simplicity, truth and warmth.

H - HEALTHY

E - ENERGY

A – ACCEPTING

L – LOVE

It's a Wonderful Life – Imagine It without You

Leaving our footprints in the sands of time helps another to find their way. Generations have been awed by the timeless film classic *It's a Wonderful Life,* starring James Stewart. Contemplating his own death, the character George Bailey looks back over his life and views what would have been different, how it would have affected everyone he knew if he hadn't been born.

Imagine that you had never been born. What would be different? Remember a couple of moments and events when your presence and actions made a positive mark in someone else's life. Embrace the treasured moments – acknowledge your value.

Write your epitaph – how you want to be remembered – for who you are and how you lived your life. Imagine the epitaph soaring in a time capsule to be read anywhere in the universe. **Truly imbibe that this is a wonderful life. Bring the feeling into the NOW and into your FUTURE dreams and plans.**

My epitaph applauds, "She giggled her way into heaven."

CHAPTER 8

BREAKTHROUGH BOOSTERS

Morph Brain Drains

Do you feel exhausted, nauseous, dizzy, or foggy-minded after a testy phone call? How about after working hours on a computer or listening to a hypochondriac, a narcissist, a drama king, or Media bombardment? You could be suffering from *Brain Drain*. These vampires siphon creative juices. They suck your life force and leave you running on empty. Physical symptoms include anxiety, migraines, nausea, and hypersensitivity to sound. Sufferers have said, "Sounds are maddening...a click of a clock is unbearable." "It's like every cell in my body compresses." The condition is similar to overload and stress, requiring downtime to rest and shake it off. You need nurturing to heal the physical aspects: vitamins, massage, exercise, tender loving care.

Feeling better requires eliminating the source of the drain: taking a bathroom break from a demeaning boss, spending less time on the computer, or avoiding unsupportive people. These psyche leeches steal your energy and use it for their own power, leaving you exhausted or feeling worse than when you first interacted with them.

Eliminate a brain-drainer by ending the situation or relationship.

Jane had a friend, an "all about me" narcissist, who was a clever avoider and never there when Jane needed help in her own life. Jane admitted, "I feel lousy after seeing her." *That is the measuring stick.* **If you don't feel good or empowered by someone, move on.** Uplifting vibes are contagious. So, find positive people who return your support and caring. Allowing emotional space can attract new, more supportive and fun-loving friends.

Brain Drain Buster

Notice what's going on at the onset of a brain drain. Are you with someone? What are your thoughts, your symptoms? Do similar circumstances trigger the drain?

I remember hanging my head out of a car window when two friends were yelling at each other. I literally could not breathe, nor could I jump out of the car on the freeway. Sometimes the drain is more insidious – ever-present in your environment – as was the case with Diane. "My mother-in-law zaps my energy," Diane complained. "She wants to control our lives. What should I do?"

Sheri, our Morph Group facilitator suggested, "Have your husband or children deal with her."

Diane shook her head, "I can't do that – she lives next door."

Sheri hissed, "When a vampire's sucking you dry, withdraw or forever lose your peace. Catch yourself being *Good Guy* or *Ms. Nice*, bending over backwards to be everyone's everything."

"Hold on," Jack interjected. "What if the culprit is my boss? He is frying my brain with scare tactics and putdowns. I used to be a thinker, an idea man. Now I'm only concerned about what he thinks."

Sheri was firm, "If the culprit is a business contact, ask them to send you emails. When the drain occurs, excuse yourself, if possible. Silently hum a tune in your head. Doodle. Open the doors or windows and breathe. Release the toxic energy that has overtaken you. Inhale your self-respect back…it's the power you need to diffuse the drain."

Yakety-Yak

The media blitz drains humankind with demoralizing, negative zingers projecting and reporting bad times, bad news. Boycott being herded into "no hope" and turn off the blasted nonsense. I went cold turkey, listened to *me*, and painted a rosier future. I showed up for friends, took hikes, and did my Pilates. By the way, stop gossiping – it's a no-no brain sucker.

When I was a teen plagued by the heaviness of life's meaning, my mother, Betty, would get in my face and smile, "Lighten up, life isn't that heavy." Betty was an upper, a positive energy-boost. She made me laugh – especially at my silly self.

A 911 Rescue Team

Have you ever been caught up in someone else's unending drama and chaos? What do you do? One such crisis period appeared to have no end game when a drug-addicted business associate, let's call her Monique, created HAvoc on a project. Even more disturbing, she seemed to be on a suicide mission, and I was there to save her. I found myself enrolled 24/7 in her at-risk-aberrations – from fielding 3:00 A.M. phone calls to picking her up when she was stranded.

After enduring sleepless nights, the mounting stress compromised my well-being. Needing immediate relief, I consulted a professional whose advice turned me around full circle: "Aren't you seeing your worst fears come to life? Aren't they happening one after another?" "Yes, exactly," I answered.

"What if the worst happens, or the drama never ends, then what?" he posed. That jolted me like a cold shower. He continued, "Are you willing to alter your behavior and how you deal with her."

I stammered, "You mean I have to change, find a new way to cope?"

He raised the stakes, "How much time are you living *her* self-destruction, and how much time are you living *your* potential?"

I got it. Absorbed in her toxic-druggie unconsciousness, I had made Monique's self-destruction my own. Through prayer and contemplation, I mustered the strength to detach from the drama. I would do what I could do, and then stop obsessing about her vulnerability and neediness.

I changed my tack and organized an intervention with friends proposing she go into rehab. She resisted – at first. Finally, after a near-death overdose, she checked into a facility. It was necessary to dissolve our business arrangement, but I let her know I was still there as a friend to support her recovery.

As time went on Monique learned to meditate. Practicing the LightHeart Breath™ she connected with the unlimited source, stillness within, expanding her capacity to be wholly present. We were able to assist her to find work and to start a new life.

Lesson learned: Don't get entangled in rescues and changing other people! It's their call to choose change. They must want and be willing to help themselves. It can be heartbreaking to detach if our child, husband, or a friend is careening down a self-destructive path. To handle the chaos we need support to manage our own stress. Participate in 12-Step programs. Learn effective coping strategies: tough love, self-love, and to trust a higher power to guide. You become anchored in understanding the pitfalls of co-dependency and become empowered to make healthier choices.

Bubble of Illusion – Control Freaks and Power Mongers

Plugged into our DNA are memories of inhumane atrocities, good and evil, the powerful over the powerless. Domination, a masculine trait, has ruled for millenniums; and humane compassion, the soft-hearted feminine nature, is reserved for poets and artists.

Control freaks (all of us have a tendency) believe we can change someone's views, opinions, and habits to ours. Whether one attempts to control life through perfectionism, intimidation, playing weak or strong, power-tripping leaves us on the short end of our potential. While in this control mode, we are in bondage, expending wasted energy on external circumstances that have no end game.

Subjugating someone else to our whims is abusive and humiliating. This hurtful control device triggers fears of being fired, loss of love, rejection. The battle of being right, winning the prize, being top dog, or allowing yourself to be hammered into a victim stance, succumbing as the underdog, can happen in a boardroom, the bedroom, or on the tennis court.

Why choose the controller's bubble of illusion over what is real? Some misnomers: "If I spend 24/7 watching over my baby, I can control how he/she grows up." "If I wear garter belts and black stockings, become the best lover, cook, and listener, I can control my husband's wanderlust." "If I eliminate everything that bothers me, I can control my happiness." "If I intimidate first, play an eye-for-an-eye, have them owe me, I'll be in control and end up on top." The subtle control in conversations, wiping out another's point of view, deeming them unworthy to listen to invalidates the human spirit.

If you play the victim you control through that stance by allowing the bully to dominate. If you pull out the crippling plug, and own up to your part in the drama, it **can** cease.

Bully-Controller

1. Do you bully-whip others and pride yourself as the intimidator? Knowingly or unknowingly you live a lie, holding onto fear-based belief that survival requires domination and the weakest link has no chance. This either/or thinking eliminates kindness, a win-win approach, and keeps you on edge ready to attack. You live a sour-puss life, in control – ever fearful that you will succumb to what you are opposing.

2. If you enjoy abusing others and feel entitled to trounce on others to win – take a look at it. What are you afraid of? What is the worst possibility? What can you lose?

3. Be aware when you hurt others. The energy field remains part of you – and you will ultimately suffer.

4. Learn to drop into compassion – for yourself first. Can you contemplate deeper and recognize your fragility.

Underdog

1. Spend little time in discussion with the abusive controlling person.

2. Don't take the abuse personally. Drop into neutral (pg.115). This is the trick for saving face, your sanity, and self-worth.

3. Set firm boundaries. Stay grounded and centered. Feel entitled – reclaim your dignity.

4. If a line is crossed that could escalate to physical abuse, seek legal and professional help.

Can you recognize the necessity for balance, for healthy compromise, for peace within and without?

Resistance Busters

What we resist will persist and bleep-out bliss. So, take a plunge into assistance. Resistance is a parasite devouring your power, smashing your dreams, dwindling hope into ashes. Fear and resistance entwine, giving rise to roadblocks and failure.

To master resistance, I view obstacles as opportunities to expand and grow. Can you say *YES* to exploring a new method? Are you willing to give up playing it safe and doing something only one way – your way? Can you release expectations or the need for guaranteed outcomes? Can you *relax* and not *try* so hard? Can you view resistance as an opportunity to discover life anew, in this moment, as a newly refreshed you?

Most of us may answer "wishful thinking" to some or all of the above questions. Or you might say, "Sure, right! I can do it. Just point me in the right direction." If you are ready, I suggest you experience the following:

Affirming Emotional Wisdom

Choose a specific goal you want to attain with a measured outcome. "I want to stop screaming at the kids." "I want to reprogram my need for cigarettes." "I want to believe I'm worth a raise."

♥

While engulfed in an emotional issue, take a deep breath; allow the feelings to be there: anger, hurt, depression, pain. Ask yourself, "What am I feeling?" Isolate the strongest sensation. Talk to it. What is it saying? For instance, "I'm sad." Ask why it is there, within you. Listen, breathe, go deeper, ask again. Let the unexpected arise.

♥

Now recall your goal, "I want to believe I'm worth a raise." Repeat this affirmation three times: "I am worth a raise." Take a break. Go for a walk. Do some gardening. Then ask yourself, "What is in my control, and what is out of my control?" Make a list of what is reasonable for you to do and what isn't. Who can assist? Seek professional advice if necessary.

Do Sayings Make It So? No – We Do!

We've all heard or used adages like *"use it or lose it"* or *"what goes around comes around."* Consciously or unconsciously, we assume adages are true; we form beliefs and live by them. Our actions will eventually prove the axiom true or false.

"You can't take it with you." It's an inevitable fact that one day we will leave this earth. Even the riches of kings, including King Tut, left their tombs behind.

♥   ♥   ♥

Marty was a warm-hearted do-gooder: a known pack rat. The adage *"a penny saved is a penny earned"* was how he operated. Marty joked, "I still have the first nickel I ever made." Operating like a 21st century barterer, his good deeds had a price attached. The paybacks ranged from, "Buy me a doughnut," to "How about a VCR?" Or, he would challenge a friend to name the price. His underlying generosity wanted a win-win. "No one should feel over their head," as he put it.

If a fan were on sale, he would buy two just in case a heat wave might occur. Unused candles were placed everywhere in his elegant home. I recall striking a match to light one when Marty leaped toward me as if I was about to set the house afire. "No! Don't! Please, I'm saving that." Curious about what occasion would warrant lighting it, I asked Marty, "For what?" He eyed me suspiciously, as if I had asked him his net worth. In an attempt to quell the strained moment, I giggled, "I know, Marty, you are saving that mermaid candle for a rainy day." He seemed satisfied to get off the hook.

Sometime later Marty became chronically ill and passed away. Regrettably, we missed sharing a sweet good-bye. Three months after his death a package arrived. I was heart-struck upon reading the card inside. It was from Marty.

"Remember when you asked me why I was saving everything and I didn't know why? I thought about it. I looked deep into my life and saw many profound things. I concluded with this. I was saving the mermaid candle for you. Just for this very moment. You have always been my spiritual touchstone. Please light it, pray, and laugh for me... wherever I am. Love, Marty."

My heart soared and rippled with gratitude. As time went on, friends related goose-bump-producing gestures that Marty had arranged. He left a college fund for a struggling teen, sent two sets of white dishes to an Orthodox Jewish bride, and created an after-party for himself filled with all the love and pizzazz that was our Marty.

Soon after Marty's passing, I contemplated the saying *"saving for a rainy day."* It conjured a fresh meaning for me. Rather than having a poverty connotation, it translated into, "Putting the right value on things can turn them into a rainbow of hope."

If the Shoe Fits, Wear It.
If it's a Tight Squeeze, Get a New Pair.

Life is like a pair of shoes. Inevitably, we outgrow phases, relationships, jobs, interests, viewpoints and habits that no longer serve us. The trick is to replace the old shoes before getting bunions. Why compromise or self-destruct by living in self-constraints?

Every day you habitually describe your *lot in life* to yourself and others. You might exaggerate, deny, obliterate, or even optimize a situation with the words you choose. This mind-set has the power to create real or imagined predicaments – cramping your progress or, conversely, propelling it.

♥ Recall a repetitive statement you use to describe your life. Recall a habitual thought or a remark you use. Think of phrase or word to describe your life. My life is like_____. Examples: Hailstorm. Weak battery. Celebration. Trapped in a dream. Erupting volcano. Rat race. Living in a ditch. Treadmill. Hole-in-one. Roller coaster. Love-Fest.

♥ What feelings, sensations and images are stirred? How does the phrase or word affect your relationship to your Self, your Higher Power, and everyone and everything in your life? Words carry vibrational frequencies, a potency to invoke emotions, alter moods, concretize beliefs, and instigate behavior. Are the words we choose serving our highest good, or are they downsizing our potential? Are we covering-up our true nature, or are we free to express it?

♥ Invent a visual phrase to uplift your predicament (profound to comical): life is like a hot fudge sundae, a Rolls Royce, a fluffy kitten. Dig deep inside for a motivator. What resonates? Slogans can express gratitude, be the catalyst to acquire a quality like patience or courage, or be the activator for attaining ways to get beyond draining thoughts and situations. Witness the intricacies of choice – how the choices affect your life. To change limited views, you can alter, delete, lighten, neutralize, and substitute positive phrases.

♥ Your slogan (or metaphor) is positive expectation in Action, a positive attitude for a positive outcome. Believe it! Examples: "*Loving is my life.*" Repeat at work, with your mate, or when stressed on a deadline. Or, "*I'm a money-magnet.*" Repeat it when paying bills, shopping for groceries, filling up the gas tank.

♥ As with affirmations, visualize your slogan's outcome as already happening. Imagine it through your senses – how you feel, what you see, taste, smell, and who is there sharing the outcome with you. Write your slogan down. Say it every day.

♥ Describe yourself as a bumper sticker. What do you project to the world or to a potential lover? "I don't do Windows, I do Diamonds." Mine is "Funny Wise Woman."

Create a Salon or Mutual Support Group

Seeking healthy environments, like-minded friends and supporters, assists our personal evolution. For several years, I enjoyed the Kindred Spirits, a group of dynamic women devoted to spiritual and personal growth. The group was co-founded by Lynn Lear, a humanitarian and philanthropist, and Marianne Williamson, best-selling author of *A Return to Love* and champion of *The Course in Miracles*.

Other members included actress/author Shirley MacLaine, whose playful nature and unique life perspective could enliven any repartee with wondrous "AHA!" blasts; Lynn Andrews, a profound spiritual teacher and critically acclaimed author of *Medicine Woman*; Dr. Hyla Cass, neuro-molecular psychiatrist and co-author of *Natural Highs*, who influenced our eating habits; and Tara Guber, a yoga master, who helped us tend to our bodies. Our bevy of top-notch women touched all walks of life from P.R. agents to criminologists.

The Kindred Spirits space was safe ground to expand and risk being my authentic self. Experiencing healing techniques, we grew together, laughed together, and cried together. We bantered, inspired, and shared our fears, dreams, plans, and schemes. Moments of intimacy made me stronger, empowered me to realize my life purpose and to actuate it.

You can develop your own salon to enlighten your spirit and mind, or join a meet-up group that shares a common interest. Maybe a hobby feeds your soul. If you enjoy sailing, join a yacht club.

Refurbishing cars? Locate classic-car aficionados. What about circus arts? Bird watching? Or belly dancing? Seek and ye' shall find your special place to bond and commune.

Coin Flips

Coin Flips is a fun and practical tool. I first discovered coin-flips with my brother Bill. As kids, we'd flip for the biggest coin: nickel beats a penny; nickel beats a dime. The winner got the nickel instead of the dime – clearly, a shady take on "winner and loser". "Heads I win. Tails you lose." Sound familiar? It's the ever-reliable flip of a coin to determine who wins.

On the other hand, the Morph Coin Flip deals with a winning or losing attitude. Habitual negative self-talk such as, "I can't do this. I'm too tired. I'm too stupid…" warrants the use of coin flips. Flip negativity (a major brain-drainer) into a positive thought.

The exercise is simple. When you think or say, "I'm stupid," for example, flip it over to, "I'm smart." Then add a positive option, "What do I need to learn about this?" When feeling "I can't," flip it to "I could." Ask an option question, "What is stopping me?" Your answer may provide a reason to go forward or may give a valid reason to put on the brakes.

Shannon stated to her Morph Group, "I'm going bankrupt." Then she coin-flipped it to "I am not bankrupt *now*. " She added the option, "What can I do to change my reality now?" Coin Flip retrains illogical thinking into the logical, the doable, the practical, and the positive.

I have contemplated the following and it is framed on my office wall.

Watch your thoughts; they become your words.
Watch your words; they become your actions.
Watch your actions; they become your habits.
Watch your habits; they become your character.
Watch your character; for it becomes your destiny.

So be it! If our true nature is reflected in our thoughts, words, and deeds, begin each day mindful of your first thought. Check in throughout the day – what are you thinking?

Be Open To Love

How can you be open to love…to bring on the Love in your life? Self-love is the anchor, the connector to infinite love. It is from our inner contentment that we love others and all sentient beings.

Self-love rocks our truth. It's not dependent on external love. We can't beg, borrow or barter it. It is not selfish. It can't be doled out in exchange for another's love. It doesn't blame, manipulate, or attempt to control. It's not driven by fear, jealousy, or rejection.

Self-love is the giver, the sustainer, and essence of your life. Self-loving scintillates, tickles, enraptures, and is magnificently there, *for you – as you*. It fills a room when you enter, warms hearts, and touches hungry souls.

♥ ♥ ♥

Tanya was a triple threat. As a legal secretary, devoted wife, and supermom, she provided loving care to others, but she didn't receive as generously as she gave. To align with her true nature, giving and taking needed to be equally balanced. Her core issue was love of Self, feeling entitled to take the goodies. She became mindful: "I will be open and be present to give and *receive* love." She began each day in meditation: in stillness, feeling peaceful within, allowing a gentle sweetness to lovingly engulf her.

Whether at work, grocery shopping, helping the kids with homework, she began sensing the love energy and joy in the event. She practiced for one week, and then reflected daily on the cognition's that surfaced. As a reminder, Tanya kept the message in her iPhone.

"Don't think I'm bonkers, but lately the beetles in my garden are friends, the kids are more loving, and even grocery shopping's fun. The group chuckled, and I asked, "And your husband – did he notice anything different?" Tanya's cheeks flushed, then she beamed, "Multiple orgasms, real intimacy…he more than noticed. We're madly in love."

Now that begs the question: what is intimacy? It includes closeness, understanding, familiarity, feeling comfortable with yourself, nature, other people. To be intimate doesn't necessarily mean love-making. But the combo of the two is special and can enhance a couple's togetherness. Wow…electrifying multiple orgasms can take us into the spiritual realm of Oneness, releasing all worldly concern; the little ego dissolves and merges with radiating Love. Tantric yoga encourages holding back the physical orgasm – expanding sensorial pleasuring and a blissful state of being. And in human terms feeling "Madly in love."

Mindful Metaphors

Mike, a Morph participant, stated, "I've been bopped off my perch." That was his description of losing his job in a downsizing. Contemplating the visual he asked, "If I'm not on a perch, where am I?" In a quandary about his next career move, *bopped* signified a pushing down, a punishment. He replaced *bopped* with *flying*. His new metaphor was "I am flying off my perch", which represented freedom, expansiveness – visualizing a destination beyond the entrapment of a 12-hour workday. Reacting to his metaphor, Mike created a business plan and started his own company.

Choose a metaphor to change a tendency or to alter a situation. Try it on for a week. "Laugh until you cry." "When in doubt, punt."

"Live Your Life As If It's Your Last Day"

Ahh…time to put things in order, get rid of excess baggage – to organize and prioritize. If you lived your life as if it were your last day, would you cut to the bottom line of what truly matters? Would you fully engage with those you love? Would you laugh more, savor moments?

Sometimes fate taps us on the shoulder signaling a wakeup call to live life to the fullest. My soul sister Darby was involved in a serious car accident and was pronounced dead at the scene with a ruptured lung. A wondrous premature meeting with fatality, or fate's folly?

Darby recounted, "I heard the word *dead* as I swirled out and hovered above my body. I could see everything – the decimated car and my body below. Timeless, I was propelled into a joyous, ecstatic, peaceful zone. Nothing mattered. My life as I knew it disappeared, leaving no regrets. All that was left was a pure essence of me. The ME I had always searched for. The wholeness I always knew was there. I was the *white light* engulfing me. Then I had a simple thought. I had recently married, and I thought, 'I would have liked to spend more time with Ken.' Instantly, without effort, I was back in my body.

"With a defibrillator in hand, the paramedic screamed, 'She made it!' Yes, I made it. From that day forward, I was no longer fearful of death. The challenge was living life here and bringing that magnificence, that feeling I had, to this crazy and convoluted world. I had that missing piece of me anchored in my being to help me live life as if every day were my last."

Panacea for Procrastination

The supporting adage is, "*Don't put off until tomorrow what you can do today.*" Avoidance of living life fully or responsibly, coupled with not attending to necessary details and commitments, demands brain-drain energy. Responsibilities don't mysteriously disappear, and wallowing in thoughts of lack, incompleteness, guilt or anxiety, zaps our reserves.

James, a sixteen-year-old procrastinator, divulged his homework avoidance tactics in a Family Morph Group. "I write great songs, practice my guitar, and even tap deep talks with my parents. If they remind me I'm slacking, I say, 'Yeah, yeah, yeah', and do nothing."

James rambled, "I can't get motivated. I know I have homework, but I avoid it. The clock's ticking down toward bedtime, and I'm online or on my cell and then I'm zonked. So, I set my alarm for an hour early wakeup to try to get it done."

He admitted falling behind in his class work. His grades suffered from not giving 100%, which lowered his expectations of his abilities, ultimately lowering his self-esteem.

What attitudes perpetuated this syndrome? How could he change it?

James discovered, "I still wanted my parents to do things for me, like getting me out of trouble, standing up for me. When I realized I was scared to do it on my own, I was ready to do something new."

Our young procrastinator adopted one simple tactic. He kept a daily to-do list and wrote a *Declaration of Commitment* to engage completely in whatever was before him, vowing to practice for thirty days. James proudly stated, "My list is like a personal trainer. When I honor it, I feel better about myself. My test scores are up. Imagine – friends call *me* for homework tips, instead of me calling them."

Desires Are a Reflecting Pool

Desires demonstrate our true nature. Maybe you want to sculpt, to be a Big Brother for at-risk youth, or to be the best CEO on the planet. It's our inner voice calling us to attain our highest purpose. These desires serve as the button of Change: they show us what we need to know about ourselves. As yearnings fester within, confusion and anxiety prevail if we fail to listen and honor our innate nature.

All desires are a reflecting pool. Ancient traditions characterized desires like lust, greed, and jealousy as thieves of the heart that rob us of our *Authentic Self* (defined as being one with God). Negative emotions tie us in knots and wreak HAvoc rather than HArmony in our lives. Jealousy about a friend's good fortune or lusting over your brother's wife or anger's all-consuming fire about losing a promotion is guaranteed to boomerang back to the sender – YOU!

If we feel jealousy, envy, anger, at being left behind by someone else's achievement, interpret it as a signpost of your purpose lying dormant. Morph it into a positive inspirational energy. Take the energy force of envy, vital energy (all energy is vital energy), and use it to propel you in the direction of your desire. Think! "If they can do it, so can I."

These potent messages are restlessly waiting to be discovered, nurtured, and manifested. **Energy flows where attention goes.** Choose the positive. Remember the *Morph Magnet*. Watch who and what you draw into your life.

Who is on your radar screen? What we focus on is what we get... and who we hang out with is who we become. How about hanging out with the best of your Self?

Reflecting Pool Within: Gaze deep into a pool or body of water. See your reflection twinkling back at you. Absorb the stillness and purifying energy.

As I gazed at the water hole, my reflection smiled back. I discovered a new friend to rejoice with.

Gentlemen – A Soft Heart Reigns

Macho men, Groucho, and tough guys have one thing in common...they seem gruff and powerful. What is power to you? What is powerless? First off gentlemen, I will repeat…gentle men. Is that an oxymoron? Certainly, NOT! In this greed-monger world we can no longer blame the patriarch – callousness is a human condition, beyond gender, race, or creed.

- ♥ **How can we turn on our heart-meter and establish the truth within?** How can we soften our hearts and reside, where authentic power reigns? **Contemplate** what you habitually say or do. Habits are reactive response, either diminishing spontaneity or igniting Awareness of infinite possibility. What possibility are you resisting or ignoring?

- ♥ **Take a moment and Breathe deeply.** Ask: "What dreams do I have on hold?" "What am I waiting for to bring me contentment?"

- ♥ **Music feeds the soul** – Singing, dancing, Mozart. Ah! Bounce out of the intellect; escape mind-babble battling your heart. The mind needs to dominate; to convince you it knows best. Who is it that listens to the mind?

- ♥ **Breathe again** – connect with the ONE that knows it is not the mind. This is your true essence...your soft place of heart. Your true Power!

- ♥ **Walk Barefoot.** Connect with the vibration of Earth's heartbeat, a grounding stillness.

- ♥ **Take Time to connect with a loved one,** a friend. You don't have to take charge or know anything special. Discover, feel, see with your heart. Hear the silence between each word, between each breath.

This is the place of authentic power...a Soft Heart, Gentle Men.

CHAPTER 9

SPIRALING INTO OPPORTUNITY

When facing a challenge, it is our great opportunity to expand awareness and to become the change. We are in an evolutionary process on the planet; catapulted by upheaval, we are moving into a new age, a quickening that requires adaptability. Imagine our ancestors riding in a horse and buggy when a Model T Ford tooted by. "That contraption is not for me," might have been the initial response. But resistance or denial will not stop our collapsing infrastructures – both personal and global. We are living in a time of emancipation from shredded values, igniting the freedom to unite. During this fiery time of creative explosion, the human race is marching into transformation. Do not be the last one to hop aboard. Be the conductor. Help us all, together, in HArmony to surrender and embrace a quantum leap of faith.

Micro-Managing Mighty Stress

Henry, a middle-aged business owner, was adept at micromanaging.

For two decades, he ran his marketing firm in a hands-on style. With an infusion of cash, the company rapidly expanded. Henry was in a quandary about how to efficiently lead his team, and found the adjustment difficult. He could not delegate or relinquish control. Waiting for Henry's involvement, his staff was under pressure, missing delivery dates, and suffering time delays. The expansion required a detached overview more than a micro style could deliver. For once in his life, confronted by viral marketing and new methods, Henry wasn't up to speed. Almost overnight, the job he once loved became an albatross, and he dreaded going into the office.

One morning, faced with backed-up appointments, phones ringing, and papers piled high waiting for approval, Henry accelerated into high anxiety. High-pitch sounds were shrill and the walls closed-in. After hyperventilating for a few moments, he called me, "Merrie Lynn, I've lost it. It's a new world, and I don't fit." From that declaration, I assisted Henry out of his comfort zone into a new life path. I suggested that he begin to ask serious questions about his priorities and get down to the truth of what was really in his way.

Re-Purpose Your Life – Lose It to Gain It All

Re-establishing priorities and his value-hierarchy expanded Henry's thinking. He asked himself, "What counts most?" The shift included creating quality personal/family time. We dealt with his fears of ageism and captured his astute assessment skills. Henry zeroed in and isolated the problem at work: "It's me. I am the problem. When I hire key personnel, it's a gut instinct. Do they have the *right stuff*? If not, I think to myself, 'pass.' Maybe harsh, but it works. If I'd been in line for CEO, I'd say 'I've done my bit and it's time to move on.' " Then, with a measured calm he added, "BUT…I do have the *right stuff* to inspire and get the best out of a team. I am a force as a motivator. It's time I became a coach."

Without hesitation, Henry relinquished his CEO position, remaining Chairman of the Board. Daily activities were no longer relegated to his office. Creativity exploded and new product lines took form, along with a burst of enthusiasm within Henry and his staff. Giving up his leadership role of twenty-five years allowed him to embrace the new and to enjoy his hard-earned success. Holding on to something that was not working created chaos. So he chose an open state of mind, opting for the good of the whole, including what best served his needs.

Bingo Bango Bongo

Henry added a Morph technique, *Bongo Emotion*, to his daily repertoire. If tempted to repeat a worn habit or quell anxiety he would play the bongos, safely banging out frustration. His tension released in minutes, followed by the pure joy of jamming. Henry's enthusiasm trickled onto Travis, his teenage son, who joined him on the drums.

Travis revealed his own motivation for jamming. "I was sick of dodging bullies at school. Now I see their faces on the drum and let out my anger, drumming. Getting it out, I get past the putdowns and feel better. I'm not a fun target to pick on anymore." Bongo release benefited Henry's work life, the bonding zone with his son, and improved Travis' life, to boot.

Life-Goals List: Your Snapshot to Play the Future Forward

In my late teens I read Napoleon's Hill's life-transforming book *Think and Grow Rich*. Filled with anticipation, I wrote the list of "what I wanted" to have a successful and happy life. It included personal, physical, career, relationships, financial, hobbies and interests – whatever I could imagine. That list came from deep within my heart. I wanted to be a good person, to be kind, generous, ethical, and help to make the world a better place. I wanted to learn to play the guitar, speak a foreign language, travel the world, live in New York, Los Angeles, London, own property with a view of the mountains, be a successful actress, make people laugh, help those in need, marry a great mate and have happy children, etc.

My treasured list was and still is a blueprint for my life. I gave myself permission to want it all and to continue to learn and grow; doing so opened a portal of truth and created a tangible destiny. Having accomplished many things on my Life-Goals List, it's clear I'll likely be well over a hundred years old before attaining all my goals. No, I don't play the guitar, as of now. But, I can whistle and do birdcalls. I never could blow outward and whistle, so with practice I learned a suck-in whistle and do interesting bird trills.

Make *your* Life-Goals List. Write all of your goals. Writing it down concretizes your dreams and sets forth the possibility into the universal databank. Review the list periodically. Check off accomplishments.

Strategy Booster: Practice – Practice – Practice!

As a varsity high school field hockey player, I was a mere 5'5" playing against girls who were six-feet tall. Being the left-wing offensive forward, I had many chances to score and did. My advantage was being closer to the ground. With the ingenuity of my brother Bill, a keen ice hockey player, we created an unprecedented offensive strategy: I spent hours going under a lowered pogo stick without my knees touching the ground (a foul in field hockey is when knees touch the ground). During my arduous practice, kids viewed the spectacle with criticism and jeers.

Totally focused I forged on, attempting to squeeze under Bill's spread legs as he taunted defensive moves. We would measure the triangle between the crotch and out-spread feet as a guideline. Each encounter built my confidence and reinforced a competitive edge. Bill prodded me to fire the ball at the net, and if I put one in, he'd bellow, "She shoots, she scores!"

Steaming to our league's playoffs, we were down to the final game for the championship. We were tied 4 to 4, needing one more goal to win. With only seconds left, most of the team had given up, assuming we would go into overtime. Not me! I was alert, time slowed down, every beat of my heart seemed an eternity. I raced for the ball and glued it to my stick. A defense player towered over me, her legs straddled apart. In a fraction of a second, I calculated how low I needed to crouch. With all my might, I scuttled between her legs, still controlling the ball, then aimed for the net and scored.

From the stands, I could hear Bill's voice announcing, "She shoots. She scores!" – repeating the very words, the very vision, he had pounded into my head during our practice sessions. There it was in all our glory; we won the championship! I learned how exhilarating it is to give my all, and then succeed.

When do you choose to give it all, play until you can't breathe because you love the game? Are you willing to create an unprecedented tactic, have joy in the process, and play while reinventing it? Can you muster your own originality to take front stage and trust it? It's your unique contribution coupled with sweat that makes you a winner. Tread the path no one has taken before. Give up the safety net of following the herd and ending up in the mediocrity-zone. Kick the ball out of the park and let someone else chase it. Lead your own way. Play the future forward.

What's Your Winning Style?

Take a moment to define your style of playing the game. Do you strive to be the best you can be, enjoy the process, relax, yet remain energized and focused? Or do you sacrifice your emotions and body to win at all costs? Is winning a do-or-die, or is it a process to enjoy?

Result-oriented competitors thrive under pressure. Winning is the motivator. Result personalities feel heightened anxiety when they lose and irrationally bloated when they win. Several losses can trigger an emotional setback, causing a fear-based syndrome. Stress management is often required to fend off disease.

Process-oriented players also enter the game to win. Yet, they are joy-based, aware of relishing the moment. They value the learning curve, as well as the outcome. Process personalities operate from a faith in Self, are not capsized by losses, and do not measure their identity by the number of wins. Rather than lock into past or future performances, they evaluate where they are now, allowing a margin of growth as a sound base.

Result-and process-oriented people both rely on practiced skills to get them through the game, to win a client, close a deal, or get the part. Attitude, determination, and commitment help them persevere. However, their motivating forces are diametrically opposed. Someone who's goal-driven races toward the big win. The trick, though, is to set smaller challenges on the way, so the goal is not the be-all-end-all. A process person may need a boost to hit the deadline, while still staying at ease.

Whatever your innate winning style, in meetings or meet-ups, bring the best of you along: cheerfulness, compassionate listening, heartfelt commitment. Focus on the highest good for all; it brings spontaneity, clarity, new vision...and true prosperity.

The Process of Play in Your Career

HUMOR is #1 in life, which includes the workplace. So what if you are a dud when it comes to cracking a joke, or if you feel like a firecracker that fizzles out when you blow the punch line? Don't fret. Just having a funny notion in your mind creates a smile. Humor diffuses threats and creates a human playground.

I developed humor to fend off emotional insecurity and eventually lecherous old producers. I learned to crack a joke in order to save face, and to laugh at their jokes in order to ease communications. Humor became my security blanket. I had a blast practicing my timing, dousing one-liners on everyone from the butcher to the cabby to the zookeeper.

Amp-up your funnies. Buy a joke book. Rehearse one or two jokes. See the humor in the moment. Watch *Seinfeld* reruns. Wiggle your nose. Having a sense of humor about yourself, about your predicaments, about the lessons in life, is the most gratifying of all spiritual gifts – it is a key to happiness.

Opportunity Awaits – The Audition, Interview, Performance

The average person interviews up to eight times in a lifetime for job changes. A salesperson may see several clients per day, may converse with twenty by phone, contact a hundred by email. A professional actor often auditions two or three times a day in a busy season. The stress-success approach to optimal performance is a pressure-cooker: sell the client, get the job, win the game. What techniques can help us do our best? How can we overcome stress, fear of failure, rejection, or the need to be accepted? How can we honor our authenticity in the process?

The interview or audition requires preparation, preparation, preparation! You need to know your stuff, be a pro, and be ready for the competition. Assuming you are *all that*, what ensures a competitive edge? To do your best! You can't control the competition. You can't control nepotism or an interviewer's bad hair day. You can control your commitment to in-depth homework, having a positive attitude, and persevering in the face of rejection.

Mastery comes through study, evaluating past successes and failures, and working with a coach. The interview or presentation may take years, months, or weeks of preparation before the actual feat. We have all heard the twenty-five year "overnight success" story. Stop whining and start winning. Speak up: brag. Spout your attributes using third party adulation. "My team made me the lead coach." "My boss said, 'I need you to handle the logistics, or it won't get done.' "

Having confidence creates an impact and leads to success.

Sponsors make the world go-around. Be your best supporter and watch who shows up to help make your dream a reality. Contemplate: self-will + grace is miracle in Action.

♥ ♥ ♥

A group of actors related their audition woes: "My hands shook so badly I couldn't read the script." "My heart beat so fast when I entered the room I know everyone could hear it." "I could tell they didn't like me the second I walked in." "When they called my name I wanted to run." "I wasn't ready. I needed more time to prepare." "If I don't get the part my agent will fire me." "All the other actors looked so relaxed. I felt the walls close in." "I need to chill."

Notice where the actor's focused their attention: a nervous physical state, comparing themselves to the competition, on the interviewer, not being good enough, and fear of rejection. They didn't focus on the Action before them.

Fear-based panics are fire-signs of failure. Dousing the jitters, chilling-out before the game, the interview, or sales presentation requires using a practiced technique. Shift erratic feelings and physical responses through relaxation techniques. Deep breathing, meditation, visualization, massage, and exercise prepare the nervous system to perform under pressure.

♥ ♥ ♥

To Chill: Meditation is my chosen daily practice. For years, I have awakened at 3:00 A.M. when all is quiet, with only the moon's gentle light and my owl hooting and watching over me. I used to toss and turn, put the pillow overhead, try to go back to sleep. Now I attune to this graceful time, close my eyes, take a few deep breaths, and allow the barrage of feelings, thoughts, and emotions to roll by – as if floating on a cloud. Within minutes the benefits are felt. Mind chatter dims into a peaceful state, the air clears, I connect to the divine within. Through prayer we speak to God. In meditation, God speaks to us.

Imagine swimming in the ocean and an undercurrent carries you beyond a range of safety. On what would you put your immediate focus? Would you panic, flailing your arms, screaming for help, or would you stay calm, calculate the shore's distance, and reserve every ounce of strength to get back? Every breath taken would count. Chaotic emotions and negative thoughts would drain your physical capacity to perform optimally. Staying calm, focused, and steady, yet having enough vital energy to get to shore, would be necessary to save your life.

All energy is the same energy: transmute it. Tension, the jitters, the adrenaline rush – it is the same energy that is required for performance. If a mood is debilitating (like dizziness, nausea, fatigue, or the urge to flee), remember it is temporary; moods change. Be mindful of emotional and physical triggers so you can Morph them into energy-boosts.

Vital Energized Mode

♥ Acknowledge your real feelings: terror, apathy, anger, panic, hyperactivity. Accept your authentic state, mood, or feelings: know you can change it. *Coin Flip* an opposite response. Turn "I feel scared" into "I am OK where I *am.*"

♥ Remind yourself: "I can be calm and focus my attention on what I choose." Then choose what to focus on.

♥ Do a physical blowout: Put your hands together, squeeze tightly, focus on the pressure. Slowly release the tension. Feel your energy expand into the present moment…the space of vital energy, your *Chi,* balanced and centered.

♥ Get your attention off yourself and onto the task: Review your lines or your client's name or perfect your new product pitch. Focus on the process of the interview and visualize a positive outcome. Give up the notion of perfection and be willing to be imperfect. And know at your core you are perfection in Action.

♥ No second-guessing: "I coulda, woulda, shoulda."

♥ To strengthen life force energy: Whisk a flat palm from the belly button straight up to your chin. Feel the shift of to vital energy. Imagine a gentle breeze. Light particles easing over you. Bathing, floating in stillness, revitalized.

Confidence Is a State of Mind

Confidence is a state of self-assurance, self-reliance. Give yourself an "Okay to Win – Okay to Lose." It's okay not to hit every ball or get every sale or to be first all the time. Confidence, your self-esteem, and personal identity will remain whatever the outcome. It's okay to collect your *no's* and to move on and say, "NEXT."

On the other hand, give yourself an "OK to Win." Winners build up a batting average and kick-start opportunities. Increasing your times up to bat elevates the *opportunity/win* margin. If you have only one client or one interview, the pressure-cooker of scoring the Big One is exasperating. Babe Ruth was remembered for his home runs, not his misses.

What can you learn from the miss or catch? What can you learn from saying, "I can do it", even if it's a first and you've never done it before.

"I Can Do It!"

I performed on *The Flip Wilson Show* as one of 49 beauty queens. Geraldine, Flip's beauty queen character, was the 50th. When the producer shouted, "Who can twirl a baton?" my hand shot up, "I can." He called me forward with another actress, leaving the others in the dust. Happily, I faked an imaginary baton, twirling my hand in mid-air. Lucky a baton wasn't on the set; I had never twirled in public, or even at home since I was six-years-old.

After rehearsal, I bought a baton at a drug store and practiced until the wee hours. The next day I twirled in an odd fashion, and the director loved it, instructing the other actress (a real cheerleader) to follow *me*. Seething, she tried. Being their favorite, I was selected to do lines with Flip. In an hilarious choreographed fight between "Miss

Miami" (me) and Flip, I accidentally pulled off his wig. It became a blooper on Johnny Carson's *The Tonight Show*. And, I became an NBC darling. From one "I can do it!" I leaped out of a bit player category and became a guest star.

Know you can do it, learn it, and perfect it – no matter what it takes. Say, "I can do it."

Make sure to stay out of the "I'll try" zone. "Try" is another excuse for not believing you can do it, and being afraid to fail. You don't *try*. Either you do it or you don't. It's a *Yes* or *No*. Either you are pregnant or you're not! Happiness comes from being open to all of life. Choose to Live in YES. And trust your heart will tell you when to say no.

Open your consciousness; stretch out your arms. Repeat, "YES! YES! YES!" Do you feel a shift of awareness? "Yes" deletes resistance, allowing an opening for miracles to flow.

Network – Network – Network

Networking amps-up the success game. The *six-degrees of separation* theory is true – someone you know knows someone you need to know. Take a risk and ask ask ask for what you need; services, contacts, assistance. From finding a good dentist to locating the best webmaster, get a referral from a happy customer. Find out what you need to know. Outsource your weak areas. Attend seminars, go to networking events, take an expert to lunch and gather information about their expertise and talent.

Effective networking entails more than business cards, having a flashy website, or being on a VIP A-list. To stay on your game and get what you want requires people skills: be interested in someone else's needs and having the entitlement to express your own. The answer to your needs may be as simple as asking someone you just met. Trust that synchronicity is supporting you wherever you are, with whomever you meet.

Practice people skills daily. Be friendly. Don't be shy in the supermarket. Talk to the butcher about farm-raised salmon vs. the attributes of wild Alaskan. Ask questions. Practice getting to the point. Cultivate the ability to be exact, to have clear intent and brevity in speech This is the art of developing your pitch speech – those critical succinct sentences to deliver about your vision, your *biz* plan, to a potential investor.

Networking is most effective when basic consideration operates over a desperate plea to get something. Don't be a beggar. Be a giver of enthusiasm and positive expectation when asking for advice, a contact, or a future meeting. I learn from everyone I meet, even if they are occasionally rude or can't be bothered. This is part of the game, so don't take it personally!

Hobnobbing for Profit and Prophet

Bruce, a CPA in a small accounting firm, splurged above his means by joining a tennis club. His intention was to hobnob with the club members and expand his client base. To better his embarrassingly soft game, he spent hours with the tennis pro. Bruce's athletic prowess was questionable, and his progress was slow. The more missed balls, the more reluctant he became to face the die-hards on the court or to mingle with them. His membership seemed a worthless investment. However, the tennis pro was relentless, foisting basic lessons at him.

One day, as Bruce was plowing through traffic, he was involved in a minor fender-bender. Concerned with the injuries of an elderly man, Bruce accompanied him to the hospital for X-rays. While there, Max, the injured man, said, "I'd like you to meet my son; he could learn a lesson or two from you. He spends his entire life only thinking how to make money. If he found me lying in the street bleeding, he'd wait until he closed the deal before he'd help me. How about meeting him at my club for dinner?"

Max, it turned out, was a business tycoon and a founding member of the tennis club: Mr. Elite personified. Bruce then recalled having seen Max on TV. The interviewer had asked him, "What makes you tick, what drives you?" Max responded, "My passion about the project and making a deal work for everyone. I could have retired at sixty, but that wasn't my nature. So, challenged by a merger, I entangled myself in the deal-from-hell. It meant a lot to me personally. I had a passion for that one, a feeling not to settle. So I kept at it."

The deal-from-hell had transformed into a hell-of-a-deal. Max reportedly made millions on the merger. And now, in awe-inspiring synchronicity, Bruce was about to meet Max's son, Arnold, for a game of tennis. Arnold turned out to be a laid-back tennis player and confided to Bruce, "It's a relief to play for fun. But, come on, my father didn't introduce us for the prospect of whacking balls. He never does anything without thinking a deal is attached. Now tell me exactly what you have in mind. Maybe we can do some business?"

Lesson learned: Bruce followed his instincts that the club would be beneficial for him, and he stayed loyal to an essential ingredient: the human touch, the caring to take a moment to help another. He demonstrated his fine character by going to the hospital with Max, rather than taking a posture of who was to blame for the accident.

Max perceived that Bruce could own-up and be there when it counted. He also knew that his son was receptive to new opportunities. Being a consummate judge of character and success potential, it was Max, the magnet of unlimited agendas, who seized the moment.

♥ ♥ ♥

Seizing the moment is an awareness used by masters in every field of endeavor. You follow an impulse, a drive, and push toward opportunity. Being clear about what you want helps to recognize and seize opportune moments. It is a go-for-broke, instantaneous recognition of possibility. The *YES!* The "go for it!" Holding back can result in lost opportunities and regrets.

How often do you join a club, make that extra phone call, or rewrite your sales pitch to advance your career or fix your plight? What effort are you willing to engage in your pursuit?

Bruce worked hard at perfecting a tennis game. Did he waste his time? Would he have met the old man and had the same results had he not joined the club? How can we trust our instincts and seize opportunity, as Max was able to do?

The key is to *show up*. Put your intention in the foreground of your consciousness, and then let your magnetizing unconscious draw it to you.

Seize the Opportunity

To seize the opportunity isn't a desperate grasp for the last straw. Opportunity alerts the winner's edge: it is the upshot to the goal. Sometimes a prospect falls into our laps, or in my case, literally walks onto our life's stage. Without any self-serving intention on my part, I found myself in a position where I had to "seize the opportunity" for my employers' public image and for my own safety.

As a young model in the Motor-City Detroit, I was the "Ford Face" in TV commercials and print ads one season, then pitching for Chevy or Chrysler the next year. Contracts included live appearances at select auto shows across the county.

At one of the shows, I was pitching a prototype that transformed into a boat, and the attendees wanted to chat or take photos with the car and me. The top brass was scheduled to view the exhibit, and as they approached, unbeknownst to me, they witnessed me smiling for a photo. I was holding one baby twin, as the mother held the other.

The executives watched me network, working the room on the company's behalf. Soon, they huddled near the staging area. I was alerted and given a cue to begin my spiel. With all the charm and pizzazz I could muster, I pushed the button to automate the car's transformation into the boat. Out of nowhere, a man in the crowd began screeching a political speech. I was on stage, still the center of attention, and I had a microphone. Knowing the performer's cardinal rule states, "The one who has the microphone has the power", I continued my pitch over his rant. Rattled by the distraction, as the car parts flipped into the boat, I reversed my lines and described the opposite – the boat turning back into the car.

Then, without warning, the ranting man pushed through the crowd and jumped onto the stage. He lunged toward me and grabbed the microphone. My mind raced in duality, "Take it back from him." "No! Get going before he hurts you." That was my moment of truth. As I gazed at the executives, then back to the man, my gut instinct opted for a damsel-in-distress persona and to hightail it off the stage. I leapt over the crowd and fell smack into the arms of the top Chevrolet honcho, my rescuer. "You're a brave woman, aren't you?" he asked, helping me to my feet.

As the poor man on stage was subdued by security, I saw how gross and foolish the action of grabbing the microphone from him would have been. My decision not to be brazen, but rather to uphold the company image, endeared me to my superiors. My role with the company changed in that moment. I was invited to help with future show concepts and to write and direct some show bits, which included a mannequin act to attract attendees to a lackluster small sedan.

My ability to remain alert paid off – I was able to uphold the company image when the moment of truth arose. Staying focused and ready for anything works miracles in the public eye – or behind closed doors when no one can see. Are you ready and willing to go for IT and to seize opportunity when it comes?

Create Your Think Tank

Admittedly, a bathtub is a great think-tank. How about spiraling outward and upping your ops and success ratio? Enlist the support of an army of helpers: your primo think-tank of advisors – all experts in their fields.

Get Real: Clarify your skills and weaknesses. Identify what elements you need to achieve your goal (marketing your product, family conflict-resolution skills, financial management, etc.). Match a successful person to each skill you need. Ask yourself, "Who do I know who has mastered or attained this acumen?" Who could benefit from your skills? Create a win-win for everyone participating.

It is advantageous to use brainstorming for issues. Set time limits so everyone to participate. Weekly or monthly meetings can prove successful. Set a timeframe that will ensure a project to completion. Your accountability will be on the line – a great motivator.

You may not need a whole brain-herd; a weekly phone call with an accountability partner may be enough keep you on track. As needed, other experts can be sought through social networking and word of mouth – a practical think-tank approach.

Glue Stick **Your Personal Brand**

Branding is a *glue stick* in your arsenal of success tricks and represents you or your biz's cohesiveness, tenacity, persistence, constancy, and unique identity. Use it to generate a favorable buzz, build alliances, and gain repeat clients. Branding is uniquely yours, so find what works. "MerrieWay.com" has an identifiable 'M' for a logo; it honors *Morphing into Unity*.

On a personal level how often do you hear, "You remind me of…" so and so? For curiosity, ask, "How do I remind you of them?" Don't take particulars to heart; the comparison is an important barometer of other's perceptions of us.

Are you frequently labeled with adjectives like *terrific, jittery, blunt*, or *outrageous*? Hearing similar feedback indicates that your personal trademark is reflecting big time (maybe positively or negatively, from the observer's standpoint). Being mindful of our tendencies is vital. How do we describe ourselves to others? What do we consciously or unconsciously telegraph to the world?

In life's play, we become enmeshed in our limited persona. We erroneously believe it to be our capacity – "Who we are is who we will always be…" – rather than acknowledging, "This is who I am *choosing* to be." With awareness, we counteract tendencies that belie our best interest.

I learned: Don't back off or apologize for your uniqueness. Come on, if it works, use it. Are you happy with the results of relationships and events you encounter? Identify those winning qualities and share them. Enjoy your personal trademark. If not, it's time for a personal redo, a makeover, new branding. What if you feel, "I don't want to seem pushy or salesy." "Being boastful turns me off." Why trade false humility for your authenticity, your power. Don't be your best-kept secret for it will land you in perpetual anonymity (no promotions, no $ bonus). Promote yourself with entitlement. Honor your talents, ambition, and potential to get what you rightfully deserve.

Write Your PR Release

Imagine you are a superstar. In your world, you are the expert! Use superlatives – *Expert Trainer, Charismatic Leader, Powerful Coach, Dynamic Speaker* – to sell yourself. Utilize a thesaurus to embellish your traits. The focus is not on getting a job – it's on you: how YOU are special. Sell yourself as a friend, lover, parent, cool person. This is for your eyes only. Are you hesitating to boast? Put Mr. or Ms. Humble on hold. You don't have to feel like Steven Spielberg or Mighty Mouse yet. Just go for it.

When you are finished, read it. Is it embarrassing, too short, unconvincing? What provoked cringing, guilt, disgust or blushing? What made you giggle, smile, feel joy or satisfaction?

Select one or two traits to embellish or delete. Practice your traits for a week. Review the list at the end of week. How did your personal traits work for you? What would you like to change?

The Magnetic Power of Conviction

Are you hesitant, afraid to step up, concerned about how you appear to others? Are you wrapped-up in self-consciousness?

A solid intention and unshakable conviction is the core of leadership. Unwavering vision boosts your ability to elicit support and participation. Enthusiasm attracts people like a charismatic pit-bull.

I've often heard, "We better say yes. Who can resist her?" People seek the energy of single-minded purpose, backed by a feasible proposition. When weighing your offer, prospective partners respond with, "Why not?" Raise the bar of what you have to offer and do what it takes to prepare yourself; then get into full gear and collect your *why-not*.

Set the Stage

Next time you are under the gun, feeling pressure to make that sale, or in a competition to perform, remember to take the ball and put it in your court.

As a producer and an actor, I've straddled both sides of the casting couch. Knowing a performer's terror, I go out of my way to make an actor comfortable, giving them their best shot. However, you may be meeting with someone who has no idea how to put themselves in your shoes. So, you need to take control; really look at the interviewer, connect, and then aim to score. Why give your power over to anyone, especially the interviewer or the competition? Own your ground.

A notable director shared his competition theory with me. "Let's say you're one of twenty ladies in the waiting room up for the same part. So you think to yourself, 'Guess I have a twenty-to-one shot'. That kind of thinking puts your mind in the long-shot mode. But, the winner-power-ratio says, 'It's them or me' – then you've got a two-to-one shot. That kind of thinking makes you one of the favorites."

Take one thing onto the interview stage: When you go through that door remember that everyone on the other side hopes you are *the One* – the answer to their problem. They want to fill the job.

The "Magical If"

Let's leap into the imagination and create positive expectation. The *Magical If* is different than the *What If* disaster thinking, which examines the pitfalls, calculates the downside, or anticipates all that could happen according to Murphy's Law.

The *Magical If* is the polar opposite. It highlights quantum possibilities of Action, positively influencing the results. It assimilates a situation **as if** it has already occurred.

Set up an imaginary scenario. What is the situation? What do you want to accomplish? What are the motivations for each person involved?

♥ Believe you attain your goal and that you are worthy of its attainment. Feelings of doubt will split your commitment and derail your efforts. Affirm aloud, "I am successfully fulfilling_____." Repeat when doubts arise. Inhale possibility. Exhale doubts.

♥ Act *as if,* think *as if,* speak *as if,* dress *as if* the result you want has already occurred.

The Secret of Keeping Counsel

Keep your own counsel. You do not have to tell everyone everything all the time. Selective disclosure saves time, HAssles, and resentments. I learned the lesson of keeping my counsel when it came to my spiritual experiences. Sharing what others could not perceive diluted my Truth in fruitless explanation. Holding the precious energy and *AHAs* within my own energy field infused me with clarity of conviction and purposeful direction.

Use discernment, discrimination, and good judgment of *who* you tell *what*. Blabbing your feelings, news and thoughts out of excitement can backfire. This includes sharing your dreams, goals, and talents. **We must uphold and protect our gifts, lest they be diminished by those who can't support our good.** If they do not support your dreams or good, bless them and move on! This opens opportunities door. Trust, by maintaining a discriminating awareness, the right ears will hear, and the world will offer itself to you.

I love the notion, "There are six billion people in this world ready to serve ME. And the kicker is I'm one of many ready to serve YOU."

Not buying the Pollyanna crusade? Are you a pragmatist hooked on the trappings of duality? "Focusing on happiness conjures sadness. Focusing on health masks the terror of sickness. How about reverse psychology? Do you trick your mind, sending it on a brief joyride while you take charge? No debates. Own what works for you.

Hellish Recipe for Un–Happiness came to me in a nightmarish frenzy, tailored for a curmudgeon's juicy delight. Down is your Up. A half-empty glass enables a killjoy stance, securing chains that bind. Delete 'Bounce Recipes' from you aura field's memory-bank.

Stop chasing Happy! Way hot to choose misery and wallow through eternity.

1. Bounce Off Walls at every opportunity. Go for emotional meltdowns.

2. Let your mind run like a rabid dog, biting at anything and anyone in its path.

3. Be a worrywart. You need all the answers.

4. Traditional knowledge is more rewarding than the fake gems inside of you.

5. Ignore intuition and innate wisdom, wholly reserved for airy-fairies.

6. Keep your heart closed.

7. Complain incessantly, and hang out with abusers.

8. Never be wrong, compromise, or give unconditionally.

9. "I Love You", three little words to avoid at all cost.

10. Shun, run from the feeling of Love. Love is fool's play.

11. Eat like a glutton. Sleep like a vampire.

12. Humor sucks. Leave folly to clowns.

13. Never laugh out loud.

Whew! BE Happy pressure is off. So, let's BE REAL…what say you?

CHAPTER 10

GROW TO KNOW

L ife-long curiosity and joy of learning is empowerment. As Confucius said, "Tell me and I will forget. Show me and I will remember. Involve me and I will understand."

Grow what you know. Have you learned anything new today? Has an enlightened new concept crossed your mind? As adults, we become less open to the new or unknown. It's unsettling when our rhythms are challenged and our fixed ways of handling the world upset. Maintaining the curiosity of a child, seeing with fresh eyes, hearing with new ears makes each moment a revelation.

Seeing in a New Way

In the land of the *Cyclops*, the woman with an eye in the back of her head was Queen! Seeing is a 360-degree possibility. Seeing with our minds-eye, sensing with every pore in our body is intuitive sight. Focus on a situation in which you are struggling. Put aside all knowledge, assumptions, and preconceptions about it. Wiggle your toes. Tap your nose. Blink fast. Wave your arms. Now you're in a ready and completely fresh state of awareness.

- ♥ Think about the situation like a baby, as if you know nothing about it. Blink fast.

- ♥ Observe the situation. What do you notice about it? Tap your nose.

- ♥ Write down your impressions, even the most basic or obvious ones. Wiggle your toes.

- ♥ What characteristics are familiar, what do they remind you of? Jump up and down.

- ♥ How have you (or others) handled your query? Wave your arms and pretend to fly like a bird.

♥ ♥ ♥

Adept learners know their learning skills and maximize them. To increase innate capacity, identify your strengths; be aware of how you learn. Knowing your weaknesses gives a head start to incorporate different skills and stretch your learning aptitude. Whether you tend to be either dominant or a combination of visual (see it on the page), auditory (hear it, spoken), kinesthetic (hands-on, movement), verbal/linguistic (reading and lecture), or people-oriented, you can, with practice, enhance a learning style that doesn't come naturally.

Kelly, a self-proclaimed klutz, was uncoordinated, not athletically inclined. Yet, her clumsiness earned her the nickname of "Quick Snatch" for her amazing retrieval of objects she dropped or bumped-into before they crashed.

If you frequently bump into walls, smash or crash objects, it's time to boost kinesthetic awareness. We learned to ride a bike through repeated practice. The ability is recorded in our visceral/physical memory bank as an innate life skill to be called upon at any time. An athlete can be in motion while simultaneously utilizing a mental strategy to win the game.

Choose a physical sport or exercise and then practice, practice, practice. A simple game of hopscotch (a definite balance challenger), rowing a boat (practice paddling with both arms promoting ambidextrous ability), a game of Ping-Pong (increases eye-hand coordination), swimming, dribbling a basketball – these activities will add to your physical memory and adaptability bankroll. A learning skill spills over into other areas, adding to peak performance.

Emotional IQ/Intra-Learner

We learn through sensing, having feelings about something, and connecting viscerally and experientially. *Emotional Intelligence* informs the attitudinal part of learning. Our attitude can be positive in one area of our abilities and negative in another. You might say, "I'm smart in math, but forget directions…I'm an idiot." Expectations regarding your abilities are a conditioned response based on past experience. The belief, "I am a good (or poor) learner," registers as an emotional memory that was formed by where we were, what happened, and how we felt at the time. It has an energetic life of its own within our emotional database.

Admittedly, I have been geographically challenged. A GPS is great in a car, but it doesn't help when you're walking. Using landmarks helped me find my way. In Philadelphia, from my hotel I spotted a clock, *"Great, I thought, I'll be able to find my way back."* Coming home,

I was lost, exasperated, and exhausted – I couldn't believe it, the clock was four-sided. Now, I've learned to read a map. I even carry a compass! They call me Ms. Magoo.

Deconstruct Negative Learning Associations

- ♥ Recall the place and time associated with your first negative sensation.
- ♥ Allow your breathing to slow down. Envision where you were, who was there, what was said. See yourself in the experience; notice your sensations, thoughts, and feelings.
- ♥ Let your impressions run through your mind. Jot them down in your Morph Journal.
- ♥ Now, Morph it! Recreate it as a positive experience. You can also choose a more positive time and recreate it as a learning model.

My memory became photographic when I used images for associations, and my math aptitude increased by learning the simple technique of rounding off numbers. Both abilities improved recall and processing time. But, being smacked with a ruler for being left-handed seemed like a curse until I found out Einstein was left-handed and he didn't talk until he was three.

Basically I am an intuitive/quantum learner; I sense what is needed. Often I get an overview, see the context before assimilating the details. *Quantum learning* is based on taking in the whole, then recognizing the parts of the puzzle. It's working backwards, from rote learning where we learn step-by-step to solve a problem. You see the answer and then go back to prove the query, or the logical explanation. There isn't *one* right way to learn, it is unique to each of us.

The Figure-Outer

Catch Phrase: "I've got to figure this out." (Or, "I can't figure this out.") The *Figure-Outer* wants to know how something is done before they do it. They want to read all of the steps first, and then go back and follow them from the beginning. If you are a Figure-Outer, you probably want to figure out how to Morph something before you Morph it. The problem is that Morphing does not work that way. Here is why:

We learn by doing what we don't know how to do. Children learn to walk and talk that way. They babble and we respond to them, perhaps giving them some juice. They respond again, this time with an edge of frustration in their voice. We do it again – do they want to be picked-up? Do they want a blanket or some other object? By our relating with the attitude through how they are speaking, babies eventually learn to communicate in words.

When toddlers stumble, we don't criticize them for falling. We cheer their efforts. This learning curve isn't exclusive to children's developmental milestones, but to human development in general. Unfortunately, as we grow up, we encounter less support for the mistakes that are an inevitable part of learning. Consequently, we carry a lot of baggage regarding our ability to change.

Ironically, overcoming obstacles in our lives is part of the process of change itself. In our knowledge-based society, we erroneously think, "If I don't know how to do something, I can't do it." To learn, we must act *As If* we know what to do. Practice it every day, learn it, grow into it – then you'll know it.

The Knower

The *Knower* is in the same box as the Figure-Outer. The subtle difference is that the Knower thinks he or she already knows the score. If you tell a Knower something that you're sure he or she doesn't know, the Knower will usually say, "I know." Or the Knower will tell you that you are wrong, saying, "No, it is not fudge swirl; it's chocolate fudge swirl." The Knower is not committed to the process of figuring it out by him or herself, but instead is committed to being right – already knowing the answer.

Here's the truth: there are many things to change and multitudes of *right* ways to change them. If you are a Knower, you're probably thinking either "I know," or "That's right," or something on the order of, "You are wrong!"

I say, "It's all fine. No contest." Participate and discover what happens. Be open to *not having to know* – stay open to the unexpected which could be greater than being right.

Humility is the paradoxical quest of the Knower. It's been said, "Those who think they know – don't know. Those who don't know – truly know." Memorizing all the books you have read throughout your life is only partial knowledge. To know one's Self is supreme knowledge – or wisdom.

The *I Can'ter*

"I can't change anything. I can't do it. I can't get started. I can't come up with any problems. I can't come up with any solutions. I don't have enough time. I'm not smart enough. I'm overwhelmed. It's not going to do any good, anyway."

The *I can'ter* feels unworthy of changing things or having *the good life*. Every human being is worthy of having a fruitful, balanced life. So if you think you can't, maybe you could shift to, "I'm not sure I can, but I'll give it a shot." That way, you'll be knocking at opportunity's door and inviting new happenings, in spite of your I can't tendencies.

The Intuiter

These folks have to *feel it in their bones*, so to speak. They have to *get it*. They won't take anybody's word for it, and may even be leery of the 7-Step Morph because they didn't eke it out in their personal, intuitive way. They are a right brain version of the Knower. They believe their way is better, truer, and more natural. I'm certainly not putting down intuition (how could I?) or factual comprehension; I strive to use both, a 50-50 balance, rather than taking a half-brained approach to life's problems. By balancing the logical with the intuitive, we enhance our life choices for success.

Right Brain Tease – Left Brain Gets the Feedback

Creative expression opens the floodgates for the brain to reprogram its first impressions. Creativity is born out of chaos, the absurd, a disorientation causing a right brain energy spike. Breaking a pattern of habit or expectation – the stove is in the kitchen – flips the expectation when the stove ends up in the bathroom. The brain is jolted outward and searches for a coherent pattern. Discovery leads to new patterns and synthesis: right brain is expansive filled with random possibility and meets left brain logical patterning.

♥ Draw a picture of your issue, and then frame it.

♥ Write a poem about your issue. Pick a favorite poet and write in their style. Read it to a friend.

♥ Write a song or free-style. (Don't think – just let the words come out.)

You may say, "I'm not an artist, not the creative type." Guess again – living is an art form. Even when planning a vacation you juggle several elements of the process. Think about the creativity in your decisions: should you rent an RV, fly, or go by train. Where will you stay, what are the costs, what's the most fun? The decisions we make moment-to-moment in our daily routine spring from the power of creativity and artful living.

Here's what I discovered: It' so simple; when I'm working with my accountant, I'm more left brain concentration. When I'm filming "MerrieWay Day" I bring on the funnies – hopefully you'll agree or not. See that's the biggee, letting go of the result, the need for approval or being on top. That doesn't mean you're not on top of your game, you just don't need it to be whole.

Ethical Learning – An Elixir

Ethical learning is growing to live in right action: Words and deeds that improve, uplift, and support you and all others involved. How do you measure or determine what's right or wrong? Would you intentionally do harm to another? Would you lie, cheat, or steal to get ahead? Would you sacrifice your family for personal gain? What beliefs do you hold about your place, your responsibility, in our society?

Our intention here is to question, question, and question your motives, beliefs, assumptions, prejudices, and rationales that you hold for your daily actions. If a viewpoint is strong, carved in stone, examine where you first learned it. Was it from your parents, school, work ethics that were imposed or chosen? Where did you formulate how you choose to live? Here's a simple ethical answer of mine: Oops, I cheated on a test…my good fortune was that I was caught and never cheated again. Lesson learned: Crime doesn't pay.

Self-examination is not a one-time activity. To mature ethically is an ongoing life experience, up for daily and weekly internal review. The human condition is embedded in our collective awareness; we can sense the atrocities occurring at this moment or the beauty of souls being born or those departing for other realms. No one is an island unto himself. We are Spiraling outward as our future selves, carrying the best from our past with us as a teacher and a friend.

Eagle Eye Overview

Supposedly, an insect sees through layered prisms – a chair appears as a moving energy pattern that might as well be a dog or a hat. Similarly, no two people see a situation or the world identically. Depending on the angle of observation and their emotional state, witnesses of a train wreck often have conflicting memories of what they saw. In the same way, life's conditioning governs our personal viewpoint and dominates our behavior and actions. The challenge is to stake a claim of ownership – we are solely responsible for whatever we think, say, or do. If we hurt others with the lies and justifications we live by, they will ricochet back on us and keep us from living our potential in HArmony.

Our actions affect the world around us. So, in eagle-like fashion, by developing a broader viewpoint, we can merge our personal needs with the effect their attainment has upon the whole. The *Eagle Eye Overview* nurtures a pattern of growth potential reaching beyond our limited perspective. To be caught in surface details leads to a superficial understanding, black and white thinking; "I'm right. You're wrong."

Soar like an eagle and view your issue from the macro perspective. Eagle Eye sees the other's point of view. What action would serve you *and* all others involved? In your mind's Eagle Eye, what are you holding as an axiom or truth that will fade in time? For a moment, soar in your imagination and see the un-seeable. The goal is to learn new possibilities and gain a new perspective.

Eagle Eye can also focus on minutia, seeing from a distance in great detail. For our purpose it is an art form for observing life's details and innuendos. Three watchful students surrounded a great energy master as he lifted a knife to chop a cucumber. With the precision of a Japanese warrior, he sliced it in lightening speed; the cucumber fell into thin even pieces. Putting the knife down, he asked the enthralled students, "How many pieces are there?" "Fourteen," one of them replied. "Nineteen," another quipped. The third student closed his eyes, concentrating. "Twenty-two," he announced. The master nodded to him, "Count them." To the students' amazement, there were twenty-two pieces. Then the master turned over the knife, revealing one more slice. "You looked, but did you see?"

Contemplate: What appears to be true is not necessarily truth. Truth is the guidance that comes from an inner knowing, beyond the mind and senses, beyond what has been taught. It is intuiting an exactness of right action, in each moment.

Black Belt Mindset: Focus. Focus. Focus.

Training to focus, even in the worst conditions, can be a lifesaver and an edge for success. Unwavering concentration is the core of a *Black Belt Mindset*. In an age of epidemic ADHD and ADD, can we cultivate the focus of a wizard mind that can bore a hole into a brick or piece of wood through concentration?

The actor, Chuck Norris, hosted a demonstration by martial artist Grandmaster Yu, a 10th degree black belt. A fifteen-minute breathing technique preceded a startling explosion of concentrated power. As Master Yu breathed, every breath filled him with an undoubting energy field. One could feel it as he expanded. Then, without the leverage of a table or the ground, he held eight bricks in one hand and busted through them with the other. Master Yu perceived solid objects as penetrable electrostatic charges. His concentration was mind-boggling. Chuck Norris took the stage acknowledging, "You've witnessed the only man in the world to complete this feat."

To produce the Black Belt Mindset requires the discipline to practice. Doubt or excuses become secondary to the tenacity to continue beyond failure. Operating in a Black Belt Mindset requires total involvement, a second-by-second commitment to persevere beyond distraction. It is self-will balanced with non-doer-ship, operating from the Chi, or *in the zone*. In this state, one rides the ebb and flow of strength and steadfastness, coupled with total certainty that the energy manifested will reach the target.

Black Belt Mindset is an entity unto itself – multidimensional in nature – a force that is intertwined with our life's work. Belief in the power of focused energy reframes your inner dialogue and your behavior to create results beyond past limitations.

Quantum Leaps

During a Boy Scout "Jamboree" weekend, 750 youth participated in an individual relay, involving ten challenges from running across logs to scaling a wall. Byron took his number, intensely watching those who were competing before him. His eyes were fixed in concentration and his body seemed to catch every nuance of the runners, calculating their off-footing and wasted movements.

When it was Byron's turn, I watched as he ran effortlessly, leaping, bounding, and climbing, not missing a beat, with perfect footing. The time tally put Byron in first place. It was amazing. Later in the day, Byron said, "The head scoutmaster asked me if I would run it again, against his son. He felt his kid could beat me."

Shocked by the scoutmaster's underhanded audacity and lack of sportsmanship, I asked, "What did you do – you didn't?" Byron was direct. "I told him, 'Sir, I already did that.' And I walked away." In awe of his composure, Byron demonstrated a true black belt mind. He owned his talent and his truth, even when confronted with a sour-grape adult. Byron was a black belt in *Tae Kwon Do* and a national gold medalist, under the tutelage of Grandmaster Yu. Byron had learned that balance is the key – not over-efforting – and with a keen awareness of tension, a fearless state ensues, pushing limits with ease. On this edge, quantum leaps are possible. Integration and assimilation of what is learned leads to mastery.

Find the *Yes* – Get off Your Butt and Dust Off!

Over dinner, Ryan bewailed that his firm was going into Chapter 11. Downsizing was necessary, and he could not bear discharging his long-time loyal employees. He sensed impending lawsuits or an investor takeover. Even his brother-in-law, an investment partner, fell into a hyperventilating meltdown over the potential bankruptcy. Anxiety cluttered Ryan's usually clear mind, preventing him from operating at his optimum. Chaos reigned, and everyone blamed him for the firm's downfall.

With empathy, I listened to the hurt and frustration of this dear man who had been my Rock of Gibraltar through many convoluted times in my life. Holding his hand, I could not muster words of comfort. Recalling Ryan's love of poetry, I spontaneously recited portions of Rudyard Kipling's poem, "If."

"If you can keep your head when all about you are losing theirs and blaming it on you; If you can trust yourself (Ryan joined in) when all men doubt you, yet make allowance for their doubting too… If you can watch the things you gave your life to broken, and stoop and build 'em up with worn out tools…" At this line, Ryan stopped cold. With tears in his eyes he said, "That's what hurts. I gave my life to this."

As he rattled on, spilling a part of his soul, his mood shifted at lightning speed from remorse to conviction toward excitement. "We don't have worn-out tools. We're the best – the best team ever. This is just a setback. I'm calling Joe." Ryan began reciting one brilliant solution after the other. I just sat there awestruck, nodding my head. "Yep, Ryan, sounds good." Then he exclaimed his famous, "Why not? Find the *YES* in the situation and win." It was clear the old Ryan was back in action stronger than ever.

Working through the challenges, Ryan and his team leveraged the right formula to salvage the company. He would have done it without Kipling's inspiration, but I witnessed a spontaneous learning curve, an instantaneous transformation, as Ryan leaped out of his mind trap into the powerful communion with a symbolic parable.

Explore the ever-present symbols and guideposts, and then play with them. Let's assume for a moment that everything happens for a reason, and that life's moments are more than randomly strung together. Could it be that everyone you meet has a purpose in your life? The rude salesperson could be showing you your rudeness. The sweet chirping bird could be serenading your sweetness, or the chance to comfort the lonely could be a way of opening your heart.

By choosing to have positive expectations in life's adventure, partaking of it will be surprise-filled (even when you are the observer of the Action). Synchronicity happens when you are attuned to life's purposeful signs. When aware, you will notice that they occur daily for your pleasure.

The following is an excerpt from a card attached to roses that Ryan sent to me after our fateful dinner:

Thought I'd share a favorite quote from "How Did I Die" by Edmund Vance Cook.

You are beaten to earth.
Well, well, what's that?
Come up with a smiling face.
It's nothing against you to fall down flat,
But to lie there – that's disgrace.

I'm up & running, Ryan

You cannot separate your Intention from your Action or your Action from your Commitment. Witnessing the perfection in the life-learning process, we are transforming from second-to-second. I've discovered that MY LIFE is my greatest lesson!

What have I learned about learning? I still have a lot to learn. You are only young once, but you can be immature forever.

PART III

You Are Not Alone

"Gazing from the mountaintop, how amazing. You have grown to see Illusion's dust, accepting truth without excuse. Bouncing even higher…BE-ing….you soar into ONEness: Forgiving, embracing, sharing, and loving."

In the **First couple of Minutes when meeting someone new** you have instantaneous access to a quantum field of information. Like an electrical current much is revealed and communicated.

- ♥ You viscerally know everything about the person.

- ♥ The mind light-speeds and intuitively computes familiarities and differences, likes and dislikes.

- ♥ You perceive what the relationship will become or not, how it will serve you and the other person or not.

- ♥ Whether it's a potential love-mate, friend, or biz contact – you sense the emotional, intellectual, and trajectory of the relationship from the get-go.

Pay heed to the information, in lies your myriad of choice. Often there's a lesson to be learned, processed, or emotional baggage to be deleted.

- ♥ Marriage partners often say, "I knew instantly she was my one and only, we've been married 40 years." "It was doomed from the start, I knew it."

- ♥ Life is not a fete complete. We can grow and change the perceived path, and weather the storm into a nourishing and fulfilling relationship.

But if you know you fall for bad boys or heart torching ladies, and when the attraction is like a moth to a flame, I was given sound advice, "Run the other way and don't look back!

CHAPTER 11

ARTFUL COMMUNICATION

How well do you communicate with yourself? How do you talk to yourself inside your head (*self-talk*)? Thoughts are powerful activators, the raw material that builds our reality. The mind is fickle, your thoughts random. In moments, a mere thought can spew an apocalyptic meltdown, send a warm heart aflutter, or succumb to nitpicky criticisms. Communication affects our reality, whether it comes from inside or outside our Self.

♥ For balance and HArmony, keep track of your thoughts: Which self-talk causes worry and which causes relief? "This is an impossible situation." Or, "It's tough right now. I think I can Morph it."

♥ Be aware of THOUGHTS THAT HINDER or THOUGHTS THAT HELP. Are you tearing-down or building-up most of the time?

♥ At the end of the day, review your thoughts. Which thoughts brought unrest or pain, peace or joy?

♥ Before going to sleep, change *hindering thoughts* into *helping thoughts*.

Restate your thoughts about your problems in a way that will bring you (and others) Harmony.

♥ Keep track of your reality: watch how your self-talk communication affects your actions. Pay extra attention when you switch a hindering thought into a helping one. How does your life change? Practice for a week or two.

When my negative mind is super-charged, I talk to it as if it's a child. "Cut that – let's think of something fun. How about tap dancing?" Be gentle yet firm. If you are fearful to start a new job, meet that blind date, or flunk a test, say to yourself, "OK. I hear you are worried and scared. Let's think positive!" "I'll bring a box of chocolates or Lotto tickets to share on my new job."

Or, if you are dealing with a more serious problem, self-talk rationally: "Yes, I know bankruptcy is a solution. It could be a rash move. How will I function with years of bad credit? I'll check with my accountant and debtors and explain my circumstance." Don't allow negative mind chatter or precipitating emotions to rule your Actions. Communicate helping thoughts to yourself and ways that will work *for* you and not *against* you.

Write in your Morph Journal. Take five minutes each day to write whatever comes into your mind. Re-read it. CHANGE the hindering thoughts into helping thoughts.

What do you want to happen in your life? Use your thoughts to create exactly what you want. And don't stop – not until you have changed every negative whisper into a positive command. Be prepared for many exciting discoveries about yourself and your New World.

Developing the Gift Of Gab

So what happens when the talk turns outward instead of inward? "I'm a tongue-tied idiot when I have to speak in front of group." "I can't remember what I want to say, even on a one-to-one." "Everyone is talking away and I'm at a loss for words." "I'm not even sure why they're all laughing. I'm usually the last one to get the joke – if I ever get it."

Some people are quick verbalizers who were born with the gift of gab: the salesperson who can sell ice in the winter or the great orator who captivates the audience. So, you aren't one of these folks? Move into the can-do zone with the following:

♥ If you're shy, have been humiliated in the past, or teased for speaking up – get the attention off yourself. Put it on the other person.

♥ If you're assigned to give a verbal presentation to your boss and co-workers, practice OUT LOUD. Memorize it. IMPROV IT. Practice in the mirror. Get it down.

♥ Do you want to sharpen your vocal skills? Do a tongue/mind-twister. "I thought a thought. But the thought I thought I thought wasn't the thought I thought I thought. If the thought I thought I thought had been the thought I thought, I wouldn't have thought it."

♥ Singing is a great vocal tool. Sing in the car. Sing in the shower – the reverberation is awesome. "I sing, even though none shall hear me."

Listen and Learn

You can't teach others to listen, but you can learn to listen. You can't teach others to be kind, but you can be kind, thoughtful, aware, caring, less self-absorbed. Notice how easy it is to talk to someone who cares about you – you feel understood. Give others that gift – understand them. Give up the expectation that they will be able to understand you. Feeling understood and being heard is the core of communication and compatibility. For one day, practice being interested in others. Discover how suddenly they find YOU so very interesting.

When it no longer matters if we stutter, forget what we were going to say, or need to say it right, our rejection incidences are reduced. I received a mega-dose of that lesson – it was my turn to lighten up.

"Let's Talk"

Wacky teen-dom had arrived. Hormones and an allergic reaction to Mom were raging. Byron's daily attire included earphones; he bopped around avoiding my harangues and power struggles. We weren't communicating. It was my problem because it bothered me more than it did him.

Intent on making amends Byron finally belted, "Mom, let's make-up before we start to talk." I smiled, tentatively waiting. He searched my face, dissecting every visible age-line, and he softened his tone. "See, I know you want to be a good parent and you are a good parent. But I need you to stop being the way you think you should be, protecting me. It's time you trusted me to grow on my own."

I was surprised…this was new. Was my boy growing into a man? Byron continued with conviction, "When something's up for me, it's okay to hear your take on it, but I have to make my own decisions. Hey, you're smart, you probably know what's best, but it's time I found some things out for myself." My face registered "What things"?

Reading me, he assured, "Not drugs or anything like that. Let me show you what I mean." With a pencil, he drew a stick figure. "See, this is me." His intonation registered with a profound knowing. Then he drew a circle. "This is the big world." Then he drew a line from himself to the world. "I have to connect...I have a lot to figure out about this world. I need to explore and discover things that you may not know or have seen."

Relieved, I nodded in recognition and understanding. Feeling safe and understood, he confided, "When you give me advice, it's like an order that I have to do it your way. Even if you are right, I can't hear it anymore. I want options and want to look at what's best for me. I need to learn that now. There are a lot of things I want to do in this world, even if I don't know them yet...or even if I don't do them right."

Sensing his need for freedom of Self, I knew I had to let go. He was right. I had been holding on, scared he would be devoured by life's difficulties.

With a simple sweetness Byron urged, "Maybe you could think of me as a friend. Talk to me as a wise friend, as you would do with another kid." My eyes shined as I witnessed his vulnerability and greatness.

In an earnest tone he continued, "Please start to trust me, trust my judgment, and let me grow my own way. Then maybe I can really trust myself. "On that note, he got up and gave me the biggest hug in weeks. Looking deep into my eyes, he pierced my heart by smiling and saying, "This is the best conversation we ever had." And then he bopped away.

I was stunned. I hadn't said a single word. I had listened with an open heart, without judgment, learning to be his friend. We shared the highest level of communication – which is *duplication*. In it, the speaker and listener merge into a flow state, exchanging innermost truths, concerns, and assets. Our shared understanding and trust was the doorway into this feeling of oneness.

Communicating with a teen requires a simple, "ACT, DON'T YAK."

Basically, don't ramble on. State your case simply, clearly and get on with it. If it is about doing homework, don't read the riot act or rattle on about consequences or badger with threats. State your case. "It is our agreement that we all do our part. When are you getting to your homework?" Leave it at that. There will be consequences if they choose to avoid it. Make sure they agree upfront, or they will power battle until you drop.

Unwritten Response: The *What* Underneath Words and Emotions

Communication requires many subtleties. We can listen actively, antennas up, empathetically hearing the emotion, the intention behind the words, what isn't being said, the pauses, breathing patterns, body language, and so on. Listening with every pore provides a safety net of trust – the open door to sharing.

Listen for dominating communication styles. Listen closely for a few minutes when someone speaks. Note speech patterns. Are they visual, kinesthetic, auditory, or mental references? We typically overlap, but one style usually dominates. Determine another's style, and choose words that speak to it. You will be heard and understood more clearly.

♥ A visual person uses words such as, "I see. Let me look at it."

♥ A kinesthetic relates to feelings. "I feel we should go ahead. Let's stay in touch."

♥ An auditory person will phrase, "I hear you. Sounds good. Let's talk."

♥ Mental dominants say, "Let me think about it. Wrap my head around it."

Also listen for the core motivator. Some people rally for ego gratification, the attainment of individual kudos. Others are motivated for the concern of the whole. Listening to how others frame their words reveals the dominant core motivator. You can then speak to their motivator or choose to keep it as an observation for your own clarity.

The Art of Body Language and Gestures

Poker-faced-deadpans can win a game of poker. And a stiff competitor can read your face and body language. How good are you at reading the non-verbal response?

"I don't get along that well with people. They seem to march to a different drummer." "It's like I'm always left out." "I can't read what people want from me." "I don't get the joke." Do you prefer to work alone? Do you feel you don't fit in? If so, one way to relate better is to read body language or unsaid responses.

♥ Watch a movie with the sound turned-off. Read the body language. Can you interpret if the character is telling the truth or what emotion they are experiencing? Are they getting what they want? Use this technique whenever possible. Also, watch body language while you are talking with someone. These unsaid responses are clues to underlying agendas. Focusing outside of yourself takes the attention off you and opens up better communication channels.

♥ If you perceive the needs of another, risk bringing it out into the open and say, "I feel you want me to hold you." Or, "I believe you're telling me you want to quit your job."

♥ Take a stab at authentic communication or skillful discussion. If you are wrong, the other person will usually tell you. And, if you are right, they might still hide the fact. By risking rejection and reaching out, giving up being right or pleasing, you will be heard. Dropping judgment encourages others to open up and to accept you.

Posture Clues

♥ Be present, open, curious, and receptive. Showing interest, you lean forward, focus on the other person. Practice intensive listening even if you are bored or distracted.

♥ Notice when you are covering your heart and solar plexus (the emotion region) – disconnecting, shutting off input or output. Crossed arms/legs are signals of cutting off, protecting, defending.

♥ Feel the resistant energy. Clench your fists. Notice the effort it takes to hold this stance.

♥ Give a free hug. Feel the freedom of expansion.

Tactile Clues

Touch relays a warm, friendly, caring signal. With a partner, practice by saying, "You really helped." Now touch their hand or arm and repeat, "You really helped." How was it different by touching? Did you experience the personal heart connection? Intuit when it is appropriate to get into another's personal space. During an introduction, instead of robotically gripping, use a softer touch, acknowledging the unique person. Touch is a heart-to-heart opener and connector.

Communication Tips

Rather than blame statements such as, "When you play the music loud you give me a headache," begin a sentence by stating your needs. "I need you to stop playing the music so loud – it makes me nervous." It's easier to hear someone who does not blame, harangue, or nag.

For clarity, acknowledge you heard what was said. If you're unsure, repeat what you believe you heard. "I think I heard you say…" keeps communication lines open and flowing.

Be aware of rambling on without completing a thought. While giving directions or vital information, stop occasionally to ask, "Is that clear or understandable?" The mind wants completion; therefore, rattling on can be confusing and others will miss the point.

Invoke high-level communication at will. Eye contact encourages empathy. Add non-judgment, a "there goes I" perception, and a willingness to be there unconditionally – not having a need to fix the person.

Speaking and Listening from the Heart

To transform interactions with friends and family, speak from your heart to their heart. Begin with a compassionate awareness, breathing into the space of the heart. Open, expand. See a cord that connects your heart to their heart. Allow. Listen without expectation, judgment, or a know-it-all stance. You instinctively know when to speak and when to be silent. When you speak from your heart others hear your intentional vibration and open more easily.

Of course, mind-to-mind connection is necessary in teaching and communicating data. Use patience and a willingness to repeat yourself, as everyone processes information differently; it pays off and builds trust.

Knowing everyone processes information differently gives us an effective edge. Speak and listen empathetically: "I hear you're upset." Don't project your own psyche's baggage: "That's not how I do it"; tune-in and engage in higher-level, meaningful communication.

We all struggle to identify or communicate authentic feelings. We grimace, become dumbfounded, bothered, and tongue-tied. If this happens to you, take note of your breathing. Where in your body do you feel constriction or tension? Take a calming breath. "Hold on a sec, I'm having a mind-glitch." And then go on.

Being truthful keeps communication lines open, even when you're unnerved. By lying to yourself, suppressing, or faking it, one day you will forget the truth. Acknowledging doubts and sharing feelings is an emotional release and a step toward connecting to others – and ourselves.

Morph Reactive Response

Can you determine when you're listening with your reactive mind, the emotional re-stimulator? You deliver a pat response, or reel in fear or angst. The moment is exaggerated with the fight-or-flight instinct. Your verbal response is extreme – either internalized or blasting outward. This treadmill-loop reaction requires self-intervention, a cease-fire to acquire control. Remember: inappropriate response is not the only option. Tell your reactive self, "Stop that NOW! I'm in charge."

Reacting vs. Responding

Reacting fires a past emotional charge that projects your personal biography. Responding answers the moment's

reality in present time. As a daily practice, Morph habitual reactions into real responses. Contemplate your reactive issues: Why am I bothered by this? What do I expect that I am not getting: Respect? Understanding? Agreement? Am I giving what I want to receive? If not, what can I do to react differently? In time, these questions are reinforced, creating the new conditioned response. **Remember: changing our reactions – changes the outcome.**

Pay attention to when you are closing off or being open to others.

- ♥ COVERT: Be aware if you or someone else is hiding or covering feelings. Remaining hidden, you (or they) can be unaccountable. Is a friend, family member, or business associate operating with a covert agenda? Check your intention during encounters; is it duplicitous or serving your upliftment?

- ♥ OVERT: Are you up-front, open, and accessible to others? Are you willing to let your emotions, feelings, and attitudes be known? Can you own-up to your agenda? Do you examine your intention and make it known? Can you say what your bottom line is? Overt communication helps to create an atmosphere in which people feel safe and understood.

- ♥ Balance the extremes of overt and covert response. Consider your intent. Is it to shame or one-up? Or is it to connect, create HArmony, and resolution? It's not about being liked or disliked; it's about expressing yourself in a way that people can hear. Instead of saying, "You flunked the test. You should have studied, stupid." You say, "I'm sorry you didn't pass. How can we help you do better on the next test?"

TRIGGERS – ZAP Communicating

Knee-jerk reactions *wail-out* from emotional histrionics, misreading another's intention. We may feel put upon by unwarranted demands. If the mother says, "Please do the dishes," the teenage daughter or son might explode, "You know I have finals this week! Don't ask me to do anything."

Giving into knee-jerk reactions is responding with frustration rather than from respect. Becoming hostile and blaming may trigger the other person to react in the same way, and the entire interaction can escalate into a major conflict. We say hurtful "id-kill," below-the-belt remarks that can escalate into physical violence.

One way to de-escalate a situation before it blows up is *Instant Re-Take*. In film or TV acting, the re-take gives another chance to improve the scene on camera. The actor, techies, or director, correct their mistakes and make adjustments. It also works for communication glitches.

Instant Re-Take

Before you begin, share with family members or cohorts what you are doing.

1. In the middle of an unpleasant encounter, say, "Instant Re-Take."
2. Say, "Pause"- and hit an imaginary "Pause" button in the air.
3. Nail the offender to respond another way. In more formal situations say, "Maybe we could start again."

I use it with customer service representatives who stand their ground even when they are wrong. At an impasse, you can say, "Let's start again," and then demonstrate a different point of view. If you've been reactive or raised your voice, speak in a softer tone. Do your best to see the other person's point, too, not just to get your own way, but also to create a win-win.

Summarize What Has Been Said

A communication breakdown does not forge bonds; it alienates, and breeds irreparable misunderstandings. Cultivate the habit of summarizing, paraphrasing, giving feedback. "I think this is what you said. Correct me if I am wrong…" "Before you continue, I want to make sure I understand what you are saying."

Ask Clarifying Questions: Inquiry develops understanding. When you don't understand something, it is important to ask clarifying questions. Asking demonstrates you are interested and are seeking mutual understanding.

- ♥ "What are the details?" (Who? What? When?) "I'd like to hear more."

- ♥ "What was your reaction? How did you feel?"

- ♥ "Is there anything else you need to say about this situation?"

- ♥ "I'm unclear about_____. Please repeat that idea."

Think of communication breakdowns you experienced in the past. Which of the skills listed above would have helped you? Which skill will you practice today?

Fly On the Wall – Detachment

For one day, one hour, or one minute, practice being a fly-on-the-wall. This is a lesson in detachment. Contribute your opinion only if it is absolutely necessary. Stay focused on the M.O. (mode of operation) of those around you. This practice tempers the tendency to overreact, to have a need to fix or control a situation.

It's not necessary to announce what you are doing, but it could be beneficial to play *Fly-on-the-Wall* in relationships at home, with friends, or at work. If you do tell others what you are doing and they want to play, take turns and provide feedback.

Echo La La

Two men met at the bus stop. "What's your name?" asked the first man. "Don't bother me," the second man answered. The first man retorted, "No." Once again the second man repeated, "Don't bother me." Both men began screaming in a jousting flurry, "Don't bother me!" "No!" Finally, the first man, breathless and exasperated, yelled, "What do you think, I'm stupid? My parents called me No a billion times. Don't you think I know my name?" With that admonishment, the second man relented and put out his hand to shake. "Pleased to meet you, *No*. I'm *Don't Bother Me*."

If you're a parent, you've probably said "No" a gazillion times, as well as, "Don't bother me!" and the snappish, "Hurry up!" another quadrillion.

How can we instill confidence and understanding with a habitual barrage of *no-no's*, rushing, and putting our kids on hold? It's not surprising children grow up to believe they're not worth our time or that they are "too stupid to do anything." We haven't learned to explain a no or a situation or give positive frequent affirmations.

I took it to heart when a communication specialist said, "Just affirm with words like *good work, good job*, especially when the tot spills her juice trying to drink it with clumsy little hands."

The analytical mind finds complementing more difficult than criticizing. Statistics reveal that parents (possibly friends, cohorts) spout 50 negative comments to one positive. Delivering an equal balance of positive to negative isn't necessary. But do FOCUS on your delivery tone and cultivate the habit of increasing the daily numbers of affirming comments. A child, friend, spouse, employee, or a co-worker wants to hear they are on the right track, doing something correctly and becoming independent. This is the precursor to high self-esteem.

Morphing Messages

"Constructive criticism" is an oxymoron if we continually point out mistakes, rather than dialoguing *how-tos* for improvement. As my son grew into his teen years, I recognized it was a tender and complicated age. More than ever, teens need compliments to take hold, and the negatives zing like daggers, wounding their fragile spirits.

♥ Turn praise into encouragement. It's great to tell people how well they are doing. To motivate them we need to encourage them.

♥ Morph negative messages into positive ones. Cut the one-upmanship and bullying.

♥ Instead of blaming someone who made a mistake, say, "How do you feel about that?" Putting it in their court and out of your judgment opens possible dialogue for rectifying a situation.

♥ Remember, the underlying tone conveys volumes. I could say, "Dinner is ready," and underneath feel, "I hate cooking for you unappreciative brats." Such underlying intents are communicated without love; it hurts, frustrates and makes us wonder if maybe the potato salad might be spiced with arsenic.

♥ Saying kind words is mirrored back. It's the best infusion of caring we can give. We either inspire or harm. Choose your words wisely.

Active Listening

Quite often, we think we are listening, but the speaker doesn't feel heard. Psychologist Carl Rogers identified the term *Active Listening*, which means being sensitive to the other person's verbal and nonverbal messages. As in paraphrasing, the listener empathetically reflects back the message.

My sister-in-law, Jan, is a great listener, and I know I am a great talker. Jan's patience is a heart-opener; she has great insight that puts matters into perspective. Instead of rattling on and on. I feel I am truly being heard.

While Jan and I were having a conversation on our cell phones, I was overly anxious to get out what I had to say. I kept interrupting and talking over her. Matter-of-factly Jan said, "When on a cell phone only one person can talk at a time or both voices are basically cancelled out." "Probably satellite beams," I replied. There was silence at the other end of the line. Then, her intent registered and I admitted, "My interrupting is a rude, grating annoyance isn't it?" I committed to improve my *Active Listening* skills, talking less and listening empathically.

Who does most of the talking? Are you listening most of the time? Are you talking most of the time? Do people (including you) go off on monologue-tangents, or do you include others, allowing them to respond, to have input? Talking your point of view is *advocating*. Do you need to repeat what you know or are you interested in learning more? Learning requires inquiry. The ideal conversation balance is 50% advocacy (making your point) to 50% inquiry (learning more).

How do you respond to messages or statements? Do you criticize the content (what the other person has said) and form a judgment (how they said it)? Do you dismiss it, or do you ask questions before responding?

Do you feel heard? Respectfully inform, "I'm not sure you heard me." Consider if your words, tone of voice, and gestures are pushing buttons and turning off their listening abilities, or engaging them.

Communicating Clearly

When you are the Speaker:

♥ Meet the other person where they are.

♥ Maintain eye contact. Honor them.

♥ Use clear, concise language as much as possible. Be aware of tone. Is it negatively charged, neutral, kind, caring?

♥ Disclose your own feelings, as well as your thoughts.

♥ Encourage questions and comments. Be open-minded. Resist resistance.

♥ Give the person time to think about what you are saying. Don't rush a response.

♥ Keep your voice calm when you are upset.

♥ Take hostility, judgment, blame, and criticism out of the conversation.

♥ Welcome polarization. Show respect for the other person, even when you disagree. You can say, "I see how you could feel that way." There is no need to say, "But I feel…" *Buts* put us on the defensive. Instead, say, "Can you see my point of view?"

When you are the Listener:

♥ Value and show interest in what the other person is saying by nodding, moving forward, and asking questions. Be patient.

♥ Don't interrupt or snap-back a response. Suspend assumptions. Listen without thinking.

♥ Listen for unspoken ideas or feelings; comment to the speaker, "You sound hurt, frustrated, elated."

♥ Concentrate on what is being said. Hear the speaker's point of view – not yours.

For instance, when discussing moving to a new house, Asha's 4 year old son Lucian, fixed on her with big, imaginative eyes: "How 'bout we get our tools so we can build a shrinker machine – we'll shrink the whole family that lives in this house, then we can sail in this tiny little Lego ship to an island in the middle of the ocean. Then we can build a new house there. Whatya think?"

Communication is an art form – it can create loving relationships and outright battles. Practice, practice, practice your communication skills until you can teach by example, rather than preaching.

CHAPTER 12

BRING ON RELATIONSHIPS

What is the most important relationship we have in this life? You may answer, "a higher power," "my husband/wife," or "me." We are in relationship with everything in the universe. Relationships are not confined to other people. We have a relationship with our thoughts, feelings, environment, work, nature, pets, finances, health, and so on. How we relate to these inner and outer influences affects our attitudes, behaviors, and quality of life.

Good Company vs. Harmful Company

Company in this context refers to the people we spend time with, as well as our time spent alone with our thoughts and actions. *Good Company* consists of people who uplift us, and thinking thoughts and performing deeds that inspire. This becomes an act of discernment, choosing what is best for our highest good.

We recognize harmful company when we perceive bad vibes, negative gossiping, narcissism, or an energy drain. In good company our best qualities shine – we feel empowered and positive about ourselves.

Comparing ourselves to others is self-sabotage. Allowing their opinions to trigger feelings of inadequacy zaps our power. Check your innermost reactions to others with the following exercise:

"I See a Person Who Makes Me Feel..."

I learned this technique from Lieux Dressler at her *Acting Playhouse* in Hollywood. My cohorts were actresses Debra Winger, Lynda Carter, Cassandra Peterson (*Elvira*), and TV Executive Producer Marcy Carsey (*Cosby* and *That 70's Show*). With that creative group, "I See a Person Who Makes Me Feel" was the ultimate ego-buster challenge for me. How to move from inferiority or feigned superiority to equal was a feat.

♥ Sit opposite a partner, facing him. Take turns telling your partner how he makes you feel.

♥ Narrow your impressions to three comments. Pick an inferior, an equal, and a superior feeling that you have about yourself that surfaced while looking at your partner. Begin with, "I see a person who makes me feel ____." Examples: A tall person could make you "feel small". Sensing compassion in the person could make you "feel understood". Their blonde hair could make you "feel smarter".

In a Morph Group, Lee Ann played "I See a Person Who Makes Me Feel." One response from her partner startled her. "I feel superior to you because you seem so intense and serious. I feel lighted-hearted and humorous compared to you." Lee Ann was taken-aback. She recognized the past memories that had led her to become calculating and humorless.

Lee Ann wanted to release the heaviness she carried and to have more joy in her life. At our prodding, she enrolled in an improv comedy class. Through role-play, she created funny characters with a humorous spin on the "trailer-trash" life she had endured. She shared a secret, "I use Roseanne Barr as my imaginary mentor because she came from humble trash-life and turned it around."

With assistance from MerrieWay Community, Lee Ann initiated a group serving at-risk teens. They created and performed poignant, yet hilarious skits. It was her giveaway for her own attainment, and the youth gave back, performing their comedy skits, dealing with important issues like drugs and peer pressure as a community service project.

Getting Past Praise or Blame

After a rampant or subtle put-down, or after hollow flattery, take stock: are you choking on a bully's wrath or a sycophant's bizarre manipulation? Is it a control device to keep you an underling, indebted to praise? Is it someone else's projection on you?

Our loved ones can test us at every turn; trigger our response to fly off the handle, or to withdraw, hold grudges like battling two-year-olds and wield retaliatory punishments. We withhold sex or emotionally disappear in front of the TV, computer, or resort to any number of tactics that inevitably cause us to feel isolated and alone.

Banish being the brunt, kicking-post, or sponge-absorber of outside influences. Are you groveling at the random whims of others? Are you allowing them to ravage your self-esteem? If we allow others to abuse us, their cruelty ultimately becomes our own.

It's natural to want affirmation, to be liked or showered with compliments and praise. "I feel good when they love me. I feel awful when they don't." But you are in charge of yourself! **Commit to get past praise or blame as you gauge for self-worth.**

Visualize the cast of players in your life, past or present, and allow them to pass through your mind. Take notice of who makes you smile or feel warm fuzzies. Notice when your heart opens. How you feel about them; how you feel about yourself? With a mere thought of their name or visualizing their face, voice, or words, you are filled with positive energy.

♥

Recall what you learned in Morph Brain Drains: who are the people and situations in your life you deemed to be brain-drainers? Going deeper, reflect on someone who makes you cringe, twinge, or recoil. Do you shutdown, hide, or protect rather than share yourself? Notice how you feel. Are you tight-jawed, weakened, or anxious by just saying their name or bringing them into your conscious awareness?

♥

Can you see how thoughts create good or harmful company?

It's important to be your own good company. Will you embrace yourself, your strengths, and weaknesses? Will you cultivate a compassionate heart for yourself? Will you choose to accept and love yourself right now, as you are, unfolding and growing? Feel the warm fuzzies when you are alone. Catch yourself when feeling regretful or self-recriminatory. Ask, "What makes me feel good about myself? What makes me feel 'less than"?

Happiness tip: Keep the company of good thoughts and surround yourself with people you authentically enjoy. Your heart wants to soar, to love more and to connect. Know hurts can dissolve. Open. Reach out, gently touching heart to heart.

Rejection and Abuse – A Gut-Sucker

Rejection is a self-inflicted act. Are you torturing yourself by rehashing upsets over a breakup, being ignored, or being kept at arm's length? STOP IT! Emotionally detach by spending a few moments in quietude. Put your attention on your inner beauty, your inner calm.

If others are hurting you, truly being cruel, DEAL WITH IT. You may be so fearful of rejection (harboring your deep need to be accepted) that you can't express your feelings to an emotional abuser. If this is how you feel, acknowledge to yourself, "I heard his (or her) abusive putdown, the judgment of me. I know what's true and what isn't. I love myself and don't accept abuse."

Set boundaries. Let the person know how you feel and what is unacceptable verbiage or behavior. If they are unwilling to have a discussion and are quick to put the blame on you, withdraw from the situation. If the abuser is a spouse, child, or boss that is in your daily life, you may seek a mediator or third party to help find an amicable solution.

Then, leave the rejection where you found it – with them, not with you.

What Are Your BOUNDARIES?

Do you compromise for approval or acceptance? What piece of your sanity is at stake if you are not liked? What piece of yourself will you forfeit, betray, and sell short to fit in? If your answers to those questions caused you to feel frustrated, resentful, trapped, or angry, it's time to revamp your fitting-in quest.

Maybe you operate from old needs that don't serve you. Maybe you have outgrown habitually *stepping up* when no one else will. Or you're on the verge of changing your predictability: "Good ole' George will take care of that." Some of us are not bent on being liked and are quite capable to say, "I don't do airports…" when guests come to town. I offer to pay cab fare if they are truly bothered. Maybe it is time to adopt a new posture and wiggle out of the balls and chains keeping you bound in a caretaker's illusion. You know you can't please all the people all of the time. So make the boundary shift. Let's separate what is our business, emotionally, responsibly, and exactly! Why take on someone else's stuff – is it really our business? Clear the confusion, and as Mama said, "Keep your nose on minding your own biz – you'll outlive the messing busy bodies – in good health and joy."

Say "NO" To Make Room For "YES!"

A gnarly problem today is that youth have lost RESPECT (if they ever had it to begin with). Watch one episode of *The Simpsons*; listen to the disrespectful vernacular in a rap song or the inanity on reality shows. The media is helping to shape a future generation of sound-bite communicators that resemble caveman grunts.

Ellen's dilemma: Her son Jake spent four hours a day on his computer, surfing social communities, playing games and the rest of the cyber drill. They negotiated daily as this fourteen-year-old ran circles around both of his parents. Jake was an A student and very smart but found his peers difficult to relate to. Where did that leave him in the social mix? Communicating with kids online had given him a presence, a fit-in with the crowd credential. From Jake's perspective, even four hours wasn't enough time to play online.

Ellen called for advice because I had been down the same road with a teen son. Asking the MerrieWay Community for assistance is not new. We have been around for years, helping parents and youth to get a communication grip. "What should I do?" Ellen asked. "I told him I would ground him. Jake said 'fine'. I told him he'd have to make his own dinners. Jake said 'fine.' I told him I'd take his computer away if he didn't get off it. Jake said 'fine.' Nothing bothers him."

Of course nothing bothered Jake – because he knew Ellen wouldn't follow through with any of her threats. Ellen was the one bothered; she had the angst and the problem.

So, we started with acknowledging that she needed to learn to set real boundaries, with consequences that would be enforced. Her solution with Jake, who agreed mainly to get her off his back, was for him to spend only two hours on the computer each day. One minute over and he would lose use of the computer for three days. After losing it twice, the enforcement kicked in, and Jake started timing himself. Together they nipped his potential addiction to gaming on the internet, and Ellen learned to keep her boundaries in line.

However, it wasn't easy. After his first infraction, Jake threatened to move down the road to live with his older brother. Of course, at fourteen, he's not emancipated, and that would be runaway status. But, Ellen and her husband let Jake run wild in his imagination with his scheme. In addition, he was told, "When you come back, the rules will be the same." Bearing that in mind, he decided to give it a go, and accept the two-hour limit – converting a *No* to a *Yes*!

All of our Actions spill over and influence our life quality – like an oozing creeping crud if they're harmful to us, or like a warm delicious fresh baked apple pie if they are beneficial to us. (Leaving out the cholesterol from whip cream – for me, that is.)

Only the Lonely – My Relationship with Me!

Single? You're not alone, in the sense that fewer than half of American households contain married couples. As a statistic most of us spend more than half of our life alone. As part of the single-set, we face the options of trolling dating sites, showing-up at singles mixers, or finding ourselves mercifully being fixed-up on blind dates by sympathetic friends. Ever since I first saw *Cinderella*, I still carry the sensation embedded in my psyche that my prince is on his way, ending my aloneness. A common plea: "Don't I deserve the great guy to put my energy behind – to make him greater? And, I'll happily accept his great energy behind me!"

If you aren't married or dating, you may be considered the one "who always shows up alone" at parties and events. Married couples give you the pathetic eye of pity. Thank God I was married once, and then, sadly, divorced – like two-thirds of the population. Before I go into the expected drone, "I'm so lonely. I'm afraid I'll be alone forever. No one will ever want me..." bit, I am going to posture an undeniable truth: You don't have to be afraid of being alone and surely don't want to be pitied. How does that sit with you?

There is a panacea for this condition of aloneness, which does not infer loneliness. It's connecting with the unconditional love inside of you. Living in self-love, you treat yourself like someone you really care about. That means dropping the inner critic and becoming your loving champion and #1 fan.

Lucky for me, I'm having a ball doing comedy – a great healing tool on the planet. I am still growing the funny-lady within me. I've realized that when I raise myself – not to grow up, but to grow happy, happier, the happiest with me – offers a special time to share with someone who has done the same. I discovered a profound togetherness emerges, a time to play joyfully with my soul mate...embracing the thick and thin.

Loving yourself as your own best friend helps embrace loneliness? I choose to fill life with my favorite goodies. That means taking responsibility for how I want life to be and creating the means to do it.

I use strength builders to enhance my relationship with myself: my daily ritual is to find ways to feel content with me. I'm getting so good at playing, frolicking, and dancing barefoot under the stars. Joy's magic is sprinkling into more and more moments – instilling greater self-awareness and personal fulfillment. Life's unfolding is teaching my happy muscle, expanding appreciation of all that is.

Bottom line, why bother attracting someone else if you're not showing up for yourself? Develop a strong inner support system, like meditating, exercise, good eating habits, and giving yourself kudos, patting yourself on the back and saying, "Good job!" when you've finished the assignment or cooked a yummy meal. This beats stressing over your weight, feeling unentitled, and lying to yourself with thoughts of "I'm not enough."

I decided I *am* enough. If anything, I'm too much fun. (How's that possible?)

"I'm going to find my Soul Mate"

Love melts hurt, cleanses pent-up feelings, and resolves aloneness. Love is your best friend, your heart guide, your light on the path.

Dottie, a Morph Group participant who was at a life crossroad, admitted, "I'm starved for love." With courage, bouncing through her regrets, shame, and pain, she landed proud with a clear-minded vision. Approaching mid-life (at 40), finding a soul mate became Dottie's quest. Recovering from two failed marriages, she took a stance, "No more dependent weak men in my life. I'm fed-up being a badgering witch… disrespecting them. My guy will be secure and successful in his own right." With an open mind, she visualized her ideal relationship. She listed a personal inventory of admirable traits to cultivate in herself to attract a man she wanted. "I will be loving, express kind words and deeds, be willing to compromise, and not take intimacy as a personal threat. I'm going to treat my man the way I want to be treated." Her list was exacting.

Creating a collage, she pasted photos of her dream man, wedding pictures, a honeymoon in Paris and the house they would live in. Sharing her masterpiece she declared, "My soul mate is somewhere in this big world waiting for me."

Dottie recently recapped, "I went on with my life, putting kindness as a priority. I opened up, enjoying myself. At night I reviewed my day, seeing what I would do differently; and I learned to appreciate my efforts. Six months later, Ted showed up and took me by surprise – he swept me off my feet. I felt natural with him, and loving him back came easily. Visiting his home for the first time, I entered the elegant living room and stood in amazement. It was a duplicate of what I out-pictured in my collage. Then, I got a surprise bonus with Ted – we work together!" Dottie laughed, "We've written a book about finding your destined love. It's so great – we're happily married and sharing our good fortune as matchmakers."

What's distinctive about Dottie's love-quest is that she gathered within **herself** the qualities she wanted in a mate. Dottie described her tactic: "I focused on changing my abrasive, demanding, unsympathetic ways into a more tolerant, caring, and loving nature. If I caught myself snapping at someone, condemning, or criticizing, I'd put a dollar in a bowl. I still do it. I built up enough cash to buy a ticket to Hawaii, where I met Ted." Dottie's amazing approach worked for her, and it could very well work for you – or anybody – whether it is attracting a life partner, a new job, new home or whatever.

Divine synchronicity appeared when Dottie became her heart's desire…a lover of love.

Raise your frequency to joy and love: Get your body moving, release toxins and pent-up emotions. Balance. Be still on the breath. Reflect on rolling clouds - see the message. Listen to the surf, dance on the sand, praise others, meet LOVE everywhere.

What Does a Healthy Relationship Mean To You?

Is this really supposed to be so *adult* serious? Why not fantasize and enjoy the possibility of finding a great mate? Why not attract someone who adores you, has admirable qualities you love, is fun and easy to be with, and enjoys life to the max? I was astonished by one man's fancy: "I'm powered by a four-foot blonde and I don't mind it a bit."

♥ Can you describe your ideal relationship? Can you describe, or *image*, what makes you happy, miserable, or content? Whether in a new relationship, married, or just ending a relationship, put on your non-judgmental cap and open-up to discovery.

♥ If you are seeking a significant other, make a LifeLine [pg. 78] to observe your past significant relationships. What qualities were empowering or debilitating? Do a Future LifeLine of your ideal proposed relationship.

♥ If you are in a current relationship, do a Life-Line Challenge [pg. 79] of the most important demarcation points in the relationship; if it's falling apart, determine the point and under what circumstances the deterioration began. What was it like before? What made it worthwhile? Are you team players or opponents? What traits attracted you to your partner? Share your list and revitalize possibilities. Go on a date-date, make love, have fun, tickle each other with a feather.

Everyone wants to be loved for who we truly are. Whether gorgeous, homely, wealthy, or self-sufficient, we still want one thing: to love and be loved. This primordial need transcends the notion of romantic love. We want the love and respect of our neighbors, co-workers, and families. Can we earn their love? Do we expect their love to exist for us no matter what? Connecting to infinite Love residing within us, we become immersed in Love. Our capacity to share unconditional love becomes the heart core of all our relationships.

Love Mates

Dancing on the edge of Love, hearts touch in Ecstasy and Delight. Outpouring, Joy sprinkles Hope, tingling as ONE.

My father Phil, a German refugee, ran out of money on his way to California. Stranded in Detroit, he took a job as a shoe salesman. My mother Betty was visiting her sister in Detroit. Wobbling down the street in spike heels, she tripped on a curb and broke the heel off her shoe, directly in front of the store. Trudging inside, she locked eyes with my father. As he slipped a new shoe on her foot, there was a tingle, a familiar ring, something like: *could this be Cinderella's Prince?*

On a more somber note, less than a year before, my father had received his mother's last letter, which had been smuggled out of Auschwitz. It read, "No matter what the religion, race, or creed, it doesn't matter if you love someone – love her. After being here, I have learned LOVE is the most important thing." Piercing his aching heart, she had released him to love.

My mother was totally smitten and enthralled with this handsome man, the first Jewish man she ever met. She brought him home to Southern Illinois to meet her mother, an evangelist and hands-on healer. Ecstatic, my mother shared, "He's the first living Jewish man I've ever known." My grandmother knowingly smiled at my father and welcomed him. "Come in my son. Jesus was a Jew." She never mentioned it again and embraced him with LOVE.

We were born into this life to love and to be loved. Beyond words, beyond our cultural beliefs, grace gently raises our love tone, and frees us of fear, doubt, worry. Connecting with our inner light force, self-love projects outward in all we do and say, and affects everyone around us – magnetizing love.

Make a LOVE Intention: "I Love myself." "I am open to Love." "I am Love." I live in Love." **Or create your own intent.** Write it down. Carry it with you. Keep it visible. Repeat it out loud or silently several times a day. Repeat it 11 times like a mantra, when you feel down – ease into that Peace of Love.

Choosing Your Family

What if you knowingly chose your family in this life to work through your individual soul's needs – the lessons you incarnated to learn? Operating from that premise how you would relate to your family?

It has been said that God entrusts children to us. Knowing they are not ours elevates the parent-child relationship to the sacred. As a mother, I realized that I was the guardian of God's child, that I was given the privilege to serve that child, and that I would love him with all my heart.

A viewpoint of "not your children" inspires a deeper awareness, "caretaker of a divine Being". Do you see the light of love and the spark of wonder within your child? How do your children see you? Do you share the love within you? Are you authentic, vulnerable, real with them – being human and letting them truly see *you*?

I was struck when Byron said to me, "I don't really know anything about you. What were you like when you were young? You don't really tell me anything." I learned to take time to share my childhood stories, pranks, and anecdotes. Teens may question your experience with drugs or sex. Preaching the "Do as I say and not as I do" attitude is a pitfall.

Have an open discussion. It's tricky, be truthful, give lessons learned.

Contemplate who your children are. Do you think you *own* your children? Do you see your children fulfilling the dreams *you* have for them? Are they unfulfilled dreams you had for yourself? Look at your children for who they are rather than project your expectations on them. Tuning into the uniqueness of your child helps to choose the appropriate school or activities. See your children through their eyes.

Create a meeting to evaluate the family dynamics. Issues could include boundaries, gripes, vacation planning. Take turns; kids can conduct a meeting and direct the parents. Allow each person to express his or her view. Take time for incubation. Verbalize, write, or draw solutions.

"I get you" sparks great friendship. Hearts open, Love blossoms when you risk staying open – in moments when your lover shuts down.

What Does Family Mean to You?

If someone marries into your family, are they welcomed or considered an outsider? Were you taught that "Blood is thicker than water," meaning the genetic family is more important than others – can you see family beyond the blood-ties?

Daphne, a close friend, arranged a Thanksgiving dinner with all the trimmings at a local homeless shelter. Byron and I, along with a few friends, volunteered to bring some goodies. When we arrived, Michelle, a precious five-year-old, showed Daphne and Byron around the shelter. After dinner, everyone gathered around a stage to listen to a honky-tonk blues singer. An invisible segregation line went down the center of the room. The women and children from the shelter were sequestered on one side, and we huddled on the other. As the music rocked-out, Byron danced across the floor, taking the hand of a shelter resident, then taking a volunteer's hand, and bringing them to the dance floor. One by one, he united the two groups. When I asked him why he did it, he chuckled, "If I didn't, nobody would have met each other."

Daphne and little Michelle's magical relationship blossomed as they danced. Daphne arranged for Michelle to visit on weekends. It was all so natural, as if they had always been together. Yet, circumstances led to the child's placement in foster care. Daphne and her husband were devastated: they loved her. Negotiating through months of bureaucratic red tape, they finally became her adoptive parents.

Is your family welcoming of adopted and step-family members? In-laws? (The connotation of meddling "in-laws" need not apply. Morph that concept.) How can you make extended family members feel welcome? Do you include friends and virtual family members in holiday and family celebrations? Doing so...

- ♥ Opens the welcoming heart – the best place to live your family life.

- ♥ Teaches children to be thoughtful and concerned about others.

- ♥ Socializes your family, opening up to new influences and points of view.

♥ ♥ ♥

Seven-year-old Danny cried and was defiant when he had to leave his mother's house for his dad's. Dividing time is commonplace in divorced families, expecting the child to adapt to blended families and time-sharing. But Danny desperately wanted both of his parents to go places with him and have fun. Feeling the sadness of never knowing life with a mom and dad together, his parents honored Danny with a weekly family outing. His dad related, "We wanted to lessen Danny's separation issue and to create family memories."

Is there something in your family dynamic you would like to change? What wouldn't you change? Who have you embraced as your extended family?

A Family's Journey – Zero Tolerance to Mutiny!

During a Morph session, Cheryl melted in a flood of tears. With coaxing, she revealed, "My husband and kids are choking me to death. I want to run like hell from their scathing putdowns, ugly judgments." She felt a lack of love, abandoned. Her own thoughts were hopeless, self-recriminating. Life seemed a dysfunctional assault rather than worthwhile.

Cheryl continued her downspin. "I hit rock bottom, my lowest. After driving my kids to Day Camp, one-hundred-and-ten miles total, we ordered a pizza. Starved, they ate up most of it. One piece was left. I asked my daughter to pass it to me. She snarled, 'Mom, you're fat enough,' and then she reached for the last piece. Incensed at her lack of consideration, I erupted like a crazy person. I grabbed the pizza and flailed it at her face. As the cheese and tomatoes oozed from her hair and nose, I was transfixed. How could she ignore me? Wasn't I starving too? I didn't exist for either one of them, other than as chauffeur and maid. Out of my frustration I had reduced myself to 'all brawn, no brains' and committed an abusive act. What if it had been a knife instead of pizza?"

The family had clearly put love and respect on the backburner.

Cheryl had forfeited her dignity by sacrificing her needs. "I failed as a role model, setting myself up for abuse." Cheryl recognized she was the one with the problem. She was the one bothered by "no respect or tenderness". She lacked boundaries, delivered no consequences, and needed to develop zero-tolerance for unacceptable behavior.

Initially Cheryl executed baby steps. When her husband complained, "This steak tastes like crap," instead of biting her lip in fear of creating a full onslaught, she offered, "There's a couple more left, why don't you barbecue one?"

When her daughter called her a "bitch," she pulled over to a bus stop and told her to take the bus. When her son refused to clean his room, she didn't do it for him.

The following week, Cheryl felt that the baby steps were not consequential enough. The laundry list of abuse escalated until she declared, "I'm a tortured slave in my own home. This is an all-out mutiny, or I'll go on strike." And go on strike she did. The first order of biz was to draw up a provisional contract, listing her demands, what she deemed unacceptable (verbally and in deeds). To eliminate victimization, resentment, or blaming others, Cheryl recognized she had to be 100% responsible to herself before she could be responsible to her family.

Cheryl mutinied; she left home and spent two weeks with her sister while her family fended for themselves. The trick is to act before a physical or emotional meltdown occurs. In Cheryl's case, the timing for change preceded her breaking point. She held the trump card and declared to herself, "I am no longer a doormat."

The trial period ended, requiring a response to her demands. In a Family Morph session, Cheryl's daughter Abby recounted a disappointing episode. "Mom only remembers bugging me about the stuff I forgot to do. But I kept telling her I was reviewing for a test." Abby confronted her mother, "You wouldn't stop, so I called you a bitch. It was total overkill making me take a bus. I was so upset I failed my test."

Grasping the other point of view, Cheryl admitted, "I didn't mean to hurt you. I am sick of this push-to-shove power trip. No one listens or pays attention to me. I might as well be..." (She started to say *dead*, but perceiving it was guilt-based, stopped in mid-sentence.)

This icebreaker fueled a fiery open dialogue as the family vented a barrage of subterranean hurts. Torrents of criticism provoked defensive attacks.

"I just want to run away," Cheryl confessed.

"Mom, I can never do anything right!" Abby cried.

Cheryl's husband, Mitch, stammered, "Sometimes when I say something nasty, it's to turn you off because I just need peace and quiet."

Cheryl was amazed by how closely her family mirrored her feelings of being misunderstood. Taking responsibility for her part in the family chaos, she owned-up to being a nagging criticizer. It cleared the way for meaningful communication. Learning to listen empathetically became a family priority. Seeing, speaking, thinking of themselves and others with respect became their motto. Becoming aware of role-based expectations helped them to perceive each other anew, supporting growth and change.

Review the following practice:

♥ List the preconceived labels plastered on yourself and on those around you. Let go of *parent, sibling, boss;* it is psychologically and emotionally freeing.

♥ Choose to view another person as if you are meeting him or her for the first time. Suspend the notion of past baggage, expectations, or personal needs. Take responsibility for what you say, how you say it, and what you do.

♥ After a disagreement, when you've reacted with an ego slam, say those mending two words, "I'm sorry." (And no placating – mean it!) Work it out and talk to each other.

♥ Envision your child, husband, friend, co-worker, and self as God's creation: perfect, learning, and growing. Communicate acceptance, the knowing of their true nature, in your tone and choice of words. Greet them with loving expectation. Your whole being expands and so does theirs.

Words, words, words...SILENCE. Peace of mind rests in the stillness of your heart. Play there, revel there. Love springs into BEING – in everyone you see, in everything you hear, in everything you touch....Love as YOU.

Friendships Are Elected Relationships

Humankind's cellular memory is wired and re-circuited with a herding/clan instinct – the perpetuation factor of the species. We bond for pure pleasure, gratification of Self, and to form life-thread support systems.

There are no fast rules – no *shoulds* or *oughts* in delineating friendship. We mutually designate perimeters of acceptance or lack thereof. No guidelines define what makes a true friend, or what to do when we outgrow or lose one to varying circumstances.

Friendship is a practice of the heart, ultimately feeding our need to share, bond, and reflect life's journey. Close friends are truth meters. They call me on the b.s., hold me accountable, and hug me in spite of it. They add to my authenticity: in their company I cannot delude myself, hide emotions, shame, or guilt.

The more we've been hurt and covered it all, the harder the nutshell is to crack. With trust, we open and flow, spontaneously expressing our truth.

Fair-Weather Friends

Tina admitted she had mostly fair-weather friends. "I don't know anyone other than family I can rely on." Often excluded from her friends' exciting functions or celebrations, she said, "I'm like an afterthought." Tina gave more than she received.

Our Morph Group participants asked her how she felt about it. "Maybe I don't feel entitled to more. I value a bit of friendship rather than nothing." Fair-weather friends let you down and don't show up when you're down and out. Give up expectations from someone who doesn't meet them.

Beware of dark energy. A woman prays for everyone (and lets them know about it), yet she shows up as a controlling oppressor who can pillage and plunder when you're vulnerable, and craftily justify the willful behavior. You can't beat guilt-trippers or heart-rippers at their manipulative games. Why meet righteousness or narcissism with honey or boxing gloves? You will only walk out defeated, dejected, and punch-drunk. Blow them off with a good-witch, I mean wish!

Purely elective friends will come and go. Binding relationships shift with our interests and lifestyles, value-rifts, and life's passages. Pat, a Morph trainee, seemed confused when she asked, "How can we possibly grow together at the same rate in the same way?" It's a tough ending when all you share are past memories and have nothing left in common with your present life.

Do you talk about letting a friendship retire or allow it to wane without a word? Pat did an instant bailout when her friend betrayed her at work and snitched her client database. "I was no longer available. I refused her phone calls. There is no excuse for her deceit. She messed with my livelihood, my trust, and there was no-second chance."

During another Morph session, we continued to focus on iffy and disappointing relationships. Gwen described the sadness she felt when her supposed best friend remarried. "A whirlwind lifestyle pulled her away, and she became a fair-weather friend in an instant. I've isolated myself... I can't bear to be alone anymore..."

Sensing the relational hurts in the group and addressing Gwen, I shared, "To make peace with uncomfortable confrontations and disagreements, let them float into the waves of forgiveness. Forgiveness is a let-go-of-stuck feelings and releases the irresolvable. Forgiveness doesn't mean we accept or condone abuse, or pretend it didn't happen. It means moving on without the baggage, deleting it from our consciousness."

Hawaiian Forgiveness Prayer

Repeat the following words to make peace and dissolve lingering hurts.

Say person's name, *I am sorry for any pain I caused you. I forgive you for any pain you caused me. I forgive you. I forgive myself. Thank you.* (Repeat three times) End- *Amen!*

Middle-of-the-Night Friends

Who could you call in the middle of the night if you were in a crisis or emergency? Dillon, a med student, confided to our Morph Group, "I wouldn't have anyone to call. I don't want to dump on someone. I'd either call 911 if necessary, or I'd wait until a decent hour if it weren't life or death." Dillon revealed he had swallowed an overdose of chaos in his own life. "But I'm not a middle-of-the-night friend, either." Are you a middle-of-the-night friend? Who would you be there for? Under what circumstances would you call or reach out? Who would you reach out to?

Sheila, our Morph trainer, added, "I've learned to take people as they are. Die-hard friends hang in until the bitter end. Acquaintances are stimulating and to help me expand and grow. The trick to sustaining a relationship is not putting my expectations on a friend's capabilities. I see what they demonstrate – granted it can be disappointing. But sometimes I'm pleasantly surprised."

How Do You *Show Up?*

View your primary relationships as a parent, lover, friend, professional – how do you *show up*? Are you constantly nagging, finding fault, seeing the negative, or needing to be right?

Let's Morph the showing up part of the equation:

♥ Do you dwell on the downside, showing-up with *naysayer-doom-slayer*? If so, practice expecting positive outcomes. Give raves and compliments to yourself and others each day.

♥ Give up that humble, less-than attitude. Build self-esteem and support others by showing up positive.

♥ Instead of nagging, say it once. "Clean up your room, please." Options: Have a consequence if they don't. Do it yourself. Exchange chores (have them do dishes, you clean the room). Let them own the problem. Close the door and let them live in gunkiness.

♥ Do you show up paranoid, untrusting, thinking the worst has happened? Get into showing up as a trusting (not blind or hind-sighted) ally.

♥ Can you let others show up as they really are? Give them the chance to demonstrate if they are kind, compassionate, rude, uncaring, mean-spirited, or loving. We all have moods and triggers – allow for human frailty in yourself and others. Patience and apologies help mend the nasties.

♥ Can you show up as the observer rather than the reactor? If you view the change in others without judgment, they can't play the same-old-same-old routine anymore. Even if they don't fess-up or change their M.O., you no longer remain the brunt of unhealthy interactions. Choose to set boundaries, or choose NOT to SHOW UP for them anymore.

♥ Morph a relationship to empower yourself. Practice for one day how you want to show up: attentive, non-judgmental, loving, firm, yet open. Watch the reactions (yours and others) to your commitment. Experiment with other ways of showing up.

What Goes Around Comes Around

Debra and I have shared a close bond for over 20 years. We have supported each other through several Life Chunk passages. Initially, I was her so-called role model, with more wisdom and life experience (a nice way to say I was older). As her confidante, I was there to soothe her growing pains, namely through a failed marriage, the birth of her son, career changes, and so on. I remember teasing her once in one of her down times, saying, "Don't worry, you'll take care of me in my old age." Even though old age has yet to arrive, the shoe has fallen on Debra's foot.

During a recent family member's crisis-illness, it was Debra who became my touchstone, supporter, and confidante. Her common sense approach helped me to find medical options; her nurturing helped soothe my emotional pain and sadness. Without judgments, Debra became a safe sounding board, allowing me to release anxious moments, and to handle the ongoing stress while I was coping with the daunting task of being a caregiver. If ever the adage "*What goes around comes around*" proved to be true, it was this time, when being there for a friend was returned beyond measure.

Reach out...let a friend give. Receive. Trust empowers mutual respect; builds character. Have gratitude for sharing your need, once hidden in unworthiness or pride, now liberated and free.

Do you maintain old friendships for nurturing? Or, are you caught in a time warp kowtowing to people because "you owe them," "feel you have to," or even more telling, are afraid to risk the rejection of making a new friend? You are evolving and changing and so are your acquaintances and friends. If they hold on to *how you were* and cannot support *who you are now* – let go.

Birthday and Holiday Blues

On the day you were born, the angels sang. Do you remember your heart song? Breathe deep. Inner rhythm gently rocks, rings true. Guiding... in perfect HArmony.

John F. Kennedy was assassinated on my birthday, November 22 – a devastating demarcation and sad day for all Americans. From that moment on, I sent gifts and cards to friends when my heart told me to. No one seemed to get it. "It's not my birthday," was the common response. I gave up explaining it, yet I am forever heartily moved to celebrate everyday, 365 days a year, as your birthday and mine.

♥ ♥ ♥

Turning 40, Scott decided to spend his birthday alone, ignoring the relevance of sharing it with friends. He lit the barbecue, threw a hamburger on the fire, and then wept. Appalled at being so down, he questioned his existence. "What happened to me in the past forty years? I live in a big house and I'm completely alone."

Scott chose to put his career above all else. His social life consisted of lavish business dinners or functions to promote new clients. His discipline of a daily trip to the gym, a racquetball game with a couple of guys, was the extent of his connection to others. Scott suddenly grasped how his friends had faded away and how he'd lost contact. The realization that he had not been a friend was clear: it took up too much time to listen to other's problems and frivolities.

As the hamburger burnt to a crisp on the grill before him, a transformation took place in Scott's heart. "I need to relearn how to become a friend." The next morning he felt great. He chartered a fresh course, now on a mission to make new friends and balance his life.

What do you provide to your friends? What do they provide to you? What attributes are necessary in your friendships? Do you offer the same attributes, qualities and ethics as a friend?

Celebrating Our Friends

Take five to bless, mourn, or fondly remember those who have traversed your life. Maybe they've treaded a different path, shifted gears, moved on.

- ♥ Invite the images/faces of friends (who helped shape your life) to flash before you. Recall moments of camaraderie. Digest your memory reverie.

- ♥ Do you have an old friend you would like to contact? Call, email, or send a note to someone you miss or appreciate. Have a Friendship Party. Each friend brings a friend…expanding the connection, the One-ness, life's great celebration.

"Don't you wish life was as simple as the advice we give others?

We love someone. We care about them. We want their happiness; we want them to be OK. So we try to fix, do or say what we hope will help. "Just leave the abusive creep." "Just stop drinking." "Just get a nose job, already." We offer bold panaceas without understanding the root cause.

Are you having a twinge of doubt, unease, or cognition? Pay heed to the subtlety. Life's lessons are wrapped up in moments of discovery.

Oops, I'm on rewind, "Don't you wish life was as simple as the advice we give other's?"

CHAPTER 13

SPIRIT AND HEART CONNECTIONS

Moving into HArmony and HAppiness, we delve into truth and simplicity: a vital awareness of being whole ("wholly"). Your breath connects your mind, heart, and spirit. How do you breathe? Is it a long, deep breath, or a series of shallow intakes? To still the mind and relax the body let's check in and retune breath.

Practice LightHeart™ in-breath technique, breathing in deep for eight counts, holding four, and breathing out long for eight counts. This is a recharge technique.

***So Hum*, an ancient mantra, is the natural sound of the breath**. Just say the word silently and notice how it is in-sync with your natural breathing. Repeat *So* on the in-breath, and *Hum* on the out-breath. Continue breathing naturally while repeating the words as you breathe. You can practice for a few minutes before meditating to quiet the mind and invoke silence. If you are stressed during the day, silently repeat, *So Hum* as a stress-busting heart opener.

The breath connects body, mind and spirit. Exercises throughout the book invite deep breathing to focus, calm, ground, and expand awareness. Breath is our reliable support, weaving a golden life thread... bringing us home to our truth.

Take My Breath Away

Mara at only 17 was a top competitor for a modeling layout in *Vogue* magazine. Cooking a celebratory dinner, she was heating oil in a very hot skillet. Lifting the heavy pot, it flipped into the air and oil spewed everywhere. In a quick response, she raised an arm to cover her face. It was too late. The skin on her face and arms were seriously burned. Mara's next recollection was several days later when she awakened in a hospital with third-degree burns. Lying in bed, wrapped in gauze with slits for eyes, she was blind.

Mara recalled, "Every breath was excruciating. I slept for minutes on the hour, not through the night. My breath was my torturer…and my lifeline. There was no way I could avoid breathing, so I focused my attention on it. Using my breath as a calming agent, I seemingly left my body. The pain was gone for the most part. I imagined my life continuing, doing photo sessions like before. My inner world was magical, full, and gratifying."

After several skin grafts and eye surgery, Mara's face is scar-free, and miraculously, she can see again. "By making friends with my breath, I was given internal sight. That led me to mustering an imaginary life from a hospital bed, inspiring me to live a positive future. That certainty brought me to the real thing – my great blessing." Mara didn't go for the final skin grafts to repair her underarm. She explained, "I left the purplish wrinkled skin there as a reminder, as my trademark, my tattoo of gratitude."

Mara's focus on her breath put her in a state of Oneness and healing. Her ongoing gratitude for that gift has led her to support the arts and humane issues.

Focus on Flame – Center Yourself

Focusing enables us to stay calm and centered. It nips anxiety in the bud and increases our inner awareness. Focusing on the flame of a candle (or on the flickering in a fireplace) can be used as sacred time to develop that calm.

♥ Prepare a quiet space. Light a candle.

♥ Take three deep breaths. Fix your eyes on the candle. Breathe naturally with the rhythm of the flame. As the candle continues to flicker and change rhythms, be aware of your breath.

♥ Continue gazing at the candle, allowing thoughts, images, and impressions to be absorbed in the flame.

♥ Shift your focus inside yourself. Then focus on the space between the eyebrows (known as the *third eye*). Picture an inner flame on that spot, and let your awareness rest there. After a moment, shift your focus back and forth between the inner and outer flames so that the flame is inside and outside of you.

♥ Slowly bring your awareness back to the breath. You may feel a need to stretch your arms, legs, or back. Reflect on your experience.

Intuition – Destiny's Companion

Searching, burning in the flames of doubt, a voice within called out. "Where are you, oh Truthsayer? Come show your face." A thunderous awakening shook my core of being, a heart piercing echo comforted. "I am here, all you are seeking. I AM...YOU...LOVE ME.

Intuition is the voice of the Self that we are seeking. It's an inner knowing, relaying the unexpected answer, one that may be completely out of the norm yet resonates within you. Intuition guides you into right action without your logical understanding of why it is so. The mind doesn't consciously compute the information, but your intuition senses the truth.

The trick is to become familiar and comfortable with your intuition – sufficiently trusting of it – and then to listen when it speaks. We often call it a *hunch* or *gut reaction*. You feel it and it keeps nudging you. It's difficult to deny or go against. And, when you do, your decision may regrettably backfire. When you follow it, life resonates with right action, bringing optimum outcomes.

Donna was visiting my home on an extremely hot day. Temperatures rose to over 100 degrees; the air-conditioning was worthless. Spending half of the day in and out of the pool, she complained of a constant throb in her head. "It's like a wound in my temple." Not wanting to alarm her, I hid my concern because if it became worse I was prepared to rush her to the ER. In fact, I envisioned taking her there.

Unexpectedly she began wailing, "Something's happened to Jaime," referring to her teenage daughter. She called home. Just as she had suspected, Jaime had fallen down a flight of steps, suffering a head injury near her right temple. Luckily, it was a minor injury and she would be all right.

On the way to the hospital Donna confided, "Thank God it's over. I dreamed it, prayed on it, felt it all week." Donna's intuition had alerted her that an incident would occur, and it would not be life threatening.

Sometimes we are alerted, without an ability to affect the situation we perceive. As a psychic preparation, it helps to face the oncoming event if and when it does occur.

Divine Intervention – Intuitive Grace

On January 16, 1994, our friend Gene invited Byron and me to his home for dinner. After a tiring workday, I was a bit resistant. Byron was convincing. "Oh, please Mom, I love Gene's salads." So, off we went.

After dinner, at around 9:00, we were deep in conversation when a voice reverberated in my head saying "Don't go home, don't drive." Upon hearing the words, a feeling of drowsiness swept over me. How peculiar, as we were only five minutes from home, yet I felt glued. I could not move out of my chair. I said to Gene, "I feel woozy, like I can't drive." He responded, "Don't go home. Use the guest room."

Our Sheltie, Caruso, was with us that night, which was rare. So Byron, the dog, and I slept in the guestroom. At 4:32 a.m., January 17, all hell broke loose. The rooms were shaking so violently I feared the walls would collapse. A file cabinet careened against the bed, tumbling within inches of our heads. In the pitch-black darkness, objects were crashing and ricocheting all around us. Living in California, we were often jolted by earth tremors, but this time my mind raced, "This is the big one." We were trapped in the fervor of a major earthquake, pummeling with a forceful vengeance. In spite of the chaos, a part of me felt so safe.

Caruso jumped on the bed and dashed under the covers. I threw myself over Byron, protecting him from any blow. The tumult seemed to go on endlessly. Finally, the shaking subsided. After a brief silence, Gene called out through the darkness, "Are you okay?"

He guided us outside to his motor home. A total blackout from power failure had cut off phones and electricity. With help from a generator, Gene turned on a radio and put on a teakettle. We sat back and waited for the news. Northridge had been the epicenter of the quake, and we were only a few miles away. As dawn approached, we saw evidence of the extent of the damage. Fires burned in the distance; sirens screeched through the streets. I was in no rush to go home.

My house was in the hills, so I waited until noon before I was ready to venture out. Driving through the streets, I was shocked: the devastation was incomprehensible. Buildings had completely collapsed. Trees and power lines were down, and large cracks cut through the roads. People huddled in the streets. Cars were crushed and fallen trees had demolished garages.

Approaching the front of my house, I could see blown-out windows and charred debris. I took a deep breath and said to myself, "Be brave," and then I went inside. We could barely open the door. The house was three-feet deep in rubble. Every breakable item, every dish, every fragile keepsake, was broken. Byron screeched, "Mom, look! The piano slid across the room. Oh, wow! The oven blew out of the wall!"

Barely able to step over the debris, I made my way to my bedroom. Standing in the doorway, I faced my bed in horror. A large art deco mirror had sheared through the mattress exactly where I would have been sleeping. Had I been there, I'd have been terribly maimed or killed.

Chilled to the bone, I recalled the voice ringing within me: "Don't go home. Don't drive." I started to sob. I knew the deep intuitive part of me had spared my life. Byron gasped at the sight, gently squeezing my hand and said, "Aren't you lucky I wanted to go to Gene's?" By the knowing tone in his voice, it was clear that he too had been guided that night by more than wanting a salad.

As the days went on, miraculous stories of intuition surfaced. One woman claimed, "My two-year-old son awakened minutes before the quake and ran into our bed. His room was smashed into rubble."

Know that your inner voice is always with you: the great keeper of destiny's gate.

Rekindle Intuition

The intuitive voice is your inner companion. It has clarity, a distinctive zing that differs from the chattering analytical mind. This inner voice guides you in various ways – sometimes gently, other times with vigor – prodding you to listen. It operates in the *Morphic* field, at a frequency beyond time and space as we know it. It traverses all linear concepts and is eternally present. It has been said the inner voice is the voice of God or of the power that sustains all life. If only we would be quiet (meditation helps), we would hear the unbounded wisdom that resides within our true nature. Intuition is ever present, whether we sense it as spiritually connected or not.

Synchronicity is a result of following intuition, such as being "in the right place at the right time." Synchronicity appears when you are attuned to life's purposeful signs; when you are aware, they occur daily for your pleasure.

Become alert to unusual, seemingly coincidental moments: Maybe you're seeking an answer to a question, and then a friend calls unexpectedly with the needed information. You've been thinking about something and within 24 hours, the event occurs. Or you say, "I just have a feeling about that person."

Our inner voice also operates on the most mundane levels; the phone rings and you know who is calling; or you have a feeling that something's not right, and you discover your car was just towed. Traversing in the realms of the unknown, your gut becomes a trusted guide.

Avoid the tendency to qualify hunches, sensations, or intuitive doorknockers with, "That's ridiculous, how could that be?" Beware of all of the *buts*, which are just an onslaught of blocks rushing in from your analytical mind to question or disprove your truth. If a sensation, vivid image, foreboding, or anticipatory thought alerts you, do not ignore or dismiss it. Just watch what occurs. Prepare, if need be.

Example: You notice your keys on the restaurant table. It's a focused quick glance – the perception of the keys. The ignited awareness has a different quality than generally scanning the table and spotting the keys. Learn to recognize the subtle, sharp distinction as an imminent message.

Let's assume that you ignore the observation of the keys, and you leave them on the table when you go to the restroom. When you return, the keys are gone. After searching for them, you discover the waitress has picked them up for safekeeping. Lucky for you. Your car is safe. Nevertheless, you missed the INTUITIVE CUE.

Overlooking opportunity or warnings in everyday occurrence is the result of not following your intuitive cue. Every day we perceive thousands of sensorial inputs of information and images. Be receptive. Often in the midst of crisis, a deep calm feeling takes over; your awareness is heightened, alerting you to clues that are vital for your welfare.

I was jogging with a buddy when my mind flashed a picture of a diamond ring. The vision was seemingly nonsensical because I didn't have a diamond ring. The image lingered and I wondered, "Am I going to get engaged, get a ring, or what?"

The next day, while driving home from the studio, I noticed a car at the bottom of my driveway. The trunk was open and a well-dressed man was closing it. I registered a strange feeling. Easing to the entryway, I saw a sliding door was ajar. Leery, I cautiously went inside. The house had been ransacked, an obvious burglary. The drawers in a dresser were askew, and to my dismay, my mother's jewelry was gone. I shuddered, "Mother's diamond ring is missing."

I had the intuitive clue, the vision of a diamond, but I never considered mother's ring to be my own. If I had listened to the intuitive message, I might have considered putting it into a safety deposit box.

Being highly sensitive, I was accustomed to delving deeper and asking questions from within. In a reflective state, I asked my higher consciousness, "Is there any additional information I need to know about my mother's ring? Where it might be or should I let it go?" The immediate answer I received was "jewelry store." No other leading images, sensations, or clues followed. I contemplated the meaning. "Should I buy another ring or what?" In the weeks that followed, in my spare time, I perused jewelry stores and an occasional pawnshop. I couldn't kid myself; I was aimlessly searching for mother's ring. I decided if I found a similar one, I would buy it.

Zipping down a sidewalk in Beverly Hills on the way to meet a friend for lunch, I was magnetized to a posh jeweler's display window. My heart flew into my throat. There it was: the exact duplicate of mother's antique ring. I immediately went into the store. The jeweler related that he had purchased the ring approximately a month earlier. A red-tape quagmire ensued to decipher if the ring was actually mother's. It was. I finally retrieved it – legally. When I'm not flaunting my keepsake, it's tucked away in my safe secret spot – the bank deposit box.

You don't have to be a witch, a soothsayer, or a shaman Goddess to experience these moments. Everyone has intuitive abilities. What were the results when you didn't listen to your inner voice? What were the results when you did?

Invoking Intuition – Developing the Skill

♥ Be mindful of physical setting. Indoors: select soothing music, scented candles. Outdoors: light a bonfire, gaze at rolling clouds, listen to a babbling brook. Invite new insight to reveal core truth.

♥ Clear your mind: Deep breathe for two minutes to gain clarity on your query: a situation, relationship, or direction to take. Ask questions like, "What do I know?" "What can I do? "What else do I need to know?" Allow your intuition to surface, with a feeling, sensation, image.

♥ Gauge whether you feel light or heavy inside. Lightness: a YES possibility. Heaviness: pause, before moving forward.

♥ Inner Physician: Close your eyes. Tune into your body. Do a mental scan from head to toe. Visualize each organ. Let the organ or body part speak to you. If it's not feeling healthy, ask why? Send positive, loving, healing energy to that part of the body.

♥ If you feel queasy, chilled, or nauseous around someone or when thinking of a situation, listen to your body. It could be a warning. Stay aware.

♥ Practice:
  • Ask someone to give you the name of a person you don't know and describe him or her. Don't think. Just do it.
  • For Mastermind guidance – Dialogue with Intuition.

Trust inner Knowing ... Don't squelch your innate gift.

Paranormal is Normal

I remember a moment, a flashpoint, at six-years-old, when I made the decision to conceal who and what I was really was. At a dinner party in my parent's home, I listened to two bantering adults. I knew what they were going to say before they said it. Whether defined as intuition, a sixth sense, ESP, or clairaudience is unimportant compared to what happened next: sensing one of the women was lying, I snickered, "That's not what happened; you weren't even home that night." (Such brash statements didn't exactly endear me to adults.) "Get that brat out of here," she seethed. My father flashed a wicked glare my way, sending me to my room.

He punished me for my seeming lack of respect, but from a child's inexperienced point of view, my intuitive sense suffered a devastating blow. I erroneously heard a life-altering message to "conceal my inner truth." I safely hid behind giggles, pratfalls, fluttering eyelashes, and playing Little Miss Cute, assuming that any divergence would lead to disapproval, criticism and even punishment. It's so sad that many of us at an early age make life-damaging decisions, forming crippling patterns.

Can you recall a unique quality that was squelched and dimmed like a solar eclipse? Or an experience that shut you down when it created embarrassment, HAvoc, or misunderstood intent? In my case, the creative energy to perceive something beyond the norm was suppressed as an outward expression (with my father), yet it remained enlivened, a reliable companion in my inner secret world.

The Art of Reading People

In everyday business transactions, interacting with family, friends, and meeting new people, it helps to decipher why they are doing or saying something. Determine their agenda – and what they *aren't* saying?

Pay attention to mannerisms; observe vocal pitch, speech patterns, inflections, body dialogue, breathing patterns, and so on. For example, if someone diverts their eyes, it could be a sign that they are lying. A wet brow could indicate fear or the need to hide or cover-up something.

Police officers, security guards, psychologists, detectives, salespeople, insurance investigators, beauticians, writers, etc. often develop people-reading skills and an acute intuitive sense as a routine part of their job. *Sherlock Holmes* rallies as a favorite among a bevy of acclaimed detectives and sleuths. Steadily, he proved through logic and observation the uncanny ability to hone in on the culprit. "It was the way he rolled the newspaper: the same way the killer folded her dressing gown," he might say.

I am not suggesting that you become suspicious of every nuance to decipher a person's intent. But, Sherlock's incriminating clues were often found through following a hunch. A hunch is the product of your wide base of knowledge, your broad-scoped life experiences cataloged as a sum-total, imbued in your brain for retrieval when necessary. It is the ultimate in common sense. Intuition helps you to make the proper assessment of a situation or the right-on deduction.

Beware of the tendency to "read the garbage", the limitations, the negatives in other people's minds. It's a waste of time to dwell or play in those realms. It is more uplifting to spend time in contemplation of your own mind.

Heart Strings

"Follow your heart." Listen to your heart – it has a mind of its own. Often stifled by mind-babble, the head and heart seem to disagree. A tug of war indicates you don't know what you want. If you feel a tugging at your heartstrings or your mind, step back before acting. Give it a break. Ask clarifying questions. When leading from the heart's intelligence, your life's purpose blooms, continuously expanding. You live in love…and then loving relationships and experiences are more easily attained.

Connecting With Your Heart

Love the one you're with. It starts with you – your constant companion. Love is a constant – it's always there in every moment…waiting for you, in you, and all around.

Are you your best friend, worst enemy, greatest supporter, or greatest recriminator? How you feel about yourself affects the vibrations when you enter a room. Others may love or hate us, but greatest harm comes when we don't love the Self. Why? We project our image upon others and situations, whether in work, romance, or friendship. We duplicate our self-image onto every encounter in our existence. If we are unhappy, we spread sadness. If we are joyous, we spread laughter. If we love, we spread hope.

Explore the power of connecting with your heart. Among the seven *chakras* (energy meridians) in the body, the heart *chakra* is the focal point. All of the energy meridians are connected, and our heart vibrates in every cell of the body, synchronizing bodily rhythms. (It's not only the place where love lives, but where inspiration and joy are manifested.) So then, what to do with the broken heart, sad heart, mourning heart, greedy heart, or the heavy heart? **Cry your heart out.** It feels good to dump the pain, the weight of the world, the disappointments, frustrations, and confusion. Even gratefulness and joy produce tears.

During a Morph Group session, Benji, a teen, shared his experience. "I was twelve the last time I cried in front of anyone. I hurt my leg real bad playing soccer. I was lying on the ground in the worst pain. I guess I was crying out loud. Then coach screamed at me, 'Stop crying like a baby. Take it like a man'. I felt so embarrassed in front of everyone. The kids called me a *wuss*. It was right then that I promised myself no matter how bad something felt, I'd never show it. I turned a part of my heart off that day."

Willie, another teen, said, "I never remembered crying, only wimp's cry. But, when my dad sobbed like a baby at his mom's funeral and I held him in my arms, something snapped. I knew we cry because it's human, it saves you." Willie, in that moment, gave himself permission to cry.

It takes courage, superseding gender, to be real, authentic. It's wise to go beyond an adolescent society's customs that don't support the most basic human and natural instincts. However, to avoid becoming a slobbering wailer, I have learned to discriminate and ferret out safe places to vent.

Is it okay to be vulnerable, to soften your heart? To be yourself without apology? When we hold others in contempt and blame them for our state, we make a crusty mess and become hard to life. I find strength in allowing a soft heart. In the revelation, I see, hear, and touch a gentle knowing...teaching the simple, the blessed. Are you yearning to flow in this truth? Be still inside, and know you are!

Wrap Your Heart Around It

Reach into your heart. Unresolved hurts lay dormant, waiting for release. Maybe you are mourning the loss of a relationship or a pet, or harboring other disappointments. Take a few deep breaths. On the exhalation, release any pent-up hurts. Let the images arise and float by until one pops out at you. Let it speak out loud. Yell it out, if you choose. What is it telling you? Watch your body sensations, your thoughts. Do you feel numb, nervous, or queasy? Are you resisting, tensing your muscles, or holding back? If tears well up, let them go. Flow with your release. It's a blessing.

♥ Being true and honest with yourself is the precursor to HArmony and HAppiness. If you are in the midst of an argument, feeling resentful or judgmental toward another, a situation, or yourself, it's time to wrap your heart around it. Practice engaging the power of the heart, the empathetic guide for wholeness and well-being.

♥ If the conflict is immediate and involves others, use a simple statement such as, "I need a couple of minutes to think, cool down. Take a break." When you feel calmer, place your hand over your heart and feel the beat.

♥ Imagine a white string of light encircling your heart space. Allow the light to warm you. Say three times, "I am wrapping my heart around_____ (state the situation) for the highest good of all."

♥ Observe feelings or thoughts – without attachment.

♥ Has anything changed in your perception? Are you ready to initiate or engage the other person on a better footing? Do you need more time? If so, save face and let them know.

When in disharmony, operating from the heart center helps us to do the right thing. We experience our true loving spirit, an opening, a healing doorway that allows others to feel safe and understood. Heart connection begins a string of magical events. From watching a sunrise to helping a child take a first step – doubt ceases, worry dims beyond all challenge. Imagine that.

Compassion – The Gateway to Human Freedom

Compassion is a liberating force from separateness and self-centeredness: it's a connector, embracing all beings as the same. Compassion is an active energy; its very nature wants to reach out to suffering and to help. Reach out. Touch hearts. Open to Truth…whatever the perfect storm.

♥ ♥ ♥

While swimming in my pool, Ilene let out an excruciating screech. As I turned to face her, I noticed a lizard flailing on the surface of the water. "Toss it out of the pool or it'll drown," I quickly responded.

Her face grimaced with fear, "I can't! I can't!" Without hesitating, I swam to the little lizard, scooped it in my hand, and tossed it to safety on the pool deck. Instantly I thought, "Did I throw it too hard?" It wasn't moving. A horrible feeling of dread swept through me as I whimpered, "Oh no, maybe I killed it."

Ilene was intent. "No, no. Look, its head is moving."

Somewhat relieved, I said, "Maybe it's just drying off or hiding from us, hoping to blend in with the bricks."

Our attention remained fixated on the little creature. I silently prayed for it, hoping I hadn't hurt it and that it would live. I was aware that the prayer was for me, for my ignorance, for my lack of awareness, and the twinge of apprehension I felt in the moment that I touched it. "Could it hurt me, how slimy is it?" I was praying for my human frailty as well as for the lizard's thin thread between life and death.

Compassion for all of us permeated my heart: one, for the little lizard fighting for its life; two, for Ilene, whose fear of touching the creature was greater than the fear of its drowning; and three, for my limited perception and me. I thought Ilene was weak until I contemplated, "What if it had been a rattlesnake. Would I have touched it?" And, I had compassion for my pain of possibly hurting the lizard.

Ten minutes later, the little creature was gone from its spot. It was odd, neither Ilene nor I saw it slip away. It happened in the blink of an eye. All that remained was an opening of our hearts and the gentle awareness of living in compassion.

Similar to empathy, compassion can evoke a detached witness state, like a mirror that is removed from the images before it. Compassion is always with you as the very essence of your presence. It is recognizing, allowing something to *be* there as it *is*, and to have full regard and respect for its potential.

Most simply, it's the power of kindness when you're in a funk and someone says, "Hang in there – everything will be alright." We trust. A space opens, diluting confusion and doubt; "What am I going to do?" An inner guide brings clarity, intervention, a respite. It erodes what must go and blesses its departure.

Compassion co-exists with *ecstasy* (which has its root in the Greek word *exstasis*, which means, "Out of oneself or part of the whole.") To experience ecstasy we must connect beyond limited feelings of lack, compulsion, and fear.

Knowing that fear is a mere movement of the mind, compassion embraces fear. It asks, "Did all of your fears happen? Which ones did? Which ones didn't? Were they gentler, greater, smaller than you imagined?" Did you learn, "This too shall pass?"

To have true compassion for others you must have it for yourself. It's not a pity, a "poor me" victim, or "less than" state. It witnesses everything as temporary, changeable, transmutable – as a condition that is *human*. It embraces all conditions, whether "good" or "bad". It dissolves limited perceptions, viewpoints, prejudices, and judgments of self and others.

This is a time for self inquiry. Contemplate a situation when you closed off and were not compassionate. Allow thoughts, feelings, sensations to come up. What beliefs did you hold? Would you choose to alter your response?

Recall a moment when you felt compassion for yourself or something or someone. How did you react or respond?

Practice the Art of Compassion

♥ Care about yourself – your health, your state of mind, your material and spiritual balance. Do not put down or denigrate YOU.

♥ Initiate help for your needs, quandaries, and concerns. Allow others to care for you. Expand your capacity to give and take, to listen and be heard.

♥ Who said that giving is better than the get? Receive full circle. Say YES. Offerings open the Good. Abundance flows.

♥ Open your heart to the gentle pulsation of all life, including tender caring, sorrow, pain, inequities, illness, intolerance, hatred, ignorance, addiction – any place where compassion is needed for change.

Every day we are challenged to live compassionately. Two young men stepped over a sun-parched homeless man lying in the street. One man scathed, "Kick him to the curb." His friend's heart melted. "But for the grace of God, there go I," he thought. Without judgments, he wondered, "How did that soul get there? What pain, disappointment, or illness had paved the street…as his home?"

Common-Sensible Living

We have examined the philosophical, the esoteric – now let's illuminate compassion as your hardcore companion.

Honoring Consequences: If your employee is a slacker, can't be trained, then fire him or her. Give the reasons in an effort to shed light. Bless that person to learn, knowing their life choices and lessons ride with them.

Tough Love: My mother's heart flipped as she watched my brother and I leap across one building's rooftop – ten-stories high – onto the next building. She knew we were not super heroes and could plunge into oblivion. After screeching the riot act, she took away the "cookie jar", and sent us to our rooms, literally grounding us. Administering tough love, setting boundaries, creating the awareness and reality of consequences for our actions was our mother's compassionate teaching.

Compassion is life's root system – the inter-connector of all growth – ending the separation from others and our Self.

Rituals of the Sacred Heart

Today we celebrate loved ones with gifts and parties, yet sacred rituals are rare. A ritual connects us to life's significant passages and nourishes the core of our spirit. Our ancestors, regardless of cultural heritage, performed sacred rituals through dance, song, drumming, prayer, play-acting, and chanting. Celebrations honored marriage, entering into manhood or womanhood, fertility rites, vision quests, birth and death, with the intent to bestow blessings and safe rites of passage.

On a special occasion, reflect on its significance. What events in your life brought you to this moment? What are you asking for, what acknowledgment, what blessing? How will you express the process of the ritual? Let your imagination soar.

Provide Opportunities for Rites of Passage

Teens view getting a driver's license, a first kiss, celebrating prom night, or graduation, as signposts of maturity. The *Bar Mitzvah* and *Bat Mitzvah*, a Jewish tradition, signifies entry into manhood and womanhood. Your teen might yearn (unwittingly) to delineate this passage. Puberty and adolescence bring with it confusion about leaving childhood behind. Caught in a pre-adulthood world they feel frustrated, exasperated, and slightly deluded. They believe no one can understand them, not even their peers. To them, no one else has traversed the foggy conditions they are experiencing.

You can offer-up a listening ear. Listen with every pore of your body and mind. No solutions or comments are necessary. Allow a safe space for him/her to express their concerns. Allow trust creative thoughts to surface beyond negative or self-deprecating attitudes.

Mom and Dad: Tune into your heart, look into your child's eyes, the window of the soul. You will know what to do, what to say, how to be. Connecting, they will see you, feel you, and listen with trust.

Create Teen Rituals

Honor first car: Gather family and friends to honor the driver and the car. Fill a bowl with water. Sprinkle water on front, sides, rear of car. Bless the car and driver to journey safe. To travel new paths to adventure. Present car keys to the teen. "These keys will be used as a symbol of this journey, to go to places of interest and carry this blessing forward" (choose your own words). The ritual can end with the family going for a ride with the teen driving.

Leaving home (moving into a college dorm or apartment)**:** Open a window symbolizing inner and outer conditions. Bless the new place for peaceful living. Honor the adventure of learning, making new friends, growing strong, confident, self-sufficient, having fun. End the ritual by closing the window, sealing the intentions of the Blessing.

Adults typically experience rites of passage at marriage, giving birth, mid-life, retirement, and our final passage from this life – death. Allow freedom from every day toiling to observe life's transition. It's okay not to know what's up next for you. In prayer, ask for guidance, purpose, direction. Bless and release life's weight. Give thanks for all circumstances and people in your life and gifts you've come to share.

Parents, honor letting go.

Youth, accept the divine privilege to open and receive the new.

Ritual – Bring On Your LightHeart™ Song

To honor rites of passage, gather with friends. To bring on your HeartSong play bells, chimes, drums, even a flute adds flavor. Dance in free flow movement, eyes open or closed.

♥

Follow a lead beat, one-two heartbeat. Feel the mind quiet and permeate a lightness of being. In that flow sway and dance. Allow feelings to guide rhythm changes. As emotions release, discover the joy and freedom within yourself. Continue until you naturally stop, and then reflect upon your experience. Feel the Oneness connecting to others – in sync and in tune with life's unfolding passage. Symbolizing the gathering: offer friends a token of gratitude.

CHAPTER 14

TAPPING THE SPARK OF
THE DIVINE

The enlightened ONE is just that – *en-light*. Spirituality and lightheartedness are not separate. When the practices, whatever they are (Qigong, meditation, you name it), are incorporated into everyday living, the benefits are divine.

All spiritual traditions have proclaimed that within each of us is a place of peace, strength, wisdom and love – a quiet place where we can go to experience our true, essential nature. The ancient Greeks referred to this nature as *entheos*, which means "the God within." *Entheos* is the source of our word *enthusiasm*, which is akin to feeling infused with divine excitement, brimming with God's energy. In the *Ming Dynasty* in China, an epigram described this inner divinity as follows: "The spirit of man communes with Heaven; the omnipotence of Heaven resides in man. Is the distance between Heaven and man very great?"

All of us have been in touch with the spark of the Divine, whether communing with nature, listening to music, or having the experience of going beyond ourselves – often athletes often talk of playing "in the zone". What connects you to God within or an inner divine spark?

LightHeart Tapping™

One way to free up and to connect with your spiritual DNA is by *LightHeart Tapping™*.

♥ Repeat affirmations of good health, prosperity, and love. "I love my life. I love myself." "I Love my husband/wife...."

♥ During the affirmations, play soothing, yet uplifting music.

♥ Take your two pointer fingers and tap the top of your head, and then gently tap your forehead between the eyebrows, your cheeks, your shoulders. Spontaneously tap various parts of your body, as you feel inclined. Continue tapping with the intent of healing energy permeating your body, mind, and spirit.

LightHeart Path Retreat™

The LightHeart *Retreat* can be celebrated in solitude or with your family and community. The basics are what I call the *5 R & R's*: Renew. Regroup. Revitalize. Revisit. Relax.

The retreat was born out of a need to explore the events occurring at lightning speed during the creation of the Morph Process. Our funding was in place, projects were lined-up, manuals were ready to be written, videos needed to be produced, teachers had to be trained, a staff was to be hired, etc. These gear-ups were happening simultaneously; we were entering into the unknown, traversing new territory. Being at the helm of this new venture, everyone looked to me for direction. As clear as the Morph vision was to me, the basic plan was propelled by gut instincts and flying by the seat of my pants. I was overwhelmed, needing a break to step back, revitalize myself, and reevaluate our team's mission strategy.

While in retreat, sitting on a brook's edge I watched minnows leap to the water's surface then dive back down. Similarly, I had been diving to my depths of concern and surfacing for a refreshing breath of air. Momentarily, I watched a flock of birds in formation; the leader guided the journey, swooping over and under, changing position, in perfection, in unison. The formation lined up differently and a new leader emerged, trusting natural rhythm, with minimum effort, maximum results.

In a burst of inspiration, I saw my plan unfold – we would initially create Morph curriculums that I would co-write with educators. Workshops would be delegated to facilitators in the schools, and so on.

Bird Formation

To find a purposeful direction, stand with your feet grounded into the surface. Extend your arms at your side. Start flapping, like a bird's wings in flight. Move your body, swaying, lifting into the air. Relax your arms, as if gliding. Feel the freedom, the ease of soaring, effortless motion. Begin walking in that ease. How do you feel? Is there a shift in awareness? Do you feel lighter, more grounded, freer? Can you see the light of purpose, possibilities before you? Write down your impressions, ideas, sensations, and feelings.

Create Your LightHeart Path™ Retreat

Set your timeframe: a daytrip, overnight, or weekend. Select an environment that will spiritually and psychologically nurture and revitalize you. Spend a day at the beach, take a long drive or go for a walk in the woods. Spend time alone before you bring together those who may also share your vision, mission, or issue.

What season or climate is it? Reflect on what that season means to you. What important events occurred during this time of year?

If it's Fall, are you at a time of reaping in your life? Is it Winter, the time of stillness and reflection? Is it Spring, the time of renewal and inspiration? Or Summer, the time of change and light? What issue keeps popping up? Absorb the energy of the season, remaining open to your feelings and thoughts. Discover how to be free, learning through reflection what you are willing to let go of and what newness you can create.

You and your loved one can opt for a couples retreat. Away from the maddening crowd, enjoy a romantic haven to explore the sensual pleasures inspired by nature. Go barefoot, grounding your body. With the crickets singing a love song, cuddle by a bonfire, make love under the stars, and rekindle that magic spark.

Become aware of your day and night dreams. Is there a revelation, a blossoming freshness bursting forth?

Dreamtime
In the still of the night, the dreamer spoke, "I love you."

Part of my self-growth process includes exploration of the *dreamtime*. I apprenticed with Clara Stewart Flagg who, with her husband Kilton Stewart, an anthropologist, explored the *Senoi* tribe's dream culture. The Senoi, an ancient tribe, lived in the jungles of central Malaysia and used dreams as the basis of their culture. Every day they shared and analyzed their dreams, creating themes on how to live harmoniously. Negative feelings in a dream (such as anger, jealousy, etc.) were confronted by imaginary helpers (dream beings) to assist and defeat the predators. The tribe had had no violent crimes for more than 200 years. To this day, people who visit the Senoi say that they still do not need jails or police.

During dream-work with Clara, my dreams became so animated and vivid that my waking hours paled into a slow humdrum by comparison. I was unearthing vital information and learning key lessons about myself. Dreaming my future wedding day busted marriage fears I had of entrapment, boredom, and making a big mistake. Shortly thereafter, I took my trip down the aisle. It was free-spirited and loving, ceremoniously outside in nature, on the edge of a breathtakingly beautiful ocean-side cliff. Cheerfully I boasted and toasted, "Just in case I change my mind, I can dive off."

Senoi's Approach to Dreams

♥ **Face Your Problems**. The Senoi believed you rule your dream world, that you can face the dragon in a bad dream rather than running away from it. You can attack the dream beings, or transform whatever is causing the fear in your dream.

♥ **Love Your Enemies.** If you harm someone in a dream, tell the person in the waking world (if possible), and apologize for your Action. Do a kind deed for them and give yourself a gift.

♥ Share Your Feelings. If someone in your life does something harmful or beneficial to you in a dream, share it with him/her, or bounce it off someone else.

♥ **Learn to Recognize Your Friends.** A true friend will not intentionally harm you, even in a dream. It is symbolic if a friend appears to be your enemy or harms you in a dream. The enemy wears a mask of the friend. Understanding this symbolism diminishes holding negative feelings about that person.

The Senoi's belief was that positive themes and future visions occur through dream sharing. Their view suggested by sharing our dreams, we would solve our problems without arguments, fights, or wars.

In the dreams, the Senoi asked the dream beings to give them a gift notion to bring back in real life. As a ritual in their waking state, they made dream inspired creations: a sculpture out of clay, a dream- painting, or composing a song or a play depicting a provocative dream.

Choose a creative expression for a current dream... Use *dream associations*. Define specific aspects: Are people, places, events in the dream sending a message? What is the dream's theme? It's meaning? What is the lesson?

Have you had the dream before? If so, when? How was the dream different this time?

Ask, "What do I think my dream is telling me? What in my waking life might this dream connect to? Did I have a problem in my dream? Is there something I want to remember or share about this dream? Am I getting a message to do something based on this dream?"

What is revealed that we don't ordinarily face or admit? Our *shadow self teaches us to see beyond our hidden fears and concerns.* Traversing the underworld, dreams unearth fearful qualities in order for you to uproot and admit to them, embrace them, go through them, and conquer them. Our shadow self is always with us whether we perceive it or not. Our hidden, dark tendencies are part of our whole self. What we cover up, what we choose not to show to the world, is still part of us. To embrace the shadow we must stand in the light of all we are, without judgment. It's from this vantage point we can alter our darker tendencies.

When I am overwhelmed, I practice the following for relief and balance:

Place your hands in front of you. Snapping them like a Pac Man, begin to devour regrets, painful memories, and feelings. Keep snapping your hands as the sensations mount, until you see they are all snapped-up. Then take both hands and with deliberate intent, toss the residual energy debris down the rabbit hole, Zero infinity beyond space and time.

24/7

No cop-outs! Let's face it. YOU LIVE YOU 24/7. Waking and dreaming – no matter what the thoughts, feelings, or emotions – they're yours. It's your life. When we get the 24/7 reality, we can't blame anyone else if we derail, are in a madness-frenzy, or hit rock bottom. The point is for us to take responsibility for our life track.

Many of us are oblivious or discount the fact that we are living a 24/7 conscious existence. Our waking world can be shadowed and influenced by our dream-state.

In spite of the inherent stress as a CEO of a major corporation, Sid arrived each day at his office filled with peace and an infectious enthusiasm. He genuinely up-toned the mood and productivity level of the entire work force.

Leon was Sid's chauffeur; he spent leisurely time shining the limousine in-between jaunts driving Sid to meetings. However, Leon's curmudgeon disposition festered in thought and deed. He often unmercifully badgered underlings, although he managed to be pleasantly efficient in front of Sid.

Years passed and the two men grew old. On Leon's deathbed, he couldn't contain his irritability. "Damn you," he shouted at nurses, and cursed his life. In his last hours, he quieted, barely able to talk. His only visitor arrived. It was Sid. Upon seeing him, Leon bemoaned, "All these years you've been so happy, so generous, so kind, while I've been a wretched cruel man. What makes you the way you are?"

Sid replied, "Every night I dream I'm a chauffeur polishing my car and listening to fine music… so lucky to have no stress. When I wake up I am grateful and ecstatic to be alive."

Leon was perplexed. "How strange. Every night when I go to sleep I dream I'm the executive of a large company. I'm so stressed and afraid of failing that I wake up frustrated and miserable."

How ironic that the polar opposite messages in Leon's and Sid's dream-state affected their daily living. The lesson is to stay aware of our 24/7 consciousness, and to use dream messages for our personal growth and wellness.

Sweet Dreams

♥ Be mindful of your sleep state. We spend one-third of our lives sleeping (one-third of our 24/7 consciousness).

♥ Remember your dream. Volumes of books and manuals have been written about dream interpretation, but the best and most useful interpretation is your own. It resonates as truth. Consider: all parts of the dream are you – the feelings, the people, the animate and inanimate objects. Ask each part of the dream a question: "Why are you here? What can you teach me about myself?" If dreaming about flying, recall how you felt. Were you exhilarated, fearful, cautious? What does flying represent to you?

♥ Keep a log of dreams. Look for repetitious themes.

♥ Upon awakening, reflect upon your initial response. Define the theme (lost love, feeling powerless, a rebirth), and learn what it means to you.

♥ You can reenter your dream and dream it again. As your last thought before going to sleep, simply state, "I want to repeat that dream. I will reenter my dream."

♥ Change the outcome. Do you want to change the outcome? You can change it. Who is remembering it? You are. You are the dreamer (or the witness) of the dream. You are in control of having the outcome you choose. Simply say, "I will change the outcome."

♥ Bring back a gift from a dream. It can be a lesson, a truth, an Action to perform, or a learned quality or skill. Translate the gift into a blessing for everyday life.

♥ ♥ ♥

Our dreams often affect our first awareness upon awakening. We might feel sluggish, invigorated, or peaceful. Be mindful of those first moments upon awakening. Choose a positive and affirming thought to begin your day. For example, choose gratitude for your life or turn the day over to God. Practice choosing good thoughts throughout the day. See how they affect you by the day's end.

In your mind's eye, play a movie of your day before going to sleep. What did your actions teach you? What would you change if you could? What was the most precious moment? Have gratitude as your last thought before going to sleep.

Ellie's Dream Journal

Ellie, a LightHeart Path™ participant, could not sustain a relationship. She found herself involved with companions who were duplicitous in their intentions, selfish, and afraid of intimacy. She always tried to please, and in the process, her true loving nature was forsaken.

Ellie read her dream out loud in our retreat. "I was very young… in my parent's home. I needed someone to make my lunch and help me get ready for school. I wandered through our house looking for my parents. I kept calling, 'Mommy, please HEAR me. Mommy, please SEE me. Take CARE of me… Daddy can you hear me?' I felt so scared because no one came. I felt sad that no one answered. I was all alone…just wanting someone to take care of me."

Questions Ellie asked were, "Do I listen to myself? Can I see myself as I really am, with my assets and liabilities? Can I take care of myself?"

Ellie's dream clearly indicated that she was alone and wanted someone to care for her. When Ellie was 13, her mother died, so Ellie learned to fend for herself at a very early age. Her independent nature often thwarted relationships, and so she moved on to the next. She examined her attitude as an avoidance or fear of abandonment.

To expand her options, Ellie imagined her dream with the knowledge that she could change it. This time, when she called for her mother, she appeared and made lunch. They hugged. With that simple gesture, Ellie brought a gift back. She would challenge the isolated, alone feelings when they surfaced. "I'll tell them to 'bugger off', and will tell myself, 'I trust I can be there for someone and allow them to be there for me.'"

To actualize her judgment and trust in herself, Ellie practiced a simple technique:

When in doubt, pause. Take a break. Commune with nature. Express your doubts, trepidations, fears, and acknowledge them. Ask, "What is this feeling telling me? What is the rest of the issue?" Remember the platitude, "This too shall pass. It is only a feeling. I am not the feeling."

Talking LightHeart Circle™ – Free your Mind and Spirit

In the same way the Senoi's *were* enlightened by connecting their dreams with the tribe, the *Talking LIGHTHeart Circle™* can engender the same healing effect within the context of a small group. We speak our true feelings, concerns, and *what's up* for us at any given time. Our circle can include anyone we choose, or we may want to participate in a group run by a professional facilitator.

Several years ago, Phil Lane Jr. (who carries the Lakota Peace Pipe), presented a talking stick to me during our *Medicine Woman* group, initiated by Lynn Andrews. I discovered the power of speaking from the heart without self-recrimination or apology and refraining from judgment when listening.

To begin: Assemble your group. Sit in a circle, on the floor, in chairs or in an outdoor setting. Choose an object to be held by the speaker. It can be a stone, stick, flower. The circle's purpose or subject matter can vary from expressing personal issues to altruistic desires.

When you are the speaker, hold the object, tune-in to yourself, then speak without thinking, without caring about sounding right, smart, or coherent. Speak from the heart; let your inner voice give the message.

As the listener, listen with every pore of your being. Don't judge or plan ahead or think about what you would like to say next. Be in tune with the speaker. As the talking object passes from person to person, the energy transmutes with unexpected revelation. Talking LightHeart Circle™ is revelatory and satisfying, uplifting our spirits. It's as if one voice speaks our collective truth.

LightHeart™ Sanctuary

Like a kid hiding in a tree house or the yogi meditating on the mountaintop, the LightHeart™ *Sanctuary* is your inner-secret space. By creating mental images, you'll be drawn into a state of tranquility that will provide a familiar, serene place to visit at will.

♥ Imagine a beautiful place that you enjoy, such as a forest, a lake, a mountaintop, or even an imaginary garden…any peaceful, beautiful environment.

♥ Imagine the sky, the flowers, their color and fragrance, the taste of a fruit, the caress of a breeze against your cheek, the warmth of the sun. Now focus your awareness on one beautiful thing in your Inner-Sanctuary – a plant, a gentle animal.

♥ Play, relax, and enjoy the serenity.

Acknowledge your secret place you can revisit at any time. Many *AHA!* moments surface when we tune into our Inner Sanctuary. Often, our calling/purpose is enlightened during these private, quiet moments.

♥ ♥ ♥

In my serenity, walking happily on the trail, I felt a sharp pain in my toe. Removing my shoe I found the agitator, a tiny pebble. Tossing the pebble, in my sightline was the glorious rock rose bush. Mesmerized I spoke to it. "Son, speak to me of God." And the rock rose blossom, bursting sunlit tendrils, bubble-gum pink petals, each petal graced with a crimson heart answered my call. I named the rock rose *Byron's Buds*.

PART IV

In The Flow

*"Flow like the river. It's Ok to float, paddle,
or ride the wave's crest. Each moment when
you are truly present...doubts, hurts,
misunderstandings dissolve.
You sense, you trust. Expanding into joy,
celebrating the miraculous.
Flowing in the heart of the river...
flowing as YOU."*

Albert Einstein said, "I have no special talents. I am only passionately curious."

Out of curiosity 'Creative Intelligence' is born. It exists in every particle of the universe. When we go deep within our being, we connect with all that is. We can access what is, what always has been, and we can IMAGINE the glory of what could be.

In this open ended space YOU ARE RECEPTIVE and FREE.

- ♥ You see the whole picture and understand how parts interconnect to form the whole.

- ♥ You connect and communicate viscerally with your surroundings and with people you encounter.

- ♥ Out of Creativity you are reborn in the moment, filled with passionate curiosity.

In response to Albert, "I have no special talents. I am living inspirational habits."

CHAPTER 15

LIFE AS AN IMPROV – THE PLAY OF LIFE

"Your Talent Lies in Your Choice"

I was on stage being critiqued by Stella Adler, famed acting coach of Marlon Brando. "Why are you wearing those clodhopper shoes?" She railed at me, "The character is a dilettante, not a farmer's daughter." Bug-eyed, I drew a blank. Stella penetrated my stupor, "*Dah*-ling, don't you know, your talent lies in your choice!" Choice meant the character's intention, mannerisms – knowing their emotional score. For an actor, this is a key lesson to contemplate.

Making precise choices on stage trickled into my daily awareness and translated into, **"Your talent in *life* lies in *choosing* how you live it."** What you eat determines your health; the company you choose, choices you make in business, or choosing a mate, influence your lifestyle.

The power of choice is the foundation of creativity. Within you are dynamic, powerful energies that make things happen, propelling change. Every moment, how we act, react, and interact with the people and events in our lives is based on our free will to choose. We create our existence from moment-to-moment, manifesting, expanding, learning, and growing. The most important talent you have in living your life is expressing your innate, energetic force.

Bounce out of the norm. Lift off the limitations you place on yourself and how you define yourself; mom, dad, son, plumber, CPA. Be creatively centered. No matter what or who we are, we are creative transformers.

You are the expert of your life. You are trained to be the expert. Part of the training process is to look at all of your experiences, within and without. Choose the best, leave the rest. One way to achieve this is to renew your commitment to change and grow. The people I have known who don't take action and have weak commitment believe they can't succeed. You really CAN change your ways. If you follow your flow, your heart within, an enlightened transformation is inevitable. Life is a rhythmic sequence of moments strung together. The beats are more than a simple drum roll; they resound with the pulsation of the life force. When you are in step with that rhythm, joy and health are bountiful.

Rhythms of HArmony – A Healer

The *Mayans* said, "**The world sings us into being, and we are its song**." Your sweet melody and rhythm can illuminate your world. From the natural rhythm of your heartbeat (that is always with you), to the magnificent seasonal changes (the rhythm of a storm, hard or gentle), rhythms are part of nature's symphony.

One morning I heard a loud *swoosh*. Caught by the unusual sounds I gazed out of the window. To my delight, two Mallard ducks were swimming in the pool. I watched the gentle rhythm as they paddled, gliding across the water as if on glass. The serene images filled my day with gentleness. I practiced gliding through the day like a graceful duck. I enjoyed donning the duckling rhythm of swimming, and I even attempted waddling.

Be mindful of rhythms: Observe the rhythm of flames on a grill, hum of your computer. Listen to the flutter of leaves, the stillness of the moment, the silent rhythm. Creative observation: Whether you are drinking a cup of tea or writing a weekly report, allow total absorption in rhythm of the activity. **This is where joy and excellence live together in HArmony. This is meditation in Action.**

Joanne is an awesome example of creative observation and communing with people, animals, and nature's bounty. Whenever I feel blue, uninspired, or even if I feel great, she lifts my spirit higher with one of her awesome encounters. On her majestic retreat site in Hawaii, she tends a meddlesome goat, chases off intruding wild pigs, and peacefully watches her sheep graze the overgrowth on the land. She dines on the property's succulent papayas and mango's, savoring the fresh *Noni* juice (an anti-aging elixir). What a life!

From swimming in rhythm with the dolphins to listening to the sound of whales pounding their tales in the ocean like drum-rolls, she hears, tastes, and smells the beauty in life. She breathes in the invigorating morning mist. Even in downtown Los Angeles, she'll be the one to hear the feral kitty's cry from under a stoop, pick it up, cuddle it until it purrs and licks her face. Let's take heart from Joanne's creative observation and learn to embrace nature's bountiful rhythms and HArmony.

Musical Rhythms – Morph Your Moods and Physical State

Musical rhythms can change attitudes, emotions, and are effectively used in treatments for a variety of physical and psychological ailments.

Notice daily internal rhythms: when you feel rushed, sluggish, anxious or happy. Be mindful of your breath's rhythm from slow to hyperventilating. In this particular exercise, you can experiment with music as your healing agent for the heart, body, and mind.

♥ Pick three different rhythms: slow dance to a ballad, a faster rhythm, such as swing/blues, and the fastest – a rumba or hard rock.

♥ Play each one for three to five minutes. Sway, clap, dance, or move to the tempo. Become absorbed in the rhythm. Note how each one changes your mood and physical sensations.

♥ Use your physiology to help you. When stressed, practice the slower rhythm. When sluggish, move to the medium or faster rhythms. When over-charged, use the faster mode to release, and then switch to the slower rhythm to relax.

A friend had a raging headache. Together we rhythmically breathed into the pain, dropped into silence. In that place of miracles, a calm resonance penetrated, every molecule listened, shifting frequency – the pain gently melted away.

Rigidity vs. Creativity

Are you rigid? If so, in what area? Maybe it feels comfortable and familiar. Do you ever feel, "It's okay just the way it is. Who has time to start over and learn the new stuff?"

Whatever happened to spontaneity? Do you have a childlike

quality that just dives in and asks questions later? Remember a moment when spontaneity reigned in your life. Were you seemingly reckless, putting the expected on hold?

The coin flip of rigidity is creativity. The truth is – creativity resides within everyone. The myth is – creativity is a reserved gift of the genius, the artist, or children. Who said there is only one right way to do something? Who said that creativity is meant only for children with curious minds or an artist on a scaffle painting the Sistine Chapel? As long as we are breathing we are creating in the moment. We make choices what to wear, what to eat – to butter our bread or to eat it dry. If you hear a rigid voice, "You can't sing, dance, or frolic with the dolphins" – pay no heed. Sing, dance and frolic with the dolphins and the voice will be dimmed – it will no longer dictate your path.

♥ ♥ ♥

No matter how old you are, you can keep the childlike wonder of creativity alive. This scintillating pulsation resides inside of you. Creativity is a blast of invention, trial and error, taking risks to grow, to dream, to bring the impossible into possibility, playful and flowing. This zone of expanded awareness is where genius resides. It is not afraid of mistakes; it learns, experiments, and corrects. Albert Einstein failed often, yet he plunged on with steadfast purpose and concentration, without apology. He spoke of that magical power of infinite intelligence that supersedes facts. We can capture creativity's truth with one breath – so powerful, so mysterious, so gratifying. When in doubt I wear a cap that reads, *Einstein*.

Watch a small child at play. Notice how every object, sound, or person they come into contact with produces a creative moment. They touch, smell, feel – closing their eyes while examining something new, and brim with zeal when pursuing an undertaking. This childlike art of approaching the moment with discovery is the essence of creativity.

Appreciation, discovery, insight, and intuition are natural creative impulses. Morphing constricting attitudes toward yourself will teach you how to develop inspiration and to achieve a refreshing point of view.

Rigidity is limited perspective. Below are statements we make to justify our rigidity:

"Can't do it."	Inability to take Action
"Don't have the talent."	Weak self-esteem.
"Don't like the task."	Choosing a negative preference.
"It's not worth it."	A value judgment.
"Not interested."	Lack of inspiration/motivation.

Fear and rigidity stifle cutting loose. What to do when you're at the wall? Are you too scared to let out a primal scream and dive headfirst into a padded wall? Maybe you prefer to be a fly on the wall or to meditate with your back against the wall. Or do you have a raging urge to bust down the walls that bind and find freedom?

Freedom – Bounce off the Walls

A soundproof room padded from floor to ceiling is an ideal set-up to scream your brains out – to vent, holler, release the frustration, pain, and angst. A creative haven of truth spin – all alone, to be, think, imagine, and dream. However, unless you have an in-house recording studio or padded workout room in your home, chances are this isn't an option. The next best thing is a *Bouncy for Fun*, those bright colored room-sized tents – a kid's jump-fest.

At a kid's birthday party, my curiosity was up so I mustered courage to plunge into a bouncy tent. With shoes off, I struggled through the net door, closed my eyes and jumped into a heap of writhing bodies, rolling over on top or under, a foot, arm, or tummy. After about thirty seconds of shouts and giggles (being the average socialized adult), fun turned to fear of being bopped, socked, or bit by a roly-poly kid. I got over it by laughing – a lot.

Find a bouncy in an amusement park or at a kid's party. A trampoline is a safer bet for the timid and still gives a good bounce and releases tension, building energy. How about bouncy boots, a wild contraption I tried. You strap them on and bounce a foot high or so, leaping forward like a frog. Truly not for klutzes, you will surely land on you butt. I did. At least give a bouncy a chance and play like a kid again.

Creative Late Bloomer

Grandma Moses started painting at 87, a stellar example that within us lies untapped treasures. Rocket-launch an opportunity you may have left behind, a childhood interest or potential talent that lies dormant. It's never too late to take up the guitar, the piano, carpentry, dance. Creative exploration stimulates your brain's development and enriches life in unexpected ways. Creation begins with an impulse... are you ready to follow it?

♥ ♥ ♥

What ignites the creative, the Loveforce, magical living? Unlock the mystery of PLAY. Participate right NOW! Gaze at your palm: designs crisscrossing, patterning unique expression. Breathe deep. Look closer at the swirls of wonder, imprinting your specialness. Take creative YOU into all you see, feel, do, and say.

Write a message in your Heart. Imagine what could be. Pure elated joy**...** So it IS!

Life as an Improv...It is, Ya Know!

I'm convinced that Life is an Improv. If it weren't you would be born with a script in your hand. In the Play of Life, the actor is you. By exploring acting techniques, we can expand our capacity to flow freely, to feel empowered and play in spontaneous creativity.

I love being a clown – a comedy gal. I can do the unspeakable, say the unthinkable. I can laugh through the pain, strife, and nonsense in life. I can belly laugh through tears and release all the tension, misery, and angst from my soul. I grab a giggle, a sparkle, and a teasing glow. I stay young. I laugh a lot.

Many years ago, I was in an improvisational (Improv) comedy group run by Howard "Howie" Storm, the director of the sitcom

Mork & Mindy. Cindy Williams from *Laverne and Shirley*, Fred Grandy (*Love Boat*), and Teri Garr (*Tootsie*) were in the group. Howie's innate ability not to go for the joke and let the *funny* happen, allowed him to be the most viable director for Robin Williams, who played Mork, an alien visitor to earth. Howie let Robin fly, knowing moments before a taping that Robin would land on the mark with the most brilliant choices. He didn't control Robin's comedy genius. Instead, he had the uncanny ability to harness it and capture it as it went down.

Pam Dauber, who played Mindy, was the other genius. Robin could change a scene a hundred times with his outrageous antics, and Pam was right there, giving and taking in the moment, not thrown by Robin's spontaneity. They were a great comedic team.

Our Improv group's goal was to be as outrageous as possible and take our comedy to the zenith of our collective talent. The prerequisites were "no-holds-barred" and to have fun. I personally found an outlet for creative energy. I learned to put the *Om* in comedy…to go with the flow of self-discovery.

♥ ♥ ♥

I had the thrill of meeting Lucille Ball, my lifetime idol. Not only was she the greatest comedian of my youth, she was a mother and an executive producer. When we met, she held my hand and said, "I've seen you. You have the funnies." I was so taken, I was speechless. It was probably my Academy Award. (Of course the fat lady hasn't sung yet on that topic!) Who would know better than *Lucy* if I were funny? I had tears in my eyes. "It's because of you. It's because of watching you. You were one of my great teachers. Thank you," I gushed.

Amazing! I was invited to Lucy's one-time-only acting class. Exhilarating mastery is an understatement. A young, heavy-set woman who was starring in a TV show complained to Lucy, "I'm always typecast as a fat lady. I never get different kinds of parts."

Lucy winced, "Aren't you a fat lady? Haven't you created your niche? **Be grateful, because there are three fat ladies right behind you ready to jump into your place.**"

♥ ♥ ♥

I learned from the comedy greats how to do Improv comedy. George Burns taught me one of the most fundamental lessons in comedy. I had been invited to audition for Mr. Burns to play his niece on a TV special. The show promised to be a major stepping-stone for me because every great comedian would be there, from Bill Cosby to Steve Martin and everyone in-between.

Mr. Burns wanted to see an array of characters, so being the hardhead that I was, I included my imitation of Marlon Brando and Moe from the *Three Stooges*. With my knees wobbling in awe of this comic legend, I started my act beneath his cigar smokescreen. I imitated Marilyn Monroe, Goldie Hawn, mimicked Bette Midler, Carol Burnett (mugging and all), and saved the best for last – Brando.

Mr. Burns began coughing loudly, so I stopped in mid-sentence. He looked at me and grunted, "Go into the powder room." I was stunned. He said, "Go...go, look in the mirror and come back and tell me what you see."

I went to the ladies room. I was ready to cry. I just stood there and looked at myself. All I saw was me. What could I say? When I came back, he started in on me. "You want to work in this town?"

Oh, those familiar words. "You got to look at your face…you are a dame. You don't have a kisser like Carol Burnett; you aren't a rubber face. No mugging with that face. Anyway, my niece is a beauty…she wouldn't do those faces in public. You want to be funny? Gracie was funny. She didn't do any mugging." Then he gave me the ultimate compliment. "You've got the timing, you are funny. Now, what are you doing on Friday?"

"Nothing," I squeaked.

"Good," he said. "Go get yourself in a Bob Mackie gown. You'll be my niece." I almost fainted. Then he added with that George Burns twinkle, "If you want to, that is."

My life's journey has been about discovering the authentic self. George Burns was referring to operating from the authenticity within myself that allowed me to present a believable character. There is a range of what *authentic* means. Interpretations of adages such as, "*To thine own self be true,*" have filled up volumes of books. But, our purpose in exploring the freedom of Self, to act without limitation, hesitation, or unworthiness will require that we suspend our view of ourselves and take a leap into the Improv. Trying on different clothes and characters stretches our imagination of what can be possible to achieve and attain.

Shine Like a Star

Taking the stage in your life is Star Time. Use full-out energy with no apologies for being the center of attraction. It's your time to shine and glow. You are on the spot, in the spotlight. It's time to promote YOU, flaunt your talents, and follow your dreams.

Great speakers, politicians, and salespeople often have a charismatic star-energy that is mesmerizing. We salivate on their every word, wanting more. Realize that universal light force, the magnetizing energy is there for all of us. Even if your natural style is low-key, **the awareness of star-quality energy will up your peak performance level in all you do. Cultivate it and use it.** Practice duplicating a magnetic quality in your own communications. Watch the magnetic energy in others. Watch their reaction to you.

Live the Improv

Know when to give and when to take; that is, when to take the stage and act, and when to let go and let someone else take center stage. Sometimes in life, as onstage, you are the star of the story. Other times, you are a bit player.

♥ Take the stage – you are 100% responsible for your performance and the results. Take responsibility for your actions. You can correct, improve, and learn something from the so-called mistake without blame-gaming yourself or others. Improvise a solution or fresh start. When life feels like a prison...bounce out! Living is your playground.

♥ Allow others to make their own mistakes and learn from them. When you give over the stage to someone else, you are not responsible for the way they do it. This is especially true in relationships where co-dependency can happen when doing the Action for the other person. In business, though, if you are the boss, manager, or supervisor, you are ultimately held accountable for every mistake made by your employees. Trusting you picked the right people can be a challenge – give them a chance to grow through their mistakes.

♥ Trust that not all Action has to be preplanned. Planning certainly plays a critical part in Action, but too much planning creates rigidity, fixation, and limits possibility. Trust the flow.

♥ Learn to Bounce back fast. What looks like a setback can be transformed into a success in a second if you are open, limber, and ready. Bounce high!

♥ Flexibility – if you are a natural leader, it can be freeing to follow an Action someone else has initiated, rather than pushing your own idea. Ease up! If you are usually a follower, learn to lead by initiating a new Action. Step up!

Sometimes people will follow you, sometimes they won't. Sometimes things go your way, sometimes they don't. Don't take it personally. One of life's great lessons: Detachment comes from looking at life as a great play.

Off the Wall

Imagine stepping out of your own persona for a moment and being someone completely different. Look at life as an Improv game. Take off your habits, quirks, and personality traits have been developed and clung to by your little ego (that resists being so much more).

Choose to strip down to your bare truth, hang-up familiar habits and instantly adopt a new wardrobe and new traits. I enjoyed playing a waitress and dumping meatballs on Chevy Chase on *The Flip Wilson Show*, or tripping down the steps with Elvira at our workshop, or garbling gibberish in another role as an Italian lady batting cockroaches off the wall (and off the wall it was).

Imagine... You Are Free

For one minute - Free from 'stuff', worry, and woe.

♥ Sing, dance, play music, chant.

♥ Pick a subject. Sing your conversation with a partner.

♥ Sing your thoughts for One minute. Happy ones, heartaches, bellyaches are set Free.

Imagine and Repeat OUTLOUD ..."I AM FREE to BE ME." Sing in different voices. Mimic animals, cartoon characters, the wind, radiate Love.

Release Your inner play-mate/ kid. BE FREE !

Keys to Improv

♥ Be in the moment. Listen with your entire being – your eyes, hair, nose, and ears.

♥ Let the other person speak, and then listen to what comes out of your mouth. It may be outrageous or nonsensical. Have fun.

♥ Trust. There is no right or wrong. It's about discovery in the moment.

Improvs – The Happy Ticket

Be a Machine: Three people (in a group) come together to play this game. One at a time, each person makes a movement and sound to create a machine. Notice how each person's sound and movement complements the other parts and transforms the machine as a whole. You'll learn how this exercise reflects life in general, as we are a unique part of our family, work, and community as a whole.

Talk out of Both Sides of Your Mouth: One person stands between two people and carries on two different conversations with both people at once. The two partners pick their own subject, not revealing it, until the game starts. They speak continuously without stopping. Timeframe: 3 minutes.

Considerations: Trust you can multi-task. Answer your first response. Don't get caught up in one conversation for too long. Commit to listening and carrying on two conversations.

Switch places until each person has had a turn in the middle.

How did it feel to be one of the people on the side? Did you feel like you were in competition with the other side or in collaboration? Did you listen to the other conversation? Were you influenced by it? Did the subjects overlap? Where was your focus? On yourself? On your partner? On the third person?

Improv Review: What happened to your listening? Your ability to respond to both conversations?

Get Real – From Laughter to Tears

Everyday occurrences from the ludicrous to the sublime test our ability to be in equilibrium and get real – or to bounce off the walls and crash to the ground.

At a fundraiser at Mimi's ranch for aged horses, *MerrieWay Community* donated *Peace Smarts* manuals, and I agreed to assist in the live auction. Before going on stage, I took a quick trip to the bathroom to freshen up. Yipes! The unthinkable happened. While at the sink, a temporary cap on my front tooth popped off and whisked down the drain. Staring in the mirror at my toothless grin, I felt like Emma Lutz, my wacky character on TV. I started to laugh, guffawed, bellowing into tears. Then I took notice, only one eye was tearing, a trifling observation.

After discreetly summoning Mimi, we used chopsticks in an attempt to retrieve the lost tooth. As I watched Mimi, a stuntwoman, confidently jabbing the sticks down the drain, a quiet peace swept over me. Gently breathing, I was filled with a joyous feeling. My prima donna, have-to-look-good side took a needed break. All kinds of sugarplum solutions danced in my head: doing the auction without the tooth, going home immediately, or sitting in a darkened corner, out of sight.

Finally, with the help of an off-duty police officer who was on the premises, the tooth magically appeared by opening the drain. Oddly enough, he had watched me on TV playing Emma and felt it was surreal, like we were in a zany episode of the show. We had a great laugh, and I was able to show gratitude by offering a *Peace Smarts* manual and signing it: "To my hero for the night."

And what was that one eye tearing about? I finally concluded it was a right brain/left brain balance, and that going with the flow is a great release valve.

Playing In the Shadow and Light

Imagine Marge Simpson morphing into Homer…and Homer with his caustic delivery morphing into Marge. It is the dance of the *shadow self* and the *light self.* Some of us deny our shadow self and ignore its vital teaching. Light does not exist without darkness. Let's play with the shadows and prance in the light.

Define who is light and who is dark. Pick your character. Choose an issue or topic. Improv. Speak one at a time. Listen. Don't judge. Play it to the hilt, and then switch roles.

"Only the shadow knows." Sunlight plays tricks with shadows. Walking down the street, I love gazing at my shadow – sometimes it is squat and dwarfish, other times it's like the lanky cartoon character Olive Oil. Some of us hide behind the shadows in life, afraid of the dark side.

Stand in the sun on a sidewalk. Spot your shadow. Notice the outline, the size, and its position in relation to where you are standing. Is it bigger, smaller, amazing? Begin walking. Are you following your shadow? Is it to the side of you or behind you?

I do finger shadows on the wall, shaping birds, gremlins, fairies. Characters are magically alive on the wall's canvas, becoming friends to talk and play with.

♥ ♥ ♥

Out of the womb's watery shadow, they said I was born laughing. The lesson: allowing a smile, through the hurts and disappointments. A two-sided coin: Crying releases laughter. Laughter releases the tears.

HAHAHA – For Fun Create Laughter

For years as a comedy player, my playground was to create the funnies: laughter, giggles, and joy. What a blessed way to earn a living! Do the "HAHAHA" to release physical and emotional tight-spots and to lighten the load. Laughter is contagious, outrageous, and totally divine. So, let's have a go.

Say the word *HA* as many ways as possible. Keep saying it until you have a feeling of knowingness, a smile of recognition, or until it becomes a *HAHAHA*, the familiar precipitator of laughter. Practice the HAHAHA until it becomes a natural, guttural response. Do it until your jaw hurts. Do it through your tears. It's hard to hold on to anything after a good laugh or cry. One can lead to the other. You can't worry or be angry when you're laughing. Let it rip.

Learn to laugh through pain, through HAvoc and HAssles, and grow into HArmony and HAppiness. Laughter is a stress-buster, a tranquilizer without the side effects. A good chuckle releases tension, lowers stress hormones, and boosts our immune system. Laughter can blast through fears and dump anguish.

HaHa Healers™

A 98-year-old woman dedicated her life to laughter. She memorized jokes and shared her funnies with everyone she met. She would laugh so hard at her own jokes that she became known as an inspirational Laugh Track. Up until her final breath she spread her contagious joy, healing with HAHA's.

The great thing about laughter is that it's a proven healing agent. It loosens the mind and spawns creativity via the brain-laughter connection. In the same way the brain muscle can be developed through chess, etc., our brain has *funny-bone* muscles. Laughter pumps dopamine, a feel-good reward system chemical near the base of the skull. MRI brain scans have shown the blood flow in areas of the brain that produce intuition are the same areas of the brain that induce laughter. **Laughter can sharpen and recalibrate intuition, playing a role in social decision-making. Lighten-up; keep those gut-level hunches on target. Winds of laughter fill the day...when you open to your blessings.**

♥ ♥ ♥

My close friend Sandy was in the midst of chemotherapy and her life felt like an ongoing pity-party. On a ride home from the hospital she removed the cap concealing her hair loss. In the side view mirror she caught a glimpse of a shining bald head with fuzzy hair spikes.

She felt a tickle. "I looked like Jack Nicholson in 'The Shining'. I began making odd and funny faces, laughing at myself in the mirror. A carload of teens pulled up next to me, and I continued with the antics. They began laughing with me. It was absurd, wonderful, and so freeing. I belly-laughed so hard I almost peed my pants." Sandy decided to carry laughter with her wherever she would go. A great healing practice, it sparks a twinkle in our soul.

No-Nos & *Yes's* For Jokes and Pranks

♥ Don't use humor as a weapon – to hurt, abuse or amuse.

♥ Don't use one-upmanship or joking to boost your weak ego.

♥ Do use humor as an up-lifter, a moral boost, or to ease tension.

♥ Do use humor to entertain, help explain, and to lighten the moment.

♥ Do play a harmless prank like sending a pest a nose made out of play-dough.

There is a vibrating cord of life...a magical connection of playing life to the fullest. This is the time – Play. When you are bored, entertain yourself. Skip for a fun boost. Play with irreverence about something silly you won't actually do. I imagined I was trolling birthday parties snagging balloons for my next party.

CHAPTER 16

I LANDED ON MY FEET –
I'M MORPHING – NOW WHAT?

Who said that landing on your feet means standing firmly on the ground with imaginary roots sprouting down, embedded deep into the earth, safe and secure? Well, considering we are not trees, let's switch gears and realize the truth. AHA! Landing on your feet means, "I am comfortable in my own skin, and I have the tools to center myself."

Consider the flight you've taken while bouncing off the walls. You have experienced an inner transition to redefine yourself, to uproot negativity, fear of failure, and calm inner rumblings. Heading for a landing, you may feel suspended in mid-air, somersaulting in joy, stretching your limits, making good choices, getting positive results.

THUMP! Glide! Twirl! Landing on your feet may find you skillfully skiing down a slope, marching for world peace, or strutting down a runway in stilettos. Whatever or wherever, landing on your feet warrants celebration.

Celebrate Yourself – It's Your World

You are the center of your universe. Like the sun, others rotate around you like planets and moons. This is not narcissism; it is honoring yourself with full commitment. Only you can honor your passion, your vocation, and your daily activities as gratifying life boosters. Remember to celebrate YOU. It's not just about celebrating your birthday. Treat yourself as your best friend; give to yourself what you truly appreciate. I have an assistant who gets a massage on her lunch break. And, my CPA would not dream of missing the sunset out of his high-rise office building. Or, as I discovered on an intrinsic level, I became my champion instead of remaining my worst critic. To belittle or make yourself small is an errant no-no; it diminishes self-worth.

♥ ♥ ♥

Mr. Ellis, one of my advisors, is a successful entrepreneur. From his childhood onward, he entertained friends with fun antics. His singing voice was extraordinary, and he was once asked to audition for the Met. Each day he danced with his wife, played the piano. Or told a funny story. When I asked him, "I'm stumped, why aren't you a professional performer?" He answered simply. "It's my fun. It's how I celebrate myself." I reminded him, "I'm a professional writer and actress and I have fun doing it." Then he asked, "Do you celebrate yourself offstage as a daily ritual?" I couldn't say I did.

I literally absorbed the idea of celebrating *me* as a daily ritual. I assembled a gallery of awards and photos, showcasing my body of work as an actress, writer, and film producer, altering my notion that flaunting a gallery display was narcissistic. A long hallway is the recipient of this honor, and whenever I walk down it, I relish the gifts I've received as a performer. Beyond being plaques of commendation, they are gifts of giggles, gratitude, and reverence for the glorious opportunities that I have been given in this life. I often take a moment in prayer to send heartfelt blessings to my many cohorts. Fond memories and moments of reflection positively impact my day. I truly celebrate myself.

Happiness is not a quest, it's your birthright. Who knows better than you do whether it's a hot bubble bath, playing racquetball, or cooing with a baby that makes you happy? Celebrating yourself is up to you. Do it your way!

♥ ♥ ♥

I guest-starred on a German TV show focusing on the Academy Awards. They wanted insight why Americans are so consumed with age and looking younger? I chuckled, "The fountain of youth, the magic elixir has been around since Cleopatra and the search for the Holy Grail.." I giggled a lot. A sign of youthism. Be Happy.

At ninety-seven-years young, Sarah described her amazing longevity. "Growing up on a farm, we planted potatoes or corn at the right time of year and sowed our pickings on time. **I learned from nature to do what needs to be done – no wasted time on resisting or you might just starve."**

MerrieWay Celebrates Natural Longevity

♥ Live in the moment – NOW is timeless, beyond age.

♥ Laugh often.

♥ Forgive yourself and others.

♥ Applaud, rejoice for others – hearty admiration feels good inside.

♥ "Play life" with enthusiasm, with the abandon of a 3-year-old.

♥ Your body is your earthly temple. Treat it as sacred. Nourish it with respect, love, and great sex.

♥ Eat the fudge – it's the portion that counts.

Still Obsessing – Give Yourself a Pinch

Are you still caught in a mind-glitch, whirling in negative thoughts, panicking or obsessing with, "I'd rather die than do it." "This will never end." In the obsessing zone, the body, mind, and emotions are locked in a freeze-frame.

STOP TELLING YOUR MISERABLE STORY. Why repeat it to yourself or others? Does it help, hinder or become reactive? When tempted to dwell in a mind-loop, STOP! Reenter the present moment:

♥ Without resisting the obsessive thought or panicked emotion, let it be where it is. Begin by touching a body part (your forehead, shoulder, arm), or touch an object (a chair, wall or ground). Say the acknowledgment, "Good," as you touch each body part or object.

♥ Observe your feelings. Are you calmer, are you present in the room or place?

♥ Repeat the exercise to reduce residual feelings until you are present in the moment.

By physically externalizing our thinking and emotional obsessing, we regain our equipoise.

Ditch Day

IMAGINE waking up in the White House…with the realization, you are the President. Your day's to-do-list is pinpointed on a wall-size global map. As you scan it, one thought rings in your head, "Geography, Ugh! Can't I just go golfing!" Then it's up and at 'em, the President can't play hooky, or can she? Oops…Imagine!

Remember *Ditch Day* (cutting school with permission)? When I was a kid, we'd rally around being snowed-in. The snow would pile up a few feet and we couldn't open the front door. And best of all, we couldn't go to school.

Do you accumulate paid sick or vacation days waiting for the "right moment" to feel entitled to a day off? Is your workload overwhelming, unrelenting? Are you in high-anxiety projecting if (or when) you'll lose your job? In work reviews, does your boss allude to potential ramifications if you utilize your vacation time? Corporate, fear-based policies promote a pecking order, giving perks to supervisors for keeping you "the worker bee" in the work overload dungeon!

Taking earned vacation days healthily frees up your body-mind-spirit. Respect your need to take care of YOU – then watch your relationships, personal and professional, flourish. Don't accept guilt-trips for a needed break. **Honor yourself; claim a Ditch Day Off.**

Create Down Time

"Slow down, whistle a happy tune…then stop and smell the roses" was my mother's advice as I speeded down my success trail. "But, I have so many great things to do," I responded. "Ah, they're over the second you do them," she said and smiled with a deep knowing. "It's the little things along the way that make a great life."

As you've learned, incubation is tantamount in the creative process – a time to regroup and recharge – a time to support growth and change. Do you allow down time to just BE? To do nothing? Feeling scattered or stressed indicates needing a *You-Fix*. We all need time to enjoy our own company and presence. Sniff an aromatic flower or herb. Lay on the beach. Play with a child or a pet. Turn off the cell phone or telephone ringer. Say *no* when you have a lot on your plate. Play a sport. Talk to a friend. Whistle a happy tune. It is an upper, guaranteed you'll grin from ear to ear.

Take an Instant Vacation- Breathing into the moment changes how your life flows. It slows mind-racing NOW! Whether you're in gridlock, changing a diaper, or when the washer breaks - chill into Harmony with: **Bounce Breath**

1. Inhale…. Breathe deeply.

2. Exhale – tension, mind-loops. See it blend into the air like a Bubble, Bouncing, Bursting, and Evaporating into Stillness and Harmony.

3. Breathe again…moment expands. Affirm: "I AM Peaceful HArmony."

We have traversed the realms of creative actions and responses. Keep flowing with the liberating joy of improv' in your life. Cultivate the habit of being creatively centered. This expanded awareness leads to the axiom, *"We are creative transformers."* Before you know it, you'll find yourself in the land of HArmony and HAppiness.

Magic HArmony Module

Quick fixes do exist – we can change our attitude (whether from feeling off-kilter, PMS, or out-of-sorts) and up-tone our spirits. We can create a perfect day and fill up our dream cup with just how we want it to be.

Think of a situation (clearing the air in a relationship, manifesting a new job) and then suspend your resisting beliefs and begin to play.

Hold a hand out and cup it. Your cupped hand represents a module to contain positive attributes and images. Imagine what you want and place it in your module. Visualize the situation and place HArmony, kindness, and understanding in the module. Continue adding ingredients in the module that will support the improvement of your situation. When you are done, activate the contents by placing the module somewhere in your body – heart, stomach, between your eyebrows (or wherever).

There is no need to think about it again. Continue the activities you would ordinarily do to handle the details of your quest. If you want to find a new home, look for it and get the financing in order. Your module is active – know it and trust!

The following parable is a leap into a new perception, an altering of moral judgment, and the winning spontaneity of a delightful soul.

"Laugh 'Til I Thought I'd Die"

Back in the day, three laughing holy men traveled the countryside creating laughter among the villagers. Their contagious *lightness of being* promoted healing, cured sadness, and dissolved discontent and woe. During an auspicious holiday in the midst of a laughing jag, one of the holy men died. Without missing a beat, the other two holy men continued laughing hysterically. Appalled, the villagers cried, "How can you laugh? This is no way to mourn. How irreverent, so sacrilegious." The holy men answered, "We are laughing in his honor. He lived to laugh and his spirit laughs on in joy."

Determined to give a proper burial, the villagers set forth with a cremation ceremony. The holy men relayed their friend's final request: "For my departure, make sure it is sundown and do not touch my clothes." All agreed to follow his wish. As they lit the funeral pyre, a blasting noise erupted, and like shooting stars, a firework display lit up the sky. The holy man had packed his clothes with firecrackers. The two remaining holy men rolled in laughter, celebrating their friend's final hurrah. The villagers laughed so hard that tears of joy streamed down their faces, melting away all meaning of misperceived loss and judgment.

Inspired by the wise men, I decided to bring love and laughter in my booties, every step along the way.

There is a vibrating cord of life – a magical connection of playing life to the fullest. This is the time...Play.

MerrieWay Recipe 4 a Happy Day

♥ AHA! There is a reason to be Happy: It is your birthright, a natural way of being.

♥ SMILE 22 times: At someone, yourself, funny movie. The shortest distance between two friends is a Smile.

♥ Give 22 HUGS: A ♥ to ♥ connector with someone includes you, pets, a teddy bear.

♥ Be PLAYFUL: Sing a happy tune. Skip, bounce, blow bubble gum.

♥ Be an OPTIMIST. Give 22 COMPLIMENTS. Acknowledge yourself, too.

♥ Share or send your HAPPY THOUGHTS or words with others. Show expressions of GRATITUDE through prayer, words, and acts of kindness.

♥ Go gentle with yourself and others. Delicate is rare in this upturn world.

Visionary Heart Quest

When he was five-years-old, Byron told me, "I feel life is a dream, and someday I'll just pinch myself and wake up." Then he asked, "Where will I be, Mom, when I wake up from this life dream?" From the mouths of babes. Who could answer this timeless question? Surely, not his Mom.

Contemplating the possibility further…if life's state is like a dream, couldn't we change it if we were the *observer* in our dream? Like a witness watching our thoughts – as in lucid dreaming – we observe behaviors, attitudes, and feelings in the dream. We can then switch roles with other players (understanding the symbols and meaning).

If this life is a dream, would you take the drama of events so seriously, or would you choose to recognize life as a giant playground – the play of life, of reality, of consciousness?

What if, in the midst of a situation, you pretended, "I am dreaming." Would you be so fearful to let out your true feelings, or be so terrified of failing? Would you bounce through the obstacle, knowing that one event doesn't control your entire life? Would you let go and let your higher wisdom guide you through the dream? You've landed on your feet; will you continue to change the dream, creating new dreams, celebrating a vibrant life?

♥ ♥ ♥

AHA! We have experienced Morphing ourselves/issues into a new perception. During HAvoc or HAssles, we can reach beyond our own little world. SPIRALING OUTWARD we can unite our strengths and flourish, sharing HArmony and HAppiness with others.

CHAPTER 17

YOU ME WE – COMMUNITY'S LIGHTHEART PATH™

Spiraling Into Noah's Ark

IMAGINE the ark that set sail with a brood of animals, some carnivorous predators capable of devouring their neighbor squeezed next to them. This heavenly designed journey and mission superseded all natural survival instincts. They trusted the divine will and did not eat each other; they were content, eliminating the expected pecking order.

Similarly, in our modern age, 6 billion people are struggling to survive in a quantum world shift. We are now setting sail in commUnity with our global neighbors. Power over others and our glutton-greed to devour more than our share is swiftly becoming a song of yesterday. The new lyric is 'unity in commUnity' to embrace our global family.

Destruction of life as we have known it is Morphing into a restructuring of human values, a rebuilding of obsolete infrastructures. The loss of "having the more" is inevitable. There is an evolution to bring back simplicity, truth, and love: a dictum to work in HArmony with our neighbors near and afar. Sharing instead of accumulating and no longer hoarding what we don't need, will set us free from the bondage of hate, prejudice, and isolationism.

This grand opportunity is a purification to eliminate scarcity consciousness. We can learn and to grow into divine beings, divine families, divine communities, and divine countries that truly trust in abundance. We are free to share, to become holistically balanced in our endeavors and our plights. Life is abundant; let us abandon scarcity consciousness. A blessed world is possible.

CommUnity – You. Me. We.

*Morphing Human Family brings a co-*consciousness "We are all one." Giving to one by one supports the whole with intention of sustaining a positive future for humankind. Selfless Service is a noble act for all ages. It is the instrument of unity, the destroyer of isolationism and other 'ism's, including racism, nationalism, and religious intolerance. Giving of yourself to others brings a bonded spirit that transcends prejudice and incorporates the inner spirit of peace.

As human's BEING – we share an infinite and *collective unconscious*. Archetypal images are all captured in our cellular memory bank. No one knows how it got there, but it is there. While it's widely accepted that our fingerprints are uniquely one of a kind, findings in genome research show the human DNA is 99.3 % identical in all races – a less than one-percent difference.

Ancient fossil discoveries proves every single person in the world is descended from the same ancestors: we are the human family, nurtured by the same sacred Mother Earth. Although people of different cultures, traditions, and ethnic backgrounds still proclaim their differences, they share kinship with all human beings: we are designated caretakers of this planet. What impact does this knowledge have on our world? Could it eliminate ethnic strife and divisiveness and empower the human species as one family?

Contemplate the truth that we are all connected. Instead of focusing on our differences, let's shift-up to our similarities. Adopt an inclusive attitude. With that awareness shift, what Actions do you want to take on your global family's behalf?

Think Globally – Act Locally

Let's acknowledge inequities in our community and narrow the gap between haves and have-nots. It is paramount to help people in need and assist them to become self-sufficient. In some developing countries, the gap between haves and have-nots leads to anarchy and revolution. If this gap continues to widen, we too are at risk for a revolution. Instead, let an evolution rise from within, right now, and translate into Action. Each one of us, doing one thing for someone else, can change exponentially improve the quality of life.

As global infrastructures are deconstructing, let's reconstruct our perspective. Instead of operating out of a greed/taker mode and living in isolationism, we can participate in our own backyard. Regrouping into a sharing mode is a boon to humanity – especially during anxious times of housing foreclosures, job shortages, and financial insecurity. Start a food bank; bring warm clothes to a shelter. Forfeit accumulating - GIVE and feel entitled to RECEIVE attracts mutual abundance.

Now is the time to *Shapeshift* – what shamans call transformation. Change into someone else's hero. Be an "Angel." Be an advocate for youth, the elderly, and the disenfranchised. Speak-out against injustice, inadequate social services, and inhumane practices that rob the human spirit. Speak with compassion, so all can hear. Giving unconditionally without strings attached opens a positive energy field to flow, a helper's healthy high.

Where to Begin? Jump-Heart Activism

Make a commitment you can keep. Start with your own community or neighborhood.

Follow your own passion. What do you care about? Is it the environment, children, seniors, the arts, healthcare, crime prevention? Is it to help people who are homeless or jobless to find work? Find out where you can be of most help. Where is the need greatest? What skills or resources can you contribute?

As an African proverb says: "Each One Teach One, Each One Reach One."

Our *Peace Smarts* project has affected youth and families nationwide by fostering a peace culture. When we begin with peace inside ourselves, we can then create peaceful relationships in family, work, school, and communities at large. The *Peace Smarts* curriculum (grades 5-12) is used in schools, after-school programs, and across curriculum. We welcome your participation, a noble effort.

Mentoring

In Greek legend, Mentor was entrusted with the education of *Odysseus'* son, *Telemachus*. Mentoring is much more than "teaching" because a mentor not only imparts information, but also embodies wisdom.

There is a well-known Jewish folk tale about a woman who wanted to send her son to live with a learned rabbi. When asked why, she replied, "I want him to watch how the rabbi ties his shoes." Obviously, the son was not being sent to become the best shoe-tier in the land, but to absorb the rabbi's wisdom by watching him perform his daily routines.

Mentoring has the same goal: The mentee (or student or apprentice) learns how to perform a task, as well as how to be or act in relation to the task; therefore in relation to life. The student acquires both the knowledge that can be given directly, as well as that which is unspoken – a self-empowerment process that strengthens the learner.

Keep your voice alive. It rings truth to those who have forgotten and captures the hearts and minds of newbies…thirsty to HEAR!

In our "Morph Film Mentoring" program, veteran filmmakers relate to young people as filmmakers who have not yet made a film. If they make mistakes, they are corrected – respectfully. They participate in every facet of filmmaking, and when they have made a film, they are filmmakers.

Our Morph Teen Anchors, a talented group of savvy filmmakers, had the privilege to work with Oprah Winfrey in Philadelphia during the 1997 Presidential Summit. Standing beneath banners that said "Mentor, protect, nurture" and "Teach, serve," our youth team watched President Clinton issue a call to action through service. Colin Powell said, "We see young people in need – young people who are wondering, *Is there an American dream for me?*"

The activities featured every living president and their wives (including Bill Clinton, George Bush Sr., Jimmy Carter, Gerald Ford, and Nancy Regan "representing Ronald"). Oprah emceed the televised event, and I directed our youth team (filming the behind-the-scenes primetime coverage), who had a first-hand view of the media diva in action.

Ezra, our seventeen-year-old anchor shared, "Oprah took charge, aware of every detail from the stage lighting to handling the president's and their wives. Oprah knew her stuff and she did it with ease. I wanted to absorb her every move and make that perfection my own." During the shoot, Oprah surprised Ezra by saying, "I've been watching you – you're doing a pretty good job." Delighted with Oprah's affirmation he framed it in his heart and mind.

The Presidential Summit saga escalated and tested our Teen Anchor teams' nerve, purpose, and conviction.

Oops! A Faux Pas – "Turn Lemons into Lemonade"

Our Teen Anchors successfully taped the Presidential Summit. Prized footage included Oprah, the presidents, celebrities (Rob Reiner, Michael Bolton, LL Cool Jay, Tony Robbins), and a surprise interview with NBC's Tom Brokaw at the train station when we departed for Manhattan.

During the train ride we buzzed with exhilaration over the once in a lifetime experience. Reaching Manhattan, totally exhausted, we hopped in a taxi and headed to the hotel. As I paid the taxi driver, our crew lugged our gear onto the street. Then, to our shock and complete dismay, we discovered that the camera bag with the footage was gone. A panicked blame-fest ensued with kids and parents accusing each other. "He had it." "No, she did." "I didn't. You did." We searched in vain, called the taxi company, the train station, the hotel in Philadelphia; it was a disaster – we had lost the footage!

After a debriefing calm-down, we shifted gears and embraced a team effort. Using *Dreamstorming*, we focused on possible solutions. The next day we contacted the filmmakers who produced the event, explaining our dilemma. We ASKED for help – it was a crucial project for us. In consideration that we were a non-profit and the only youth group covering the event, they took heart and generously agreed to send us their broadcast quality version. How fortunate for us. Then the producer added, "Tell those kids, a filmmaker straps that gear to his body. Footage is history, lose it and you can't get it back."

Our youth team summed up the lesson, "Be careful, responsible, and diligent in your undertakings. If a *faux pas* happens, your fault or not, get the team on it fast and turn those 'Lemons into Lemonade.'"

MerrieWay Echoes: **"Your parents did not give the earth to you; it was loaned to you by your children."** We are the caretakers – we design the future's dream.

Youth Service Learning

When kids learn the meaning of service, their lives are enriched at an early age. Their skill-base broadens when interacting in the community infrastructure, and they learn how a society works.

In *Morph America* programs, students have served the elderly, given musical and performance events to the community, taught ESL (English as a second language) to younger kids, lobbied for educational rights, participated in drug forums, and physical and sexual abuse awareness. The common denominator breeds unity, HArmony, pride, joy, and big smiles on the participant's faces. *Morph America* has been acknowledged by two Presidential administrations. I had a meeting with George W. Bush, joining after-school programs for "No Child Left Behind."

After meeting with Bill and Hillary Clinton, my son, Byron, who served as our national youth spokesperson, shared these moving comments.

"In the East Room at the White House, as a *Morph America* representative, I met the President of the United States. When I shook President Clinton's hand, I didn't look into his eyes…I looked at his hand. This was the hand that shook President Kennedy's hand, which shook Martin Luther King's hand. Now, when I look at my own hand, I realize it is a part of history. Greeting each other with respect and shaking hands is a true honor."

One Action Begets Another

CommUnity is nature's way of keeping the soul of the tribe alive: Participation nurtures and brings joy to our spirit. One person's involvement stimulates others to come forward. What could you create for your community that your children and grandchildren could continue? Model it. It is a great gift.

At a fundraiser, Magda, a surgeon and devoted mom, shared her concern. "I was having horrific nightmares over the escalating number of youth mortalities I saw in the E.R. senselessly lost to firearms. I became driven to prevent it, so I began speaking in schools about the dangers of gun misuse. The students donated toy guns as a symbol to end gun-violence and they received a Peace Award for their efforts."

"How amazing," I said. "What did you do with the toy guns?" Magda answered, "Nothing. They're stock-piled in the garage."

Without hesitation, we donned our think-caps and the "Toy Gun Brigade" – a 3D art project – was launched. Acclaimed artists teamed with students and created mind-blowing toy gun sculptures, displayed in art galleries. Filled with enthusiasm, students lobbied their communities in support of gun control, and as advocates for peace, they vowed to boycott violent videogames. Hats-off to Magda for her selfless-service in Action!

Sage-ing Instead of Aging

If you are a senior/retiree, instead of feeling useless, out of sync, or thinking, "I don't fit in anymore," find your place to contribute. In your spare time, step-up and share your skills, whether in classrooms, libraries, or on the ball field. Sage-ing keeps you young and curious while you interact in a young person's point of view. According to a study by Howard S. Friedman, Ph.D., individuals who fulfill their responsibilities and commitments live longer than others do.

Whatever Happened to Neighborly Kindness?

Being neighborly is a lost art in crowded cities like Los Angeles, where we rarely know our neighbors. For weeks on end we are sequestered in automobiles (our second home), stifling our innate need to connect and interact. Let's make an effort to reach out, support, and talk to each other. Get off the cell phone, take off the earplugs.

Being neighborly traverses beyond fences, ingrained prejudices, and guarded hearts. It provides an opportunity to end the collective fear engulfing our society. Helping and reaching out is a gift – the out-of-bad-comes-good cycle – reducing loneliness and bringing back true friendships. Happily, in many communities, friendliness, giving, and kindness are still the practice.

♥ ♥ ♥

Beth and her husband jogged everyday and often passed an elderly woman walking a dog. Many days went by and they didn't see her, except for a glimpse of the dog peering out of the front window.

Concerned, they stopped to check on the woman, who they only knew by sight and a quick hello. They discovered that the woman had been relegated to a wheelchair, a victim of a recent stroke. Beth offered to walk the dog, ending her jog a few minutes earlier. The woman's eyes shone brightly as she mumbled, "I prayed you'd come and you did."

Spread the Love to Others

LOVE is God manifesting truth through you. The emotion of love is devotion…our finest resource. By loving ourselves, we spread that love to others. A smile, a giggle, kind words or a gesture, a listening ear resonates, reflecting purity of heart. Give Love freely to yourself. Its potency dissolves outmoded tendencies, transforming, and igniting a blissful state. Truly, no one can give Love to you or take it away – it's forever with you.

Remember to love, honor and respect your family, neighbors, your community and our planet. In loving, there are no boundaries – we see beyond our differences and the embrace our spiritual unity and dignity. By projecting loving energy and kindness to others our hearts celebrate. I have grown to realize the greatest creativity is LOVE.

Spiraling Into a LightHeart Path™

Granted, scientists have proven our DNA is 93.3% identical. Hopefully they will soon discover the missing 7% link: our heart and soul connection. We know energy transforms into Action and our thoughts transmit faster than the speed of light, traversing time and space. Opening our hearts through prayer and intention connects to everyone on the planet.

LightHeart Breath™

♥ Tune-into your breath. Inhale deep and exhale long. In the stillness, feel the vibration of your Heart. Allow the light within to permeate every cell in your being.

♥ Now expand your awareness to fill the space around your body, the room.

♥ Envision the light expanding further, sending light out into the world. Feel your heart touching other hearts, spiraling light. Feel the Love light connecting: Heart on heart immersing in the power of eternal Love, tingling in peaceful HArmony, dancing in joy.

Bounce off the Walls Land on Your Feet

CHAPTER 18

THE LAST SHOT

Sometimes we're so involved in an activity that we lose sight of essential details. We forget to turn off lights when we want to keep our energy costs down. Rewriting a proposal at the last minute, we dash around the house looking for our car keys, leaving behind our briefcase. "To err is human," wrote Shakespeare.

Parachutes – The Unforgiving Morph

On my way to Montreal in a Lear jet, turbulence tossed the plane like a rocky road in the air. As my heart flew into my throat, Chris, a seasoned 'extreme sports' photographer started to laugh, "Did I ever tell you about my thousand air jumps?" My face green with terror, I looked at him pleadingly as I shook my head, "Yes."

"Well," Chris began, "then this is the time to tell you about my bud, Petey. We were the top photographers in these air jumps, and Petey was the best ever at photographing free-falls. He'd get up there and jump with greenhorns, shooting every second in the free-fall. One afternoon we went out in separate planes, and Petey made a jump with some people. He was shooting video, getting amazing footage. When it came time to pull his cord and open his chute, he must have been stunned. He screamed inaudibly, waving his arms…he had done the irrevocable, the act of destiny. He hadn't put on his gear – there was no parachute. Needless to say, it was Petey's last jump. Amazing." Chris shook his head sadly. "The camera was found and the footage was the best he had ever shot."

At that moment, the plane lost altitude and I grabbed Chris's arm and held on tight. The plane leveled and in a moment, we were smooth sailing. Chris smiled at me, "Like I was saying…I have the footage. Would you like to see it?"

Still recovering from the bumps on our own flight, I answered, "We don't have a parachute up here, what's the difference?"

Chris stared at me for a long moment. "Petey was a *pro*, and he made a mistake. You are human; you make mistakes, but I bet none of them is like forgetting your parachute, now is it?"

I contemplated Petey and his last jump – forgetting his chute. I had done stupid things everyday. Like the time I left the door to my house wide-open and was robbed. I thought of every dumb thing I had done, but Chris was right – none of them matched forgetting a parachute

In the past, I often drove my car without buckling my seatbelt, but when I heard Petey's sad story, I resolved to buckle-up. Now, even my Sheltie dogs have a seat belt contraption. **Take time to remember, to observe with caution and exactness. Stay vigilant and pay attention to the essentials.** But when we do inevitably make a mistake, can we be a little kinder to ourselves? "It is human *to* err".

Be aware of your human frailty, and forgive your *faux pas* and lack of consciousness. Whenever you beat yourself up for making a stupid mistake, remember Petey. I am sure he would want us to know that **nothing can be as unforgiving as forgetting the parachute.**

Unfolding Journey

We might think that we are in the final chapter of *Bounce off the Walls, Land on Your Feet.* The premise "final," defies the notion that the Spiral Morph is ever-evolving from the inner-self outward to our spheres of influence, and then back again and so on. Neither you nor I are final, finished, or complete; nor is our life mission or purpose. This book will not end at the last period because we will continue to Morph (whether we are conscious of it or not). And hopefully, by this juncture, you have added a few tools to embellish your awareness toward seeking your highest good.

Your individuality is comprised of unique experience. The passing on of information, sharing your personal discoveries and inventive solutions, will metaMorphasize and continuously change. The Morph continuously Morphs itself. It is continuous, unending with new beginnings. The AHA! adventures and moments synchronize in the spiral of life.

Know What You Know

If the Morph Process seems complicated, redundant, undoable, intellectual, airy-fairy, overbearing, or even if it tastes like delicious nectar and inspires you (yet somehow did not gel or infuse within), don't fret. Incubate. Let it cook, brew, and stew. Do trust that your next encounter with a book, a friend, or while meditating, will offer continued expansion, a moment-to-moment adventure of your transformation.

Don't give up. Give up on what doesn't work. Use what does. Remember to reach for what you cannot. To see what others do not see. Miraculously, it is you who will write this final chapter and the many volumes of you – a legacy for generations to come. You will write it through your thoughts, Actions, and deeds. You will live it through your effort. Some of you will write it or record it in your Morph Journal and pass it on for others to glean your revelations.

Together we will write a new history based on kindness and humane Action. We will create it by how we live in HArmony and how respectfully we treat one another. We will reach out through community forums to support our dreams of peace and Oneness. We'll participate in interactive Webcasts, through email or inspire live conferences.

When overwhelmed by a challenge, put it to test with the 7-Step Morph. Remember, by tuning-into your heart space, quantum possibilities emerge beyond the mind, and you intuit the best solution at any given moment. Remember to be kind and patient with yourself, to pick yourself up when you bounce off the wall or to gracefully accept a hand to help you.

Try your hand with the Oracle below:

WOW – Words of Wisdom – ORACLE

You have landed on your feet – spiraling forward. One mission, one issue, may be flowing just as you wanted, and then, suddenly, another situation crops up that sends you back into your padded cell. You're once again bouncing out of control, frustrated, down and out, feeling blue, or needing an injection of inspiration.

If you have a pressing question and want an answer, go for the WOW –*Words of Wisdom Oracle,* to gain a fresh perspective.

♥ Hold *Bounce off the Walls – Land on Your Feet* in your hand.

♥ Close your eyes. Tune-in. Skim through the pages. When you feel like it, stop at a page, and open your eyes.

♥ Put your finger on a spot on the page. Whatever is there is your *WOW* message to be interpreted. Read the lines above it and the paragraph below.

♥ Close the book. Contemplate how the message applies to your question or alters your state of mind or emotions. Does it give you a flip side, another aspect to consider?

When we are open to *WOW*, wisdom appears in random forms. By celebrating yourself, you'll learn to trust your impressions, stand-up for your beliefs in the midst of adversity, and remain continually open to change. Success follows truth and you become real about what you need. Remember to seek a WOW, a pump-up of good thoughts and wisdom.

What Is the "Last Shot?"

As a filmmaker, I am aware of the subliminal power of the last shot in a movie. It's a gripping symbol, illuminating the theme or the underlying message of what the movie is about. Can you imagine the last shot of this time we have spent together? Can you conjure an image, a sensation, a provocative meaning in your heart or mind? My vision of that shot for myself is very special, totally unique.

TAKE A MOMENT AND LOOK INTO A MIRROR – THE LAST SHOT IS YOU!   Come on, give it up for you! Gaze into your eyes and inhale your specialness. Meet yourself with respect, honor, and love. Smile at the discovery. Since the brain doesn't know real laughter from faking it, just start laughing. Fake it to the max. Keep it going.

May you continue to query and ask questions in search of evolvement. As a reminder, the quality of truth's answer lies in the quality of the question. And IN GRATITUDE, may you grow strong, imbibing the lesson of life's teachings as you continually learn more about how you learn, delving deeper into your truth.

Know whatever the circumstance, the challenge, you will Land On Your Feet. Trust you are grounded and gaining self-mastery – knowing you can successfully Morph HAvoc and HAssles into HArmony and HAppiness.

HaHaHaHa! May the giggles be with you on your MerrieWay, a LightHeart Path™

-

To Be Real, Laugh, and Love!

For over a decade 'Morphing" has evolved into this offering. It takes a great team to make great things happen. Our team is so filled with enthusiasm, relentless support, and stellar skills that I am smiling with humbling **gratitude and thanks to:**

At the get-go Sheldon and Sheila Lewis, both gifted writers, helped to define the book's mission and its initial content. Your enlightened understanding of the spiritual nature of my message teemed with the practical is a gift to all.

Shauna Zurbrugg, my brilliant editor, whose precision and deep insight shaped the contents, stories, and helped to define my voice with clarity. I can't thank you enough for your patience and emotional support in the hours we spent together that kept me keeping on. Your beautiful spirit rings a happy bell in my heart.

Laura O'Loughlin edited the final version. Your creative spunk inspired amazing additions. I am grateful for your eagle eye attention to details and your perseverance. Your friendship is a delightful treasure.

Katie Bowden – Your keenness to typeset this book – and your immaculate detailing was done with ultimate professionalism. It is so fine.

Asha McLaughlin's , designed the book cover and the content's flavor. Your graceful simplicity, beauty consciousness, and talent are immeasurable. You took an abstract vision and made it real- just like you, my dear friend.

David Paul, photographer of back cover photo. Your artistic talent capturing Byron' pictures in my sacred locket is an awesome blessing, enlivening my heartfelt inspiration for writing this book.

Gloria deGaetano, my miraculous co-writer of Morphing of America. Thank you for your encouragement and your expertise is all areas of education and helping to make our curriculums a reality and successful effort.

Carol Connors, singer and two-time Academy Award nominee songwriter. You are a touchstone - prodding me to excellence. Your prophetic '*Morph America*' song is a delight and inspiration to those who hear it - the youth and choirs who sing it.

Ilene Protor – Public relation's maven and my confident. Ilene's brilliant input is a gift much appreciated. You are so special… magically beating to your stellar drum.

Gratitude to our publishing team at MediaMorphUs. Your energetic enthusiasm and insight is a key factor for our missions to enlighten, empower, and bring Unity in community. Handling our outreach, marketing, new products, and rollouts keep me in awe of the fruits of collaboration.

Bob Lorsch, your business acumen, mastermind advice, and boundless energy are immeasurable. Thank you for your integrity and commitment to inspire youth to live their potential.

Gene Adams, my business advisor, CPA. For showering light at the beginning and end of the tunnel: Love your generosity of spirit and selfless effort - keeping us on track.

Ron Dunham, whose brave conviction to share his beloved son's departure to help others cope with their loss. Thank you for your noble intent and unconditional support.

Darby Macfalane, my soul sister, and a loyal friend of the project contributed generously. Your moral support and keen measure of wisdom in the stories you shared, dedicated to uplift humanity.

To Deepika Avanti for her ongoing loving support. Keep shining that love light.

To our sponsors: Ellis Foundation, Microsoft, Lorsch Foundation, Roger Dauer, Write Brothers, Lear Foundation. And to our contributors at Girl Scouts, LAUSD, UCLA, New York Schools, Chicago Police Museum, and the scores of other wonderful MerrieWay Community alliances. Our Board members:, Norman and Lynn Lear, Phylcia Rashad, Paul Cummins, gratitude for your ongoing support.

Gratitude and admiration to my mentors and friends who have helped define what I stand for - To my spiritual teacher's inspiration to live a great life - AUM forever.

Especially to my mother, Betty, and my father, Phil – who encouraged me to believe in myself: to remain vigilant, steadfast, and to actuate my heart's desire. Bless you.

My brother Bill and sister-in-law Jan forever remain a backbone of my efforts. I love you both. Bill you know, your influence in my life is interwoven in my heart and throughout the pages of this effort.

My niece, Aimme Lou Dee, our *Morph America* web designer. I'm proud of you. You've grown into a remarkable woman and mother. I thank Matt for being your awesome husband. Hats off to Mason - your adorable son.

To Carey Fox, Byron's father. I thank you for honoring our son - and for sharing his magnificence with me in your heart and soul. Your loving nature is a strength that rests as gratitude in my innermost being… for being there… always.

To our participants and facilitators in workshops, sessions, classrooms, who have shared your heartfelt stories. Too many to mention, you know who you are. We have shared our truth, dreams, and life's foibles…growing strong together.

To my beloved Byron - I love you and will cherish you always. Being your mother is my greatest accomplishment in this life. I have honored your wish…my dear ONE. Yes, the book is published. And, I am committed to Be Real, Laugh and Love. You are my inspiration.

100% of book proceeds will benefit youth/family/educational charities.

ABOUT THE AUTHOR

Merrie Lynn Ross – a tour de force, award winning writer/ filmmaker/actor, starring in 35+ TV & Films is known as daytime's first comedienne; giggling her way into millions of viewer's hearts on ABC's "General Hospital" Internationally acclaimed as a lead child advocate, honored by Presidents' Clinton and George W, she created *"Morph America"* and *"Peace Smarts"* curriculums: serving over two million families to create a peace culture.

After a personal tragedy and discovering a way back to living in purpose, Merrie Lynn is guided to share her healing and life altering recipes. With a contagious joyous energy she shines as a beacon of light for everyone she meets.

She currently stars on 'MerrieWay Day' TV - filled with uplifting news, red-carpet folly, and fun global treks. With great passion and dedicated to empower youth, she's producing the film, "Franky… What's Next?" written by Byron Fox.

A hill-dweller in Southern California, Merrie Lynn lives with her two shelties, and enjoys a 'green healthy' life with her circle of colleagues' and loving friends.

Websites:
www.bounceoffthewalls.com
www.merrieway.com

Interactive materials, audios, tele-seminars are available for Bounce/Morph techniques.

Merrie Lynn Ross is available for media interviews, live events, lecture and motivational-speaker engagements, and workshops.

♥ ♥ ♥

Enjoy this FREE Gift!

IMAGINE GATHERING in a CommUnity that Accepts YOU!

Each ONE of us tunes into the inspirational light within. Following your lights flame, your presence inspires those in need…thirsting to hear.

We Invite You - Stay Connected to MerrieWay Community…

- We celebrate in Intimate Groups, Global Web Gatherings, and Live Energized Events.

- Bring a 'LightHeart Bounce Gathering' to your hometown.

- We entertain, train, and sustain.

For more info': www.merrieway.com

*As Millennium's Front Wave we rally **"LightHeart Bounce"** - a living lesson for Peace, Love, and Sustainability. We gather in the expansion of awareness…we know the way. One breath, one moment at a time.*

www.ingramcontent.com/pod-product-compliance
Lightning Source LLC
Chambersburg PA
CBHW021216090426
42740CB00006B/239